American Homeowner
How to Own and Protect the Dream

Steven DeSalvo

Copyright © 2015 by Ameripublish, LLC

All Rights Reserved

Reproduction or translation of any part of this book or its contents including storage in a retrieval system, or transmitted in any form or by any means, electronic, mechanical, photocopying, recording, scanning, or otherwise beyond that permitted by section 107 or 108 of the 1976 United States Copyright Act without permission of the Publisher as copyright owner is unlawful. Requests for permission or further information should be addressed to:

**Library of Congress Control Number: 2015911773
Ameripublish, LLC, Kingston, New York**

DeSalvo, Steven, 1958-
American Homeowner: How to Own and Protect the Dream
ISBN **978-0692253328**

Printed in the United States of America

This book is designed to provide accurate and authoritative information in regard to the subject matter covered. It is sold with the understanding that the author and publisher are not engaged in rendering legal, accounting, or other professional advice. **Your own individual circumstances are fact dependent.** If legal advice or other expert assistance is required, the services of a competent professional should be sought.

#HomeownerBooks

With the speed to market in publishing today this book is updated as often as necessary. To see what's been added since this version was printed visit:

AmericanHomeownerBooks.com

Free eBook Gift!
While on the website, enter your email address to receive the upcoming eBook:
American Homeowner's 101 Time and Money Saving Tips

Follow us

#HomeownerBooks hashtag on social media to follow news.
Twitter @HomeownerBooks
Facebook.com/AmericanHomeownerBooks

Steven DeSalvo is an insurance broker in Kingston, NY. In a 35 year career including real estate and banking, DeSalvo has helped hundreds of homebuyers and homeowners achieve and protect homeownership. An 18 year insurance broker, he's completed many insurance courses including the Society of Certified Insurance Counselors courses on home, auto, life & health insurance. He's a past president of National Association of Insurance & Financial Advisors local chapter. As a 30 year NY State Licensed Real Estate Broker, he's operated franchised agencies, is a Graduate of the Realtors Institute, and many real estate and appraisal courses. As a former Asst. Vice President for a NY State Chartered Bank, he worked with borrowers as Insurance and Loan Servicing Manager and saw firsthand the stress borrowers faced as he helped them get back on track with mortgage modifications when needed.

DeSalvo is past chairman of the Town of Esopus, NY Board of Assessment Review. A homeowner for over 35 years, he's bought, renovated and sold homes and investment properties. DeSalvo holds an Associate's Degree from SUNY Ulster, Bachelor of Science from the School of Business at New Paltz University and has attended many courses and seminars on homes, healthy living, energy savings, and lawns & gardening.

TABLE OF CONTENTS

Introduction

1	**Welcome to Homeownership**	1
	The American Dream, Creating Layers of Protection, Common Courtesies,	
	Moving Checklist, Recordkeeping	10
2	**Household Finances - Find the Money**	31
	Financial Security Basics	
3	**Money and Time Saving Tips**	45
	Be a Smart Consumer	
4	**Invest it Right**	61
	Keep Your Retirement Dreams in Sight	
5	**Your Mortgage, Property Taxes & Assessment**	81
	Know Your Details and How to Save	
6	**Household View of Insurance Needs**	99
	Auto & Personal Umbrella Policy	
7	**Types of Home Insurance**	113
	Open or Named Peril	
	Actual Cash Value or Replacement Cost	
8	**Review Your Insurance Policy**	129
	Home Insurance Policy at a Glance	
9	**Flood and Earthquake Insurance**	145
	Not Every Wet Basement is a Flood	
10	**Condominiums and Co-ops**	149
	Understanding Unique Coverage Needs	

11	**Dealing with Insurance Claims**	157
	Neighborly Tree Advice	
12	**Protecting the "What if?"**	173
	Life and Disability Insurance	
13	**Home Maintenance**	189
	Preventive Maintenance	
14	**Energy and Money Savings**	216
	Improvements that Return Investment	
15	**Home Improvements**	234
	Pick the Right Improvements	
	Working with Contractors	
16	**Safety & Security**	250
	Avoiding 5 Common Home Injuries	
17	**Lawn and Garden**	276
	Find Your Balance, Use of Pesticides,	
	Composting, American Flag	
18	**Foreclosure Prevention**	296
	Know the Red Flags, Get Reputable Help,	
	Avoiding Scams	
19	**Selling Your Home**	308
	Track Capital Improvements	

Summary Enjoy Many Happy Years	316
Bibliography	319
Homeownership Resources	320
Important Document Locations	327

Introduction

Homeownership in the United States is a cornerstone in building the strength of our communities. Owning a home creates independence and the security of having a place of your own. Cared for and protected your home will pay dividends for years to come as you create a nicer, healthier environment for you and your family, in paying off to own free and clear, and in the potential for increased value. Yet, all too often when the dream of owning a home is finally achieved some families find it slips away. From the first time a homeowner turns the key in the front door they're faced with decisions that well-chosen can set the stage to help create a fabulous experience. **American Homeowner** provides insight gained through decades gathering real estate and insurance knowledge, advice and homeownership research. It provides up to date information and available resources to have information right at your fingertips. It's designed to be easy to read, helpful, and inspirational to strengthen a homeowners' knowledge in what for most will be the greatest investment of their life. **American Homeowner** covers a variety of areas that both new and experienced homeowners will find saves time, lots of money and will increase enjoyment of your homeownership experience for years to come. Our goal is to reach homeowners at the earliest opportunity, to set the stage for a successful experience. Soon to be homeowners will find information very helpful, and in particular may want to review Chapters 7 and 8 on home insurance as you arrange insurance for your closing.

Introduction

If insurance is in place some of the suggestions may have you want to sit down with your agent to review coverage's further.

American Homeowner is designed to be a Quickstart, to not sit on your shelf waiting to be read *some day*. Allowing you to begin on the best footing possible day one; and as a reference each topic is designed to stand alone whenever possible. Topics include creating financial security for you and your family, insuring your home right, maintenance, money saving tips, environmental, safety and home security. To be sure, there are many more detailed books written on any one of the areas discussed. Including basic financial planning is done with the goal of reaching as many homeowners as possible at the outset, to create a solid emergency fund and build financial security. With foreclosure rates having peaked and almost a third of adults lacking an emergency fund of any kind, we can't be selective in reaching homeowners. Foreclosures happen to people of all income levels, and we're looking to protect homeownership for all. Homeowners with an emergency fund and solid financial plan in place may still find very useful information to protect their assets in the discussion; though the thought of preaching to the choir may come to mind. You may choose to dig deeper and read further in any one or all of the topics discussed.

A homeowner unpacking, settling in and picking paint colors has many areas to consider at the outset. **American Homeowner** is the first step as an easy reading overview with links to many resources along the way. There are ***Dozens of***

Introduction

Money and Time Saving Tips within the following pages that may save homeowners up to thousands of dollars. Additionally, we included a **Seasonal Maintenance Checklist** and a **Journal** to list home improvements, service records and contact info; to make your ownership experience easier during a project, when you need details later, and as a record of your capital improvements when it's time to sell. Readers of the eBook may want to keep a notebook handy for items to act on, or print Journal pages to include in your property ring binder we discuss in the Moving Checklist.

If you've just closed to buy your home the excitement is fresh, you have the keys and it feels great. But what do you do now? Reading **American Homeowner** will help ensure many years of enjoyment; from Day one, through the day you pull the door closed for the last time.

Readers with a **recent or upcoming home purchase** will find suggestions in the Moving & Recordkeeping Checklist following Chapter 1 helpful. Not all may apply to you, but pick and choose those that are appropriate, and fit them in as the timing applies.

Mid pleasures and palaces
though we may roam,
be it ever so humble,
there's no place like
HOME.

John Howard Payne
US Actor and Dramatist
1791-1852

Chapter 1

Welcome to Homeownership

Congratulations on your decision to become a homeowner…a proud homeowner. Home to you may be a traditional single family detached home, but it could also be one of many others; from condo or townhouse, to mobile home, mansion, or multi family. It can be in the heart of the city, in the suburbs, or in rural America. For the purpose of this book we'll call all "home." Your journey to homeownership may have been an easy one. Possibly though, it may have taken a great deal of time and effort, from saving enough to buy your home, to searching out properties, the mortgage process and closing. Not to mention all the effort that goes into moving and getting settled in. It's been said that nothing worthwhile is easy. In any event you can be proud of your accomplishment, whether it's your first home or one of many. There are people that will never realize this part of the ***American Dream***. Some by choice may not own, and many because of the inability to put it all together. Take a deep breath and savor the feeling. When you watch news and events worldwide take note of how many people go without a home to call their own. You are one in as many as two in three households in the United States who own their own home; up from less than half that owned their own home back in 1900. (US Housing Census)

As with many things in one's life, there may be times when you may look at ownership as a burden. Instead, realize that

Welcome to Homeownership

many things that at first glance may look like a burden are actually a blessing that shouldn't be taken for granted. There are many countries that don't allow property ownership by individuals. In addition, there are many people who retire after 20 to 30 years that never chose to buy a home. Can you picture how much further ahead they would be if they'd owned all those years with the home now paid off in retirement? Better late than never, there are benefits to homeownership at any age. So the next time you're outside on a hot summer day cutting the grass, say over and over to yourself - *"this is a blessing, this is a blessing..."* Take a sip of lemonade, and remember that you'll be the one cashing in when the home is paid off or sold, and not your landlord.

Settling In

A home of your own builds security in more ways than one. Aside from long term financial benefits, homeownership strengthens the lives of people and families. You'll note many inspirational quotes throughout **American Homeowner**. In searching out the most appropriate, many by Benjamin Franklin surfaced. Along with all of Franklin's accomplishments as a founding father of the United States and an inventor, he also published *Poor Richard's Almanack for the American Colonies*. This included seasonal forecasts and household information, as well as words of wisdom that Franklin wrote under the pen name Richard Saunders. An illustrated lithograph with 24 of these sayings was created by Oliver Pelton (1798-1882) "Poor Richard Illustrated, lessons for the young and old on industry, temperance, frugality & ... by Benjamin Franklin." The vignette that follows includes the quote: "I never saw an oft(en) removed tree, nor yet an oft(en)

Welcome to Homeownership

removed family that did so well as those that settled be." A cart is being packed with all the tenants' belongings, and a sign on the building says "This house to LET." As true then as it is today, moving from house to house whenever a landlords plans change, or rents are increased doesn't allow a family to do as well as those that are more settled, having the stability and security of homeownership.

"I never saw an oft removed tree, nor yet an oft removed family that did so well as those that settled be."

Benjamin Franklin

Welcome to Homeownership

The American Dream

The phrase *"The American Dream"* is used today in a variety of ways, very often regarding the American Dream of owning a home for oneself. The term though is about more than achieving homeownership. It's about the dream of creating a better life for you and your family. To some immigrants, simply being able to be free to openly have faith in their religion has been reason alone to come to America. To most the dream includes more than any one item, and most often includes the security owning a home.

The concept of *The American Dream* was first written about by James Truslow Adams in 1931, shortly after the crash of 1929 while the country was in the great depression. In his book, *The Epic of America,* Adams takes us through the discovery and founding of America through then present day 1931. Around the time Adams was putting finishing touches on the books ' manuscript, President Herbert Hoover was in the headlines for flipping the switch to open the Empire State Building. Americans were looking for rays of hope during difficult times. In the books concluding Epilogue, James Truslow Adams coined the phrase and wrote of the American Dream: "If, as I have said, the things already listed were all we had to contribute, America would have made no distinctive and unique gift to mankind. But there has been also the *American Dream;* that dream of a land in which life should be better and richer and fuller for every man, with opportunity for each according to his ability or achievement. It is a difficult dream for the European upper classes to interpret adequately, and too many of ourselves have grown weary and mistrustful of it. It is not a dream of

Welcome to Homeownership

motor cars and high wages merely, but a dream of social order in which each man and each woman shall be able to attain to the fullest stature of which they are innately capable, and be recognized by others for what they are, regardless of the fortuitous circumstances of birth or position....No, the American dream that has lured tens of millions of all nations to our shores in the past century has not been a dream of merely material plenty, though that has doubtless counted heavily. It has been much more than that. It has been a dream of being able to grow to fullest development..." Adams described simpler times, before the growth of big cities. "When a man staked out a clearing of land, and, knowing his wife and children needed shelter - there was no need to discuss what were the real values in a humane and satisfying life. The trees had to be chopped, the log hut built, the stumps burned and corn planted. Simplification became a habit of mind and was carried into our lives long after the clearing had become a prosperous city."

Keeping up with the Joneses

As apparent to Adams in 1931 as it is true even more so today, people need to take the time to smell the proverbial roses. Now, as a homeowner - take the time to enjoy the good earth. If you're in a condo, do the same figuratively. Take pleasure in some of the basics in life that often go unnoticed. As Adams stated it: "...how size and statistics of material development came to be more important in our eyes than quality and spiritual values; ...how we forgot to *live,* in the struggle to "make a living"..." And on being too materialistic"...the American dream itself opens all sorts of questions as to values.

Welcome to Homeownership

It is easy to say a better and richer life for all men, but what is *better* and what is *richer*?" "In this respect, as in many others, the great business leaders are likely to lead us astray rather than to guide us...The danger lies in the fact that the theory is advanced not for the purpose of creating a better type of man by increasing his leisure and the opportunity for making a wise use of it, but for the sole and avowed purpose of increasing his powers as a "consumer." He is, therefore, goaded by every possible method of pressure or cajoled to spend his wages in consuming goods. He, like the rest of us, thus appears to be getting on a treadmill in which he earns, not that he may enjoy, but that he will spend...The very foundation of the American dream of a better and richer life for all is that all, in varying degrees, shall be capable of wanting to share in it. It can never be wrought into a reality by cheap people or by "keeping up with the Joneses."

What does the promise of the American Dream look like to you? Is it materialistic - to work longer hours to get bigger, or more expensive cars - and stuff, or is the dream with less focus on material gain - having more *things*, and more about living a simple and fulfilling life? As a homeowner, would it include having the home eventually paid off in 15, 20 or 30 years to give a retirement nest egg should you sell? Thirty years may seem like a long time now, but ask anyone in that age group and you'll hear it arrives sooner than you think! With a paid off home, retirement years will be much less stressful without a mortgage.

Does the American Dream mean giving in to every whim for gadgets and stuff that you and your family want now? This, to the point that many homeowners are up to their eyeballs in consumer debt and one missed paycheck away from a

Welcome to Homeownership

foreclosure notice? As a measure of how in debt people are getting, the US Census Bureau most recent report shows that half of households owe $7,000 or more on unsecured debt like credit cards (this doesn't include secured debt like cars and home mortgages.) This is up from $5,365, so the trend is *more* debt causing more household *stress*. There's nothing wrong with enjoying the fruits of your success. The caveat though is that it should be within a budget to know you're on the right track for a prosperous future.

As American Homeowner's title suggests, our goal is to provide a guide in *How to Own and Protect the Dream*. "Our" means all the stakeholders who want to see you succeed in homeownership. This includes Realtors who believe in and strongly encourage homeownership through many initiatives; knowing that increasing homeownership strengthens communities. Banks and credit unions, who want to see you succeed and pay off your mortgage, to avoid the expense of foreclosures. As well as insurance companies who would rather see you insured correctly in the event of a claim. Each of these we know has their own profit motives, but ensuring homeowners succeed helps them succeed.

Protecting your home means in a variety of areas. **Protecting** means good maintenance, so that a simple unattached gutter drain pipe doesn't cause a flooded basement. Or so that a simple squeeze of caulk in a gap by the tub avoids water leakage - causing an uninhabitable home due to mold growing in the wall. **Protecting** means insuring your home correct, and within your budget so that if there is a major claim it can be rebuilt. To be better prepared in the event a natural disaster strikes; and so that if someone trips on your walkway

Welcome to Homeownership

and sues, you avoid losing your assets and having your income garnished. **Protecting** also means creating a financial plan to address the most common causes of foreclosure:

- **Loss of a job**
- **Divorce**
- **Medical expenses**
- **Mortgage payment increase**
- **Death**
- **Disability**
- **Increase in Taxes**
- **Unmanageable credit card and consumer debt, car loans, etc.**

There's not one magic bullet or pill that eliminates all the above along with many other possibilities. According to RealtyTrac (www.realtytrac.com) a California based company that tracks foreclosures; there are 925,932 properties in the US in some stage of foreclosure as of June, 2015. One in every 1,049 homeowners received foreclosure notices in April, 2015. At first glance this may not seem like a lot, but if this were the chances of winning tonight's lottery you'd run out and buy a ticket due to the odds being pretty good. With some planning, many common causes of foreclosure can be reduced or eliminated. Creating "**Layers of Protection**" for your home, insurance and financial well-being will help create and protect the American Dream you've worked hard to build for yourself and your family.

Welcome to Homeownership

Creating Layers of Protection
A Sturdy Three Legged Stool

In the next few chapters, we'll suggest creating **Layers of Protection** for your home and family. Think of the basis to create this protection as a sturdy three legged stool. In fact, for a moment picture yourself sitting on this stool reading this book. One leg represents protecting homeownership from a financial viewpoint, the second represents insurance to protect your home and family, and the third caring for and protecting the physical home itself. We're looking to protect your home through creating *Layers of Protection*, while at the same time building financial security and long term wealth; protection that includes financial, insurance, home maintenance and security. Examples of layers of protection would be, say in the case of having a pool: To have the pool fenced in with child proof latches, but also to have a pool alarm in the water in the event the gate was left open. Then to also have in place higher liability insurance in case you do end up being responsible for someone's injury. Another example would be to have an emergency fund saved to pay 6 to 12 months of household mortgage and expenses if you were out of work or disabled, but to consider shifting insurance priorities to have disability insurance in place should you be disabled and out of work for a length of time with your savings exhausted. The goal isn't to pay more money for insurance, but as a homeowner it may be worth considering shifting priorities. We'll discuss concerns, and you can decide which solutions are appropriate based on your circumstances *to best help you fulfill the promise of the American Dream as it means to you.*

Welcome to Homeownership

Marked Up, Worn and Tattered, to Protect the Things that Mattered

We're looking to protect the things that matter to you today. The "*ed*" was added to complete the rhyme, but also so that someday looking back you'll see that the extra effort protecting homeownership was worth it. Some books look good sitting on display in pristine condition on the coffee table or bookshelf. Often people have the ingrained feeling that books are to be kept crisp and new for the next person, probably from our school text book days. We hope this isn't that book. This should be a book that's read cover to cover, marked up and highlighted with notes that come to mind along the way. It's that first mark on the page that may be the most difficult, because you're committing to make the book yours. Then you'll find the act of personalizing the suggestions rewarding. There are also seasonal checklists with room to add items particular to your home. As mentioned in the introduction, readers of an eBook version may want to keep a notepad nearby to add notes that come to mind.

Moving Checklist & Recordkeeping

__ **Lease Termination:** Are you renting now? What steps are necessary to arrange the ending of your present lease agreement? How much notice is required in your agreement? Is the landlord holding security? Are the utility or phone companies holding security? Have the landlord walk through with you to confirm all is in order, and that there will be no issues with return of security. Breaking a lease can create the possibility of the landlord seeking payment from you for the remainder of the lease term. If your landlord refuses to return security and you feel it should be returned there may be free resources to help tenants in your area.

__ **New Insurance:** Check with your insurance agent/broker to make sure all is in order before and after the closing. Are all policies in force, do your policies have the correct new mailing address as you transition to a new address? See if there may be an insurance inspection for new policy and address any possible concerns. Inspectors look for concerns with broken & missing railings & steps, uneven walkways, hazardous tree limbs, etc. Avoid any lapses between old and new insurance to give continuous liability and contents coverage. Many insurance policies extend 100% contents coverage for 30 days into a newly acquired residence. After 30 days many drop to 10%. If staying some place in the interim between closings consider renters insurance if needed.

__ **Old Insurance Policy:** If cancelling previous homeowners or renters insurance it's normally best to cancel when fully out of the premises or sold and closed. For rentals keep in force until fully vacated, and no longer responsible by your lease or agreement. Be careful to cancel 12:01am the day after the closing, not 12:01 the day of closing as there would be no coverage if you later found a claim occurred closing day - which may have a greater chance with all the activity. Again, keep continuous coverage between old and new insurance to provide coverage for your contents and liability insurance even during a gap between occupying residences.

Welcome to Homeownership

__ **Fire/Security Box:** Have a secure fire box or safe to keep all of your important papers: title, deed when received, copy of will, title for cars, etc. Make sure the box is not stored in an area that could flood like a basement floor, or that has excessive dampness and moisture. (Page 21)

__ **Closing Statements/File:** Create a file for all of your closing papers for tax purposes this year, and for the future. Check with your tax advisor to see which of the expenses may be tax deductible on this current year tax returns, and which may be used some day when you sell the home to offset any possible capital gains tax. As a general guideline normally items like interest on your mortgage and any "points" paid to your bank that may have been treated as prepaid interest may be considered as expenses the year they are incurred. There are IRS guidelines pertaining to points that you will want to seek advice of tax professional. Expenses such as attorney fees and survey increase your "basis" of the cost of your home, and have no deduction unless to reduce a potential capital gains tax should you someday sell.

__ **School Records:** If you are moving to a new school district arrange to transfer records.

__ **Medical Records:** If changing Doctors, Dentists, and Eyeglass providers arrange to transfer medical records as appropriate.

__ **Will:** If moving out of state, check with your attorney to see if anything needs to be done, especially if property is owned in more than one state.

Welcome to Homeownership

Moving

__ **De-Clutter:** Decide what's worth moving. If there are items you will be replacing does it pay to reduce moving expense by selling some items and having a yard sale prior to the move? There are also many Facebook yard sale groups to post items for sale.

__ **Get Estimates for the Move:** Are you hiring a moving company, or renting a truck to do the move yourself? Get 3 written estimates from moving companies. Your family, friends or Realtor® may offer suggestions of reputable companies.

__ **Keep Track of Moving Expense if Deductible:** Some moving expenses may be tax deductible if for starting a new job or the move was required by your employer. Check IRS guidelines. The deduction covers the reasonable expenses you incur to transport your personal effects and household items to your new home. The cost of renting a storage unit for up to 30 days may be included if you are unable to move into your new home immediately after leaving your former home. You can also include the cost of traveling to the new location for yourself and other members of your household. If you drive to the new location in a personal vehicle, you can include the actual cost of oil, gasoline, parking fees and highway tolls. Instead of using the actual cost of gasoline and oil, the IRS permits you to calculate those costs using the standard mileage rate. For long-distance moves, you can deduct the cost of airline and train tickets. Rules include moves that may have been delayed to finish out school year and may change, verify

Welcome to Homeownership

all requirements. See IRS Publication:
www.irs.gov/publications/p521/ar02.html

__ **Moving Insurance:** See what insurance the moving company includes, if they have other options, and check with your insurance broker, especially regarding valuable items. Does the moving company insure to full replacement value, or the lower – depreciated actual cash value "ACV"? Some delicate, breakable items that you carefully pack yourself may not be covered by the movers insurance if broken, since they did not pack. Your renters or home insurance if in force may insure items in storage for the perils the policy covers such as fire, and theft, but not breakage. Make a detailed list and review with your moving company and insurance agent.

__ **Pack:** Starting with the non-essentials and clearly label all boxes. Pack essentials separate for the trip and box of essentials for day 1 in your new home.

__ **1 Day Before the Move**: Confirm details with mover.

__ **Furniture Floor Plan:** Draw a plan of where furniture will be placed to avoid confusion on moving in.

__ **Home Inventory:** Take a household inventory with support of photos/video of all your furniture, fixtures and belongings as you settle in. Many insurance agents have inventory booklets, and there are many online and as easy to use apps such as:
- **www.knowyourstuff.org** by the Insurance Information Institute.
- **www.insureuonline.org** by the National Association of Insurance Commissioners.

Welcome to Homeownership

View, upload pictures and update as needed. Include make, model and serial numbers if possible. If not web based, store the inventory in your fireproof box, or off premises in the event of a fire. It's easier to take an hour or two for an inventory now, than to have to sift through ashes in the unthinkable event of a fire or break-in and have to remember what was in the home.

__ **Mail:** Stop at the New (or Present) Post Office: to update to your new mailing address. Have the old mailing address forward mail to the new address. The post office has had moving kits with change of mailing address. The recent kits have had 10% off coupons for a national home center.

__ **Mailbox:** Make sure your name(s) and house number are on your mailbox and on the home itself. This is important to ensure delivery of mail, and also for emergency services to locate the home. Having the number display with light ensures night time visibility.

__ **Correct Address:** Update your addresses for driver's license, registration, etc. at your Department of Motor Vehicles. Many DMV's do not forward mail, even though the post office has instructions to forward. Many states require notification of change of address within 30 days or a ticket may be issued for the violation.

__ **Discontinue Deliveries:**
   Newspaper ___
   Garbage collection ___
   _____ ___

Welcome to Homeownership

Safety

__ **New Door Locks:** Will it be necessary to change all the door locks in the new home? The home seller normally delivers keys to you at the closing but who knows what other keys may be floating around with others over the years. To feel 100% secure replace all the locks. There may be an option to change only the tumbler cylinder less expensively.

__ **Deadbolt Locks:** Install deadbolt locks if needed. Many insurance companies give additional discounts for homes with deadbolts.

There's a saying that locks are meant for honest people. If a door is locked most honest people won't try to enter. Adding more secure locksets with bolt cylinders that securely lock doors will deter, or at least slow down criminal activity.

__ **Smoke Detectors throughout**, with batteries checked? If unsure of age replace with new. Many manufactures state the units do not function properly after 10 years.

__ **CO2 Detectors**, with batteries checked.

__ **Fire Extinguishers as needed:** In kitchen, garage and utility rooms as needed.

Welcome to Homeownership

Utilities

__ **Have you turned on all new** utilities in your name, meters read?

- Telephone
- Cable
- Gas
- Electric
- Trash
- Oil

__ **Have you cancelled the above old services** when appropriate, being careful to avoid freeze or other concerns?

__ **Maintenance Priority Items:** Make a priority list and take care of immediate maintenance concerns, such as making sure home is secure, locks changed if needed, small exterior holes sealed. Storms and screens opened/closed. Drain and downspouts installed correctly and directing the water far enough away from the house. A home inspector may have made you aware of concerns to address. Most inspectors will prioritize items needing immediate attention.

Welcome to Homeownership

Home Maintenance Priority Items

1	
2	
3	
4	
5	
6	
7	
8	
9	
10	
11	
12	
13	
14	
15	

__ **Winterization:** If it is winter, double check that your old home and the new home are ready, or are winterized, including outside faucets to avoid freezing. If a home is vacant, sometimes leaving sink cabinet doors slightly open will allow more heat to reach the pipes. Lack of running the water can make pipes freeze. Often, in freezing weather, allowing faucet to drip helps avoid pipes freezing. There are simple freeze warning devices to turn a lamp on as a warning or internet based to monitor homes remotely.

Welcome to Homeownership

Household Recordkeeping

If you had 5 minutes to grab things and run - what would you grab?

Starting with a plan of where to keep all your homeowner paperwork, personal and financial records helps get and keep you organized from day one. This makes life easier over the years running a household, and is invaluable in the event of a catastrophe. If you had 5 minutes to grab things and run - what would you grab? Would you know where to start? Those that have been through disasters: from household fires, to approaching wildfires, tornadoes and floodwaters would stress, very emotionally the importance of advance preparation. You'd hear of the difficulty and delays in replacing vital records such as birth certificates, passports, and social security cards - as well as original life insurance and deed records. A topic brought up by many after a disaster is the loss of family heirlooms as well as photos. A good reason to have many of the old photos scanned and saved to an online source such as Facebook, or a cloud.

USA.gov has a helpful page with suggestions for managing household records, how long and where to keep paperwork. You may want to discuss with your family attorney where documents such as your will should be kept. Many states have unique laws, for example if the will is stored in a bank safe deposit box, the box may be sealed on death making the will difficult to readily retrieve. **As a suggestion, consider four types of records to be stored in these locations:**

Welcome to Homeownership

1) Household file cabinet/desk for records that are replaceable and that you refer to often such as bills, bank and credit card statements.

2) Household and Personal Property Binder or Folders Start with two binders or folders, and include pocket pages.

Label one House, (or Real Estate, or Real Property.) Include in here any operating instructions and warranty information for items that belong to the physical house, or real estate. The items that if you were to one day sell the home you may leave for a new buyer.

Label the second Personal Property for operating instructions and warranty papers.

Receipts: Include receipt for date purchase in the event of warranty issues and returns.

As binders grow in size consider separating into additional binders or folders for ease of finding items.

Garage, **Workshop**, or **Lawn and Garden** can have their own binder as needed.

3) Safe Deposit Box in a bank: store documents in a zip lock bag in the event of water concerns.

4) Fire and Water Proof Box More important, difficult to replace papers, such as passports, vehicle titles, birth certificates, etc. can be kept in the safe deposit box or fire and water proof box at your home. Keep (ideally certified) copies of items that are in the safe deposit box at home. Bear in mind that many states have banking laws that require safe deposit boxes be sealed on death; delaying access to its contents including a will. A concern storing a will in your own firebox at home is that it may give access to the will to someone that perhaps you didn't want to see, and may not be happy by your decisions - such as them not being included. Many attorneys will keep an original will in their safe, but be sure to specify in your records what attorney is to be contacted when needed.

Welcome to Homeownership

Get to Know the Neighbors and the Neighborhood

As a new homeowner you'll want to get a feel for your new home and neighborhood. Driving in the car only lets you see so much. Take walks, jog, ride a bike to really get to know the neighbors and neighborhood well. A friendly hello goes a long way. You may also spot concerns like a loose dog that may need to be avoided. Kids are also great at exploring the area, and may find a favorite sledding hill or swimming hole. You may want to get a handle first on the area. Getting to know the neighbors:

- **Helps you know what goods and services** are available nearby.
- **Get the Scoop:** You may learn of criminal or other persons to be cautious of.
- **Strengthens and builds** a sense of community.
- **Front Porch:** Where in many neighborhoods families aren't seen, and entertaining is done in the rear yard - there is a trend toward front porches being used. Not with the old torn living room set creating a mess, but with the likes of rocking chairs, wicker set or porch swing. Making use of the front porch helps a homeowner get to know what's going on in the neighborhood.
- **Notice unusual activity**, in the area.
- **Creates a neighborhood watch** mentality.

Welcome to Homeownership

Welcome Neighbor

It's been custom that existing neighbors make the first gesture to welcome a new homeowner, though don't always count on tradition. Much has been written about being a good neighbor. Most would fall in the category of following the golden rule, and common sense.

On being a neighbor from Emily Post's Etipedia®
www.emilypost.com

Emily Post wrote *Etiquette in Society, in Business, in Politics, and at Home* in 1922. Her work is carried on by The Emily Post Institute, which she founded in 1946. Emily Post's Etipedia discusses "Neighborly Basics *Keep Things Neighborly:*" Quoting Post, "Good neighbors don't impose. But what exactly is an imposition? As you get to know neighbors and by paying attention to individual lifestyles, customs, and social cues, you'll learn their preferences." Summarizing Post, consider:

Greet neighbors whenever you see them.
Have an occasional chat.
Call ahead before visiting.
Limit visits to a reasonable amount of time.
Be considerate of neighbors' schedules. .
Don't take advantage of a neighbor's expertise or talent. .
Say thanks for any favors.
Be respectful of privacy.
Be respectful of property.

Welcome to Homeownership

Condo and townhouse owners have their own private space, but walls, ceilings, and common areas are shared. Post's *Etipedia* says that "residents should take responsibility for keeping common areas neat and litter-free and report any damage to maintenance. Designated containers should be used for trash and recycling. If the bin is overflowing, leave your trash bagged neatly and immediately report the problem to maintenance. Condo and townhouse owners accept a certain amount of noise as a fact of life. Establish quiet times in the morning and evenings. It's easier to come to an agreement ahead of time than be the subject of someone's complaint."

For Homeowners Etipedia suggests that "As a good neighbor, it's important to keep your property looking neat, and to follow any local ordinances regarding lawn care, trash disposal, and yard sales."

Have Children at Play? Etipedia comments that: "It's up to parents to keep a watchful eye: Youngsters can easily forget their manners and the rules of safety when they're curious or caught up in play."

Additional suggestions worth keeping in mind

Borrowing Tools: Return in better condition than you found, for example wipe a tool clean instead of returning with grease.

Helping Neighbors: Some neighbors prefer to keep to themselves; preferring to not help others or ask for help. There are times though that concerns, even emergencies arise where neighbors and towns may pull together to help each other. During snowstorms, hurricanes and tornadoes, power outages or a family emergency we may all need some type of assistance along the way. When one neighbor is able to help others in some way because they have a snow plow, or blower in a major snow storm is the neighborly help worth providing? If a neighbor normally clears their own driveway and they're away for a week during a snowstorm might it be a good gesture that they arrive home surprised it was clear and not 12 inches of ice, expecting nothing in return? Naturally, a person can't always be available to help all neighbors, use judgment and common sense. If you are on the receiving end of a random act of kindness by a neighbor it's worth keeping in mind and reciprocating when possible. It may be as simple as when the neighbor knocks on your door with their child, the courtesy of buying something they're selling for a cause.

Lawn and Power Equipment Noise: It may go without saying to avoid starting up the mower or chain saw at 7am on a quiet Sunday morning as the Emily Post tips suggest. In addition, keep in mind when possible to consider your neighbor at other times. If, in a conversation over the fence you become aware that this Saturday afternoon your neighbor is having a party in their yard, is it being a little considerate to avoid mowing your yard at the same time? Some times with a busy schedule finding a window to mow the lawn in between rain is difficult and power equipment needs to be run. The suggestion is brought up though to make homeowner's aware of neighbors when possible as a courtesy.

Dogs: While dogs are loved and part of the family, they often generate friction among neighbors when common courtesies aren't followed.

Welcome to Homeownership

When walking dogs, have a scooper or plastic bag in hand to pick up after as a courtesy to neighbors. Many keep the bag visible as a sign they'll be picking up after the dog. Many towns countrywide have leash laws requiring dogs to be controlled on leashes at all times. Dogs roaming loose are a concern for others safety, and even a friendly, playful dog can cause a child to crash a bike. Loose dogs often cause motor vehicle accidents, injuring people as well as often injuring or killing the dog. Dogs roaming loose frequently will seek out places on neighbors' property that other dogs "frequent" leaving a mess for the neighbors' to pick up, and ill feelings.

Having a Housewarming Party?

Bring the firewood. Many new homeowners have a housewarming party, allowing family and friends to tour their new place - often bringing a gift. The name *Housewarming Party* originated years ago, prior to homes having central heat. Guests would literally bring firewood as a gift to build fires in all the fireplaces and as a gift for the new homeowners. Many countries and cultures also have traditions that you may want to include, such as in France where the party traditionally included hanging the chimney hook to hang the cooking pot, as the last item to finish the home.

Add Some Practical Gifts to the Wish List: When you make up a wish list or guest registry for a house-warming, consider including a few practical and safety items along with the kitchenware. Though not pretty, an extra smoke or plug in CO_2 detector, kitchen fire extinguisher, or rechargeable flashlight can be important additions to a home for personal and family

Welcome to Homeownership

safety. Where historically the firewood is the namesake for a housewarming, today the fire detector may be the lifesaver. Wikipedia has interesting Housewarming details:
wikipedia.org/wiki/Housewarming party

From Dear Abby on Housewarming Parties

In Dear Abby's December 2, 2005 column a writer asked: "Is it proper for people to throw themselves a housewarming party? My husband and I are looking into buying our first home, and I'd love to have one. What, exactly, are the rules? Do you have to be newlyweds? I have never been to one or know anyone who has ever had one. Is it still done?"
Signed CURIOUS IN THE SOUTHWEST

Abby's reply was brief and to the point:

"DEAR CURIOUS: It is customary for new homeowners, after getting settled in, to invite friends and family over for a housewarming. You don't have to be newlyweds -- just new homeowners. Generally, the host and hostess send invitations to prospective guests and provide the food and beverages. And the guests bring gifts for the house. That's all there is to it! Good luck with yours."

Miss Manners on Housewarming Parties

In Miss Manners column from the Washington Post, Sunday, January 22, 2006 the appropriateness of housewarming parties was discussed by Judith Martin in a little more detail. Martin points out nuances of the intent of the invite: "That particular kind of party known as a housewarming used to be a rare event, as Miss Manners recalls. Once, perhaps twice, in a

Welcome to Homeownership

lifetime, when people made what they deemed to be a permanent move, they would be eager to direct their friends to the address where they would be entertaining them from then on. Pleased for them, the friends might bring the traditional, symbolic housewarming presents of bread and salt." According to Judith Martin: "Hoping to furnish one's quarters on other people's budgets is not a proper reason for giving a housewarming party; but Miss Manners doesn't only hear about this issue from greedy people and their targets. Polite people worry that a housewarming party always looks grabby. No, not if it is given in connection with a serious move for people who are likely to be going there often. Anything unsolicited they choose to bring may be gratefully accepted…and if the house is not new but the guests are, it is still fine to give a party. Just forget that word *housewarming*. It's a lot warmer, in that case, just to call it a party."

Welcome to Homeownership

Your New Neighbor

Once in your new home or at some point over the years you may have a new neighbor move in. While the initial time moving in is hectic and often overwhelming, a friendly and brief hello can break the ice. If appropriate, a gesture like baking some cookies or muffins; or in some cases a cold six pack may be more appropriate and remembered. If you have kids they can walk over with you to drop off the baked goods. This initial hello is easier than having months go by as a standoff is created by both neighbors wondering who should introduce first. Also, in the event of an emergency in the neighborhood it's good to know your neighbors in advance.

As a Homeowner, and the First Leg of the 3 Legged Stool

Now as a homeowner getting settled in the reality of household budgeting starts with *actual* expenses. We're able to see the true cost of owning the home monthly over the first year as items like heating and cooling costs become clear. During this first year especially, developing a household budget and establishing an emergency fund is important. Before squandering, extra money can be used to pay off outstanding debt such as student loans, credit cards and auto loans. Earlier we discussed looking at protecting homeownership like a 3 legged stool. Chapters 2 through 5 are about the financial "leg." **Chapter 2** looks at the benefit of building financial security, and places to *Find the Money* to do just that!

As a start, out of money spent monthly, **what expenses are for needs**, and what expenses are **for things you want but don't** *really* **need?**

Needs Versus Wants

Monthly Needs Expense		
Mortgage	$	
Taxes		
Home Insurance		
Utilities		
Electric		
Oil		
Gas		
Water		
Sewer		
Telephone		
Cable		
Auto Expense		
Auto Insurance		
Life Insurance		
Groceries		
Total Monthly Needs		$

Monthly Wants Expense		
	$	
Total Monthly Wants		$

Chapter 2

Household Finances - Find the Money

It seems many people spend more time planning for their *annual vacation* than for their *financial security and retirement,* which well-planned should be the longest vacation of their lifetime! Creating layers of protection for your home includes having finances in order. The goal of **American Homeowner** is to help you enjoy your home for many years, to pay it off and retire rich - or at minimum retire comfortably. But yet all too many homes today *are* lost to foreclosure, and from people of all income levels. Legal notices in classifieds of local papers nationwide advertise foreclosures of all types, from modest starter homes to mansions of the rich and famous often making headlines. It's much easier to be proactive from the beginning, than to have to deal with a looming foreclosure or tax lien on the horizon. Most tax liens add substantial and unnecessary additional expenses and legal fees, becoming difficult to dig out of. Aside from the potential of some of these liens to "jump ahead" of your banks mortgage lien and the potential to lose your home, this additional expense also puts a damper on retirement savings.

Ask anyone suffering from the stress and anxiety of foreclosure if they could have had a do-ever would they have handled homeownership differently? Most, if not all will say yes. The strain on family life and the resulting effect on personal health and marriages normally take a toll. Imagine the helpless feeling the day before having to move out of your home as your family packs up their rooms. The decisions you make today can set the course for a solid, successful homeownership track, or a derailment. Along with suggestions and tips to make your homeownership experience more rewarding and enjoyable, we also look to avoid the major reasons homes nationally get foreclosed on. Some things are beyond your immediate control, like the housing market. But most items are within your control and can be dealt with by proper planning. Caring for and having both your physical and financial houses in order will help ensure many happy years and a pleasant homeownership experience.

The Importance of a Financial Plan and a Budget

As a homeowner your needs and priorities may have changed. A good review of all income and expenses should be done to be certain you're on the right track. There are a lot of pressures today for you and your family to have the newest electronic gadgets, the best car, and the best vacation. Owning a home adds to the tug at your wallet in additional directions. Sometimes it means making tough decisions of where to spend your money, and holding off on projects that you'd like to do on your new home. You may have all finances in order and feel this section is preaching to the choir. Yet there are, as mentioned previously, a who's who of celebrities in the news facing foreclosure. If you haven't already been diligent enough to do it, the importance of creating a financial plan and budget can't be stressed enough. When a household is one paycheck away from not being able to pay the mortgage, the kids and family can't always have that hot new gadget or newest and largest flat screen TV. What would hurt them (or you) more...having to say no to something today that they "just have to have," or having to face the pain of foreclosure on the family if you over extend yourself? If, after reviewing all of your finances you feel that you could pass a "financial stress test," because you are on track, have an emergency fund and are financially secure, then it may be time to reward yourself for your hard work. This, then, without regret knowing you're staying within your planned budget. If the item is not in the budget, it may be worth saying that the expense requires the character building of cutting a few lawns or babysitting to pay for it.

The Effect of Foreclosure Stress on Good Health

We often hear of people who, after becoming disabled and out of work, fall behind on their mortgage and either sell the home or go through foreclosure; but what about the reverse? Instances where people of good, even excellent health begin having financial difficulties, fall behind on their mortgage and face foreclosure...**then** develop an illness. More and more, we're seeing the effects stress has on health. The medical community is seeing that often a major illness has been preceded by unusually stressful life events. Some types of stress are brief, such as when an animal in the wild is being chased by a predator. This burst of stress is acute and short lived while in that momentary danger.

When people go through financial difficulties, the stress is different. This type of stress...chronic stress doesn't go away. When this stress is ever present the body begins to break down.

Money and Time Saving Tips

Author Robert M. Sapolsky, professor of biology and neurology at Stanford University, and recipient of a MacArthur Foundation genius grant has researched this. His book: *Why Zebras Don't Get Ulcers: An Updated Guide to Stress, Stress Related Diseases, and Coping* looks at the science of stress. Sapolsky points out that people develop diseases because our bodies aren't designed for the constant stresses of a modern day life, like sitting in daily traffic jams and financial stresses of modern day living. Rather says Sapolsky, "...they seem more built for the kind of short-term stress faced by a zebra - like outrunning a lion."

As further evidence of the effects of stress on health, in 1967, psychiatrists Thomas Holmes and Richard Rahe looked at the records of 5,000 people; in all cases of illness a life stressor was present. The Holmes-Rahe Scale is a Life Stress Inventory of the odds of having a major health breakdown based on life events the past year. The chart that follows is from the American Institute of Stress website:
www.stress.org/holmes-rahe-stress-inventory

Money and Time Saving Tips

The Holmes-Rahe Life Stress Inventory
The Social Readjustment Rating Scale

INSTRUCTIONS: Mark down the point value of each of these life events that has happened to you during the previous year. Total these associated points.

Life Event	Mean Value
1. Death of spouse	100
2. Divorce	73
3. Marital Separation from mate	65
4. Detention in jail or other institution	63
5. Death of a close family member	63
6. Major personal injury or illness	53
7. Marriage	50
8. Being fired at work	47
9. Marital reconciliation with mate	45
10. Retirement from work	45
11. Major change in the health or behavior of a family member	44
12. Pregnancy	40
13. Sexual Difficulties	39
14. Gaining a new family member (i.e., birth, adoption, older adult moving in, etc)	39
15. Major business readjustment	39
16. Major change in financial state (i.e., a lot worse or better off than usual)	38
17. Death of a close friend	37
18. Changing to a different line of work	36
19. Major change in the number of arguments w/spouse (i.e., either a lot more or a lot less than usual regarding child rearing, personal habits, etc..)	35
20. Taking on a mortgage (for home, business, etc..)	31
21. Foreclosure on a mortgage or loan	30
22. Major change in responsibilities at work (i.e. promotion, demotion, etc.)	29
23. Son or daughter leaving home (marriage, attending college, joined mil.)	29
24. In-law troubles	29
25. Outstanding personal achievement	28
26. Spouse beginning or ceasing work outside the home	26
27. Beginning or ceasing formal schooling	26
28. Major change in living condition (new home, remodeling, deterioration of neighborhood or home etc.)	25
29. Revision of personal habits (dress manners, associations, quitting smoking)	24
30. Troubles with the boss	23
31. Major changes in working hours or conditions	20
32. Changes in residence	20
33. Changing to a new school	20
34. Major change in usual type and/or amount of recreation	19
35. Major change in church activity (i.e., a lot more or less than usual)	19
36. Major change in social activities (clubs, movies, visiting, etc.)	18
37. Taking on a loan (car, tv, freezer, etc)	17
38. Major change in sleeping habits (a lot more or a lot less than usual)	16
39. Major change in number of family get-togethers ("")	15
40. Major change in eating habits (a lot more or less food intake, or very different meal hours or surroundings)	15
41. Vacation	13
42. Major holidays	12
43. Minor violations of the law (traffic tickets, jaywalking, disturbing the peace, etc)	11

Now, add up all the points you have to find your score.

150pts or less means a relatively low amount of life change and a low susceptibility to stress-induced health breakdown.

150 to 300 pts implies about a 50% chance of a major health breakdown in the next 2 years.

300pts or more raises the odds to about 80%, according to the Holmes-Rahe statistical prediction model.

Money and Time Saving Tips

Note that on this scale, foreclosure on a mortgage is 30 points, and a major change in financial state is 38 points. Add in any of the other items that may be stressful in your life, and if your total is over 150 points the study implies there is about a 50% chance of a major health breakdown in the next two years. 300 points or more, 80% chance. Think about those you know where an illness has occurred, to see if the same appears true.

Be *proactive* now, to eliminate or minimize the financial woes all too many - even very wealthy US households face. This, with the goal of helping you lead a much less stressful life over the years. To fully live all of the *American Dream*, "that dream of a land in which life should be better and richer and fuller for every man." Having read this far, you understand that protecting the American Dream is worth every minute of reading time. Worth missing a couple of TV reality shows or ball games to protect, in order to avoid it becoming an American nightmare.

Be the Millionaire Next Door

Who are America's millionaires, and what do they look like? Surprisingly, millionaires aren't as many picture them, and many that look like millionaires, aren't. Often, for example, new college graduates with their first well-paying career position ***splurge.*** After years of scraping through college and Raman Noodle dinners, they *spend.* They buy the expensive luxury car, home (or homes,) and expensive suits. By outward appearance they look wealthy, *but never actually become wealthy.* The book, **The Millionaire Next Door: The Surprising Secrets of America's Wealthy** sheds light on characteristics of America's millionaires. The answers will surprise many, and tells how many ordinary middle class Americans become millionaires. Millionaires don't always look like millionaires. They often are your neighbors. The school teacher, janitor, and small business owners can and do become millionaires. It's done by living within their means - or more accurately living below their means, being frugal, and systematically saving. Most millionaires today are first generation rich. Being from modest backgrounds wealth is built *gradually*.

Find the Money

Look at all of your expenses. Even the seemingly "small" stuff really adds up. Author David Bach uses the term "The Latte Factor®" (2) and makes the point of how much these items add up over the years, using an online calculator on his website www.finishrich.com. Take an example of someone who picks up a cup of coffee and a hard roll 5 mornings a week, spending $3.00 daily - which is $15 a week, or $780 a year. Now suppose this was invested annually. In 30 years earning a 5% return they would have $54,413. Take this thought and carry it over to a lot of extra expenses that can be scaled back.

    Though a touchy subject and a very difficult habit to break, smokers know the cost of cigarettes well at over $8 a pack. A two pack a day habit of $16 a day over 30 years that could have been earning say 8% interest invested wisely - is depriving yourself of almost $715,000. This is without counting an increased cost for items like life insurance and health costs.

  (2) © David Bach, Author FinishRich The Latte Factor®

Money and Time Saving Tips

From the calculator at **www.finishrich.com**
$16 Daily with 8% interest earned equals:
- $ 6,307.20 in 1 year.
- $ 13,118.98 in 2 years.
- $ 20,475.69 in 3 years.
- $ 28,420.95 in 4 years.
- $ 37,001.83 in 5 years.
- $ 91,369.65 in 10 years.
- $ 171,253.81 in 15 years.
- $ 288,629.86 in 20 years.
- $ 714,499.87 in 30 years.
- $1,633,921.27 in 40 years.

Find Your Balance

You may have money to pay a landscaper to cut your lawn, or to hire a local teenager. You may also have the money to hire Lawn Doctor® to professionally apply all the lawn fertilizers seasonally. As routine maintenance tasks are needed, or home improvements undertaken which items should you do yourself and what should you pay to have done? To this, find the balance between your skill level, emergency fund/savings, and available time.

- How much savings do you have, and how much is needed?
- If there isn't at least an emergency fund in place of 6 to 12 months expenses can paying to have routine things like mowing the lawn be justified?
- Are you mechanically inclined to do some basic level home maintenance? Can you use a lawn mower, checking its oil as needed?

Money and Time Saving Tips

- Are you able to learn the skills, possibly by attending how to workshops and clinics?
- Do you have available time, or does your job and career entail long, demanding hours?
- When you are retired, at some point physical work may be difficult to do, making it necessary to hire out. In the meanwhile if you have the physical capacity now is it best to do what you can to accumulate savings for the future?

To some though hiring out can be justified. By working harder in a career, working overtime or taking on new cases, consulting or a part time job to earn income. To do what you are good at - and use this money to pay to have those that at are skilled at their trades help you at home. Is saving $1,000's at home by doing projects yourself similar to working extra part time jobs over the years to supplement household income? Saving by DIY projects can also be done as needed based on your available time, without needing to punch a clock.

Got the Music in Ya?

We know that getting on track financially will lead to a more successful homeownership experience, and richer retirement years. You may feel today that you'll never want to retire because you love what you do. It's nice though to have the ability to make continuing to work a choice you make and not to have to work out of necessity. You may even decide to retire a few years younger than your peers if financially secure. To get and stay on track financially to reach your

Money and Time Saving Tips

goals it's helpful and motivational to listen to and watch some financial programs. Radio personalities like AM Radio's Dave Ramsey **www.daveramsey.com** have grown to the point of having an almost cult following of faithful listeners, making him the frequently proclaimed third most listened to radio show in the nation. Ramsey preaches living a debt free life, except for the house. Then pay off the house. You can also learn a lot from callers to the show's financial woes to avoid costly mistakes yourself. Many people have a lot of radio time around the house and during drive time that can be occasionally used to focus on your goals. It's OK to listen to popular music radio stations, but is your financial security worth finding a balance? Some know the words to every radio song and watch every TV reality show, happily be-bopping away until they realize they are like a third of the country with no emergency fund and no retirement savings. If it's important to you to protect your home, build an emergency fund and gain financial security for your family it should be important enough to live the goal with a passion. Is it worth including some financial advice from many of the financial radio and TV shows in your mix of favorites?

You, Inc.
President and Chief Financial Officer

Spending money is *easy*. With credit card use exploding it's as easy as pressing the "easy" button to click and buy. Spending smart and within a budget takes more effort, but is worth it to protect homeownership and save for the future. Look at all household and personal expenses as you would if you were managing a budget in a business, including cable and phone.

Money and Time Saving Tips

To spend $200 a month for a cable TV bill really cuts into a budget, especially if there isn't an emergency fund in place.

Are you able to get by on basic, or an expanded basic cable and some free movies available at your local library, Netflix, or an occasional $2 redbox® DVD? Make some hard decisions and see where expenses can be cut until you are on track with all of your investments, and have an emergency fund to pay 6 to 12 months of expenses.

Sometimes as your own CFO hard decisions have to be made. If the paycheck comes in, and you're barely able to make ends meet, let alone save an emergency fund a change has to be made. It may even mean getting out of your comfort zone to get some traction. Getting rid of a large car payment...or payments, or cutting out a cable bill may make you feel you're making progress.

Try plugging in an amount you can save monthly on an item in a calculator such as on the finishrich® website and see how much that amount will equal when it's time for a child's college or your retirement.

Opportunity Cost

Money saved by digging into every dollar before it's spent is money you then have available to do something else with. $100 saved is $100 that can be used for some other purpose. It can be saved in an emergency fund, or invested for the future. The $100.00 can be put towards buying disability insurance if you're unable to work, or life insurance to allow family to stay in the home in the event of the unthinkable. The *opportunity cost* of spending the extra $100 a month on morning coffee, lunches out or extra Cable TV channels is that you wouldn't have that $100 to do other items that build and create financial security. Where can *you* save money?

Morning Coffee: Can you make a pot in the morning instead of stopping to buy every day?

Lunch: Can you brown bag lunch, or stock up when on sale and bring a canned or packaged item instead of buying out every day? It's good to support local businesses, especially if in sales but consider perhaps making buying lunch out more of an occasional or once a week treat.

Cars: A good rule of thumb for automobiles is that the value of your auto(s) should equal no more than 50% of your household income. If you earn $40,000 a year, driving a $20,000 car may be appropriate, not an $80,000 luxury car with its accompanying high maintenance cost. If you normally have a car payment can you buy a less expensive car without a loan, or have a loan payment that is $100 less? That's $100 additional monthly to grow in savings.

Loaning Others Money: Watch your finances carefully before agreeing to loan (or give) others money. If the amount you're looking to give someone in relation to your emergency fund and assets will strain your finances think twice. Is there some other way to help without giving money? Can they negotiate payments? Sometimes, helping find other resources can help more than giving money. Some of the nicest people in the world would give the shirt off their back to help others; and some of the nicest people in the world are found in foreclosure and bankruptcy court.

Money and Time Saving Tips

Business Owners: Business owners often have their personal finances intertwined with their business. When business slows, they'll pay staff before themselves. It's important to develop a budget, adjust accordingly and act swiftly. Many states have Small Business Development Centers. Often counselors are available at no cost through programs such as the SBA - Small Business Administration and SCORE - Service Core of Retired Executives. Do a business plan, and know what it costs every day to turn the key in the door to open for business. Get ahead of any change in cash flow before it affects your personal finances. Business owners are the extreme optimists, always believing the next great success is around the corner. Many business owners do have great success. The question though is "are you willing to bet the family farm on it?" Henry Ford went bankrupt five times before he started Ford Motors. Follow the business budget, have a personal budget, and avoid suddenly realizing property taxes haven't been paid in three years and facing a lien sale.

> "There are two ways of being happy: We must either diminish our wants or augment our means, either may do - the result is the same and it is for each man to decide for himself and to do that which happens to be easier."
>
> Benjamin Franklin

In **Chapter 3** we'll dig further into places in our daily lives to save money that's often otherwise wasted. Money that then can be used to pay off debt and invested to create **real** wealth.

Chapter 3

Money and Time Saving Tips
Find the Money

Look for places to save money every day. Make note and include other money saving ideas as you come across them in all areas of your life not only at home. For example with automobiles, keeping proper tire pressure in the car and changing oil and filters saves gas. Following are suggestions to consider. **As Foundation for Saving Money** keep the frame of mind in any money matter and purchases made that this is your money; you worked hard to make it. Think of how much time it took to make the money being spent. Think also of the *opportunity cost* of this money as discussed earlier. $25 isn't just saving the $25 today. It is: "what would this $25 be worth in the future if it were invested today?" Books and entire college courses are taught on the topic of consumer rights and smart money. The foundation of these five items begins our Money and Time Saving Tips. Additional suggestions are made in the upcoming chapters.

1. **Be a Smart Consumer**
2. **Comparison Shop**
3. **Shop Coupons**
4. **Get the Rain Check**
5. **Complain When Necessary**

Money and Time Saving Tips

**"Beware of little expenses.
A small leak will sink a great ship."**
Benjamin Franklin

"Benjamin Franklin 1767"
David Martin - The White House Historical Association

Money and Time Saving Tips

Be a Smart Consumer: Consider the home improvement, item or service you're buying. Is it something you really need? Is there another less expensive option to satisfy the need? Is it a rush purchase that should be thought about, needing to "sleep on it" before buying? Buyers that rush frequently end up having buyer's remorse, regretting their purchase for not having thought the process through. Often, people pay more attention to ads for products they purchased *after* the sale. After considering monthly and long term budget, if this is an item that is needed you'll feel better after your purchase knowing you researched well and bought the best product or got the best job for the right price by doing the following:

Comparison Shop: Not only to get the best price, but also to get the best product or job. For example, if looking to build an addition, getting three bids at minimum will not only show a range of price but also may uncover different, possibly better options. It may not necessarily be best to go with the lowest price. The ideas generated can be used with the builder chosen. Consider comparison shopping products by searching positive and negative feedback on Google® reviews, Consumer Reports®, and websites that search prices. Amazon.com has a price checking app, allowing the bar code on a product to be scanned by your smartphone to generate pricing at a list of stores and Amazon.com

Continue to Comparison Shop *After* the Purchase: Most stores will give you a credit to match a new price they advertise. Since you could package the item and return it to the store for a refund and buy the item at the new lower price, many will save you this trouble and simply refund the difference. Many will also match competitors' new lower advertised price.

Shop Coupons: When making purchases in stores or online:

Shop the newspaper circulars, and watch mail to utilize coupons. Friends and neighbors may also have coupons for products you use and they don't, allowing you to help each other.

Google the name of store with the word coupon before a purchase, and often it's as easy as copying and pasting a code to save substantial money online.

The Post Office has had moving kits for those needing a change of address that included 10% off coupons for Lowes Home Centers.

10% Off: Many stores routinely have at minimum 10% coupons available, often by simply asking the cashier. Many stores, including Home Depot and Lowes give 10% off for Veterans with their VA Identification. They may have a circular nearby, or have a coupon code they scan by the checkout. With the easy math 10% off on a $100 purchase is $10, on a $1,000 front door is $100.00, and on a $15,000 kitchen is $1,500 saving. It always pays to look for a coupon before buying!

Get the Rain Check: Stores often advertise a great price to generate store traffic, only for you to find out when you get there when the store opens it's already sold out. Often they did sell a lot, but frequently it can be a store using a bait and switch tactic. On getting to the store the salesperson may say that item is sold out, "but we have this other (more expensive) item." If you go to a store for an item that's a good buy, ask if they give a rain check; so that when the item is back in stock they'll honor the lower price. Pay attention and shop stores that follow good business practices.

Complain When Necessary: If you don't feel you're receiving the right value for the goods or services purchased let the business know. Mistakes happen, the mark of a good business is how well they do to make things right. Great customer service and follow up can keep a customer loyal. You'll be surprised by how many times standing your ground with a business when you know you're right will get you a refund, often more. If not, at least you know you did all possible to safeguard you money. Start by calmly letting the clerk you're dealing with know the concern, some have authority to make it right. Often, especially when a small concern arises, a simple email on the manufacturer's website or letter to home office will generate a refund, set of money off coupons, or supply of fresh product. If not corrected to your satisfaction ask for the manager and again firmly but calmly explain the concern, see if they can resolve or let them know what you feel is needed to be done. When you know your position is right, sometimes the suggestion - or threat to take it to the next level gets more action than actually going through with it. If warranted for example:

1. **Let a store manager know** that if not resolved you will be contacting their home office. They're busy, and hope you will go away. By them knowing you feel with all

Money and Time Saving Tips

conviction that their action wasn't fair, and that you'll make it your mission the next few weeks to have it rectified will get them to take action. A rental complex, refusing to return a security deposit without cause may warrant different threats than not receiving a rain check on a $5.00 item.

2. **Stating that you want the situation rectified by a date and time, or I will** : A statement such as "I see your position but disagree, and would prefer to work this out amicably. However, if I do not receive__by this Tuesday, June 15 at 5:00 I will spend my day Wednesday doing the following: 1) Complain to your home office. 2) File a complaint with our local police. 3) File a complaint with our District Attorney. 4) File a complaint with (whichever federal agencies regulates them - Federal Trade Commission, Public Service Commission, State Attorney General) If your complaint is in a written form listing each of these names, address and phone will show you will follow through. These, depending on the situation and severity. Most businesses will want to ensure they did all possible to make things right, and avoid the scrutiny, time and cost of responding to a regulator.

3. **Small Claims Court:** Again, first start calm and try to resolve the matter amicably to keep on good terms. The goal is to bridge the concern and keep a relationship with this business. If all else fails and it appears they are taking advantage, let them know that if not resolved in addition to the above you will file a

Money and Time Saving Tips

small claim action. Let them know it's the principle, no matter what the cost you will attempt to recover your money along with legal fees and other expenses. If the company you're dealing with is incorporated, they may incur the expense to pay an attorney to represent them, and also risk the additional legal expenses you are seeking. Again, it's hoped that letting them know in advance of your intent to not let this go away will resolve the matter. Most businesses are reputable, but on occasion we may find one that tries to take advantage of the situation, and hopes you'll let them. Again, it's your money.

Money Saving Tips

Avoid Known Homeowner Scams: Beware of unsolicited knocks on your door or phone calls trying to rip you off. There are legitimate companies that perform household services and are established in the community. Always check references, keeping in mind though the references can be their friends. Check Better Business Bureau, ask your friends and relatives for recommendations, and check with local authorities to see if legitimate. Some common rip offs among many:

1. **Driveway Seal Coat:** Often, a pickup truck will stop at homes saying they're seal coating a driveway on the street and have leftover. There's a chance it can be legit but begin with the assumption that it's not. Verify the company. Are they known to be local? Get references. Frequently a fly by night will spray some inferior coating, even used motor oil. This may look

Money and Time Saving Tips

OK at first but then washes away after you paid and they're long gone.

2. **Duct Cleaning:** Some scammers will arrive to clean ducts, may cut an opening but never do the duct cleaning.

3. **Chimney Cleaning:** Some may state they clean but don't; or may offer a very low price, only to point out damages to have you pay for major chimney work.

Trash Pickup: If you pay for trash pickup service, consider downsizing to a smaller container to lower the monthly bill. To do this, consider reducing your waste stream by: Separating recyclables, composting, making a conscious effort to buy products that use reduced packaging, or using a trash compactor. Self-haul to landfill on occasion, or switch to fully self-hauling to eliminate the monthly trash bill if cost effective based on landfill costs.

Barter: To save on labor costs hiring work out, keep in mind the option for example of gathering a group of friends for a painting party, or bartering to get a job done. Someone qualified for a project may also need services you offer.

Cable TV: Review bill and shop competing companies if available. See if any charges on bill can be dropped by purchasing devices like the modem, rather than including the lease cost of these items on your bill for years. Watch any promotions offered to new subscribers. Annually contact your cable company to let them know you are shopping. Having a better deal or competitors offer will often have their retention department match advertised deals to keep customers.

Money and Time Saving Tips

Frequently they will throw a choice of additional channels & features in to keep you.

Energy Savings: Money savings ideas in Chapter 14.

Garage & Storage

Canisters for Nuts & Bolts: Rather than buying canisters for garage storage of nuts & bolts, using Peanut Butter type or other plastic jars with lids work great. They aren't breakable like glass yet still allow seeing contents.

Plastic Storage Containers: Make a set of storage containers by using laundry detergent jugs. Take a utility knife to cut away an open area, leaving the handles in place. Great for miscellaneous plumbing, electrical, phone, cable and other parts.

Paint: Store Can Upside Down. Stored paint often develops a film and globs. To reduce this, store the can upside down to create an air tight seal. Make sure the lid is secure, and you may want to store on a tray, and/or in a clear plastic (such as reusing from produce) checking now and then just in case it wasn't. Instead of throwing away paint that has a few chips & globs try using inexpensive mesh or cone paint strainers (available at home centers) or an old pair of panty hose to strain the paint.

Shopping

In addition to the initial 5 foundation items, keep in mind:

Money and Time Saving Tips

Watch out For Mispricing: Often stores will ring the wrong price on products purchased whether because of human error, or computer glitch. In most cases stores will refund the overcharge, and many will give an additional bonus for catching their mistake.

Second Hand Shops/Yard Sales/Antiques: Leisurely visits to secondhand, yard sales and going antiquing may score items for the home and patio that may be better made and much less expensive than new. Some may become a craft/spray painting project to personalize. Be careful with old pre 1970 painted items if sanding to refinish due to lead paint concerns. Often buying antiques becomes an investment in items that may hold value over the years, instead of poorly made disposable items.

Closeout Stores: Often, stores that sell closeouts of windows, doors and building supplies can be a great source of items for the home.

"Would You Take $XX": When an item isn't exactly what you're looking for, and you don't want it that bad you may want to try and negotiate with the seller such as "Would you take $ amount? Most yard sales and second hand stores are used to negotiating, and include some wiggle room in their prices. If they accept your offer you saved, or they may negotiate with you. Of course there may be times the item was exactly what you wanted, and were willing to pay full price, but only you know whether or not it was exactly what you wanted. There's always the risk though in not accepting the asking price that you may end up not getting the item.

Money and Time Saving Tips

Fix It and Repair Café's: Don't be so quick to throw old items in the trash. Try fixing it yourself or seeing if a handy friend or relative can help. Repair Cafés are opening around the country, many in local church halls. From their home page: "What do you do with a chair when the leg has come loose? With a toaster that no longer works? Or a woolen jumper with moth holes? Toss it? No way!" www.repaircafe.org

Yard Sales & Recycling: You may not be a "yard sale person," but they can be useful in many ways. Having one or two a year is a good way to clear out unwanted items. Kids can earn all or a portion of the proceeds on their spring cleaning (to buy more stuff.) Yard sales can also be a way to meet your neighbors casually, learn about other homes in the neighborhood some of which may be for sale, and to pick up some bargains. There are also many ongoing Facebook yard sale groups that may be local. Items can be posted for sale, or yard sales being held can be posted. Many radio stations around the country have garage sale type shows where you can sell items free.

Avoid Landfill Cost/Find Stuff Free: Why fill your trash can, or pay to remove? The old adage applies, "One man's trash is another man's treasure." Place a free ad to find someone who may want, or look for someone who may want it by finding a local chapter of **www.freecycle.org** or through many similar Facebook Freecycle Groups. All items must be free. From a recycling standpoint, it's a shame to throw many useful items out to only clog a landfill. They can also be donated.

Money and Time Saving Tips

Remodeling? By offering the items free avoids expense of hauling away in a dumpster, and avoids the landfill. "We may not be able to affect change to the landfill issues of the world, but we can do our part. It gives some personal satisfaction to know we're minimizing our own impact, and may make a difference in how children, family and friends help the environment by your example."

Financial

Check FICO Score, and Improve: Your FICO score by Fair Isaac ranges from 300 to 850, and affects rates you'll pay on mortgages, credit cards, auto and consumer loans as well as home and auto insurance. Ideally, you'd have no loans, save and buy all items cash, have no need for loans and credit cards and have no FICO score. More likely though it's best to keep your score as high as possible in order to keep your rates as low as possible. Visit **www.myfico.com**, and click on the Learn About Scores page, and then the Improving My Score tab to learn items that will improve your score, some very quickly.

5 Year look back, Inheritance & Estate Tax: Should you, a spouse, or parent you may own a home with unexpectedly need to be in a nursing home for an extended period of time it may put their financial assets at risk. There's a five year look back into these assets, so we don't want to wait until one foot is in the nursing home door. Keep aware of how the laws will affect your assets. Get estate planning advice, and attend estate planning seminars many attorneys hold, especially if health is changing. There is planning everyone should do regardless of wealth. Will, Power of attorney, Health Care Proxy, and planning others should do depending on situation and assets. Not having a plan in place may cause a drain on financial assets and put the home at risk.

CPA/Accountant Advice Before Major Financial Moves: Often, financial changes are made only to find out that when income tax is paid the following April 15 there's a large unexpected tax bill due. We don't know what we don't know regarding tax planning. If an unusual financial event is being planned get advice in advance.

Capital Gains: If selling your primary residence or investment property, getting a tax professional's advice in advance may be in your best interest. For example, having lived in the residence two out of the past five years allows married couples to exclude up to $500,000 from federal income tax, and $250,000 for singles of the gain on the sale. A closing a few days short could trigger a gain tax. In the case of a married couple where one passes away, the surviving spouse only then has $250,000 exclusion. This exclusion for primary residence is allowed once every two years. The tax laws have many variables that apply to homes, vacation homes, investment and other property; a tax professional and planning may be able to minimize taxes due.

IRA/401K Withdrawal: Need to withdraw money out of a retirement plan? Know in advance the tax that will be due before taking the withdrawal. As a general rule, money shouldn't be withdrawn except to prevent foreclosure. Is it better to borrow against instead of withdrawing? Is it near year end with less income expected next year? Perhaps it's best to wait until after January 1st to take the withdrawal, putting this money on the New Year income in which you may be in a lower tax bracket and have an additional year before paying the tax.

IRA/401K Rollover: Rolling money from one account to another must be done following specific rules to avoid the event becoming taxable.

Income Tax Deductions and Credits

Buying your home, tax return the year of purchase: Review all closing documents with your tax advisor for any deductions. As an example, points considered prepaid interest may be deductible the year they are incurred.

Home Office Deduction: Do you have a home based business? Be careful to meet requirements of this deduction.

Home Energy Tax Credit: See if any energy saving credits are available such for purchase of certain Energy Star efficient windows and doors. Some credits were available through 2014 tax year. See if any currently apply to your projects www.irs.gov

Historic Preservation Credits and Grants: Seek if any available that may pertain to your residence.

Agriculture: Check for filing deadlines and requirements.

Money and Time Saving Tips

Moving Expenses Deductible? A variety of events including a new job can make the cost of moving and some related expenses tax deductible. There are requirements for distance from work and time frame. See IRS Publication: www.irs.gov/publications/p521/ar02.html

Think outside the box for ways to save money on a regular basis; and discuss any unique needs with a knowledgeable tax advisor. There may be deductions and credits available based on your situation.

We looked at a variety of money saving tips. These are only a few of the many areas you may find in your life. Keep your eyes open for places to save daily. In upcoming chapters we'll find others such as saving on property taxes, home mortgage and household insurance. Next, we look at ways to use these savings dollars to build up an emergency fund and long term savings. This, to help you lead a more financially stress free life, and avoid being a foreclosure statistic. Make a decision now to be proactive and plan for a secure future.

Notes

"A good home must be made, not bought."

Joyce Maynard
Domestic Affairs

Chapter 4

Invest it Right

"You've Found the Money, Invest it Right.
Build your Emergency Fund and
Keep your Retirement Dreams in Sight"

How much discussion on the topic of money and investing is warranted in a book on homeownership, without going off topic? Enough to ensure you're on the right track to financial security for your home and family. We just found lots of places to save money every day, and can continue to look for places to save in order to build financial security. Just as it's crucial for your home itself to have a solid foundation in the ground, it's just as important to have a solid foundation for your finances. The foundation for this financial security is having an **emergency fund of 6 to 12 months household expenses**; yet 29%, almost a third of all adult Americans have no emergency fund according to NeighborWorks America. The higher the unemployment rate in your region, and more difficult it may be to secure a job based on your education and industry the larger the emergency fund you may want to maintain.

Invest it Right

Where should your emergency fund be invested?

The emergency fund should be readily available when needed; an FDIC insured savings or money market account are good options. If it were invested in more volatile investments like stocks and mutual funds and needed at a time when the values are low or economy is in a recession you would have less money available. As a rule saving and investing, the higher the interest rate earned, the more risky the investment may be. Savings accounts and bank certificate of deposits (CD's) pay a lower interest rate and are not risky investments as long as they're invested with balances that include FDIC insurance. This emergency fund shouldn't be in an account that has a sales charge to invest in or take money out. As an example, as of this writing if you walked into your local bank with $10,000 to invest you'd see that interest rates paid on a savings account are less than half a percent. Lock the money into a longer term 60 month CD and the rate is up to 1.6 percent, though we don't want to tie this money up for 60 months. While we want the emergency fund itself invested conservatively, we may not want all money saved, including for retirement in low interest accounts. With the inflation rate currently running around 1.5 to 2% the interest earned in savings accounts isn't even keeping up with the increasing cost to buy things. The $10,000 a year from now will have lost purchasing power, which is like losing money. There are different types of investment risks, and this loss of buying power is an investment risk to consider. Keeping all of your money in low interest savings accounts over the course of 30 years will historically result in having much less money in retirement than investing in a mix of stock and stock mutual funds. With your emergency fund in place in savings you can then look to grow wealth in places that may generate a higher rate of return. As mentioned, the higher the rate of return, the riskier the investment may be. These riskier investments fluctuate in value, going up and down like a roller coaster. Watching these values daily can be agonizing so it's good to set up an investment plan based on your time horizon for the money being invested and monitor as needed.

To sleep more soundly, a financial advisor will suggest determining your risk tolerance. Most financial companies have risk tolerance worksheets on their websites. Requiring advisors to know their customers by asking probing questions to sense their tolerance to market value fluctuations, how you would react to seeing balances increase and drop.

Your $10,000

As an example of risk tolerance, suppose you invested $10,000 very conservatively and every monthly statement showed the value increasing by a small amount. After say three years the statement shows $10,500. No money was lost. Now suppose that same $10,000 was invested to get a higher return in stocks or mutual funds. The first statement arrived, followed by others showing the $10,000 dropped in value to $9,500. Would you pull your remaining money out and take the loss, or invest more? Now further suppose subsequent statements over the next few months and years show the value growing to $17,500 then dropping $5,000 to equal $12,500 at the end of 3 years. Would you panic that you just lost $5,000? After the three years in the first conservative investment scenario your account earned $500. In the second investment in equities, stocks and mutual funds: The account overall earned $2,500. The investment in equities earned $2,000 more than in the conservative investment. By having a conservative emergency fund in place as your financial foundation you'll be less inclined to panic and withdraw money when values drop, and able to stay the course to withdraw when profitable.

"The way to begin savings and investing...is to begin."

Your Investment Portfolio

A portfolio should include a variety of investments based on its goals. Money being saved for retirement in 30 years will have a different mix of investments than money being saved for college in 18 years. We wouldn't want the investment for college to be withdrawn at a point when stocks are low in value. Many mutual fund companies offer age based, or target dated funds that move the mix of investments to become more conservative as the date needed draws closer.

The Financial Industry Regulatory Authority (FINRA) has good information on being a smart investor. Locate their risk tolerance page that asks similar probing questions for you to determine your tolerance for risk. www.finra.org

Invest it Right

Risk Tolerance

FINRA.org suggests that both your age and your time frame for meeting financial goals play a role in determining your risk tolerance. If you're young and have a long time to meet your goals, you may have a higher risk tolerance than someone who is nearing retirement and is counting on investment income to live on for two or three decades.

But, according to FINRA "other factors may also affect your tolerance for investment risk. Your personality, personal experiences, and current financial circumstances also come into play. For instance, if you're a single parent, are responsible for the care of a sick or elderly relative, or have lived through a period of economic upheaval such as a major recession, you may be a more risk-averse, or conservative, investor. On the other hand, if you have a promising career, a generous salary, and little in the way of financial responsibilities, then you may be more comfortable in assuming greater investment risk."

Don't Panic

Above all, you need to feel comfortable with the risk you're taking. If changes in the value of your portfolio keep you tossing and turning at night, or your instinct is to sell your investments every time the stock market drops, then you may want to consider shifting to a less volatile investment mix; with a greater emphasis on more predictable, income-producing investments such as bonds and bond funds. The time horizon the money being invested will be needed also plays a role in the choice of investments. Don't be in a position where money being invested is needed to pay daily household expenses, or where a drop in value would make you panic. When values drop don't panic and sell. Ride the value back up unless the investment is in poor performing stocks or funds. When values drop, and the investments are good it may be time to buy more, not panic and sell.

$250,000 FDIC Insurance Guarantee

Bank and Credit Union accounts are normally insured by either the FDIC - Federal Deposit Insurance Corporation www.fdic.gov or the NCUA - National Credit Union Administration www.ncua.gov . Accounts are guaranteed up to $250,000 per depositor, per insured bank, for each account ownership category. The FDIC.gov website has a helpful YouTube video on their deposit page www.fdic.gov/deposit/deposits/ that explains how deposit insurance works. The $250,000 amount of guarantee may seem to some like an amount of savings that they have no concern being at risk for exceeding. On a regular basis though, through any combination of diligent savings, selling home or rental property for a gain; (sadly) inheritance, receiving life insurance proceeds as a beneficiary; or perhaps selling a business people often have over $250,000 at risk sitting in one account at one bank. The $250,000 FDIC insurance per depositor may be able to be applied to all your money by a combination of having accounts at more than one financial institution, and in more than one type of account ownership category. This following overview is from the FDIC.gov website:

Invest it Right

The Federal Deposit Insurance Corporation (FDIC) is an independent agency of the United States government that protects the funds depositors place in banks and savings associations. FDIC insurance is backed by the full faith and credit of the United States government. Since the FDIC was established in 1933, no depositor has lost a penny of FDIC-insured funds. FDIC insurance covers all deposit accounts, including:

- **Checking Accounts**
- **Savings Accounts**
- **Money Market Deposit Accounts**
- **Certificates of Deposit**

FDIC Insurance does not cover other financial products and services that banks may offer, such as stocks, bonds, mutual funds, life insurance policies, annuities or securities. The standard insurance amount is $250,000 per depositor, per insured bank, for each ownership category.

Receiving over $250,000? If you find yourself in a position of going to be receiving over $250,000 it may be worth considering having more than one check cut payable to you, and depositing in more than one bank or ownership category to avoid exceeding the $250,000 guarantee even for a few days. This often occurs after the sale of a home or business, and on receipt of a life insurance settlement. Discuss options with banker and advisors in advance to avoid exceeding the guarantee, putting funds over $250,000 at risk in the event of bank insolvency.

Invest it Right

Grow your money with tax free or tax deferred investments
With the security of a fully funded emergency fund and having no consumer debt except your mortgage payment savings will grow. Today, over half of Americans have no idea how much they'll need to retire[2]. Yet, we have no trouble buying a lot of sometimes unneeded "things" without giving it a second thought. Start kids out early to understand the concept of money. As they earn, teach them to save some, spend some, and keep charity in mind as appropriate. Being frugal and investing from the outset they'll be more on board with you over the years.

There's a lot of great information and calculators for building savings, retirement and home budget calculators, and teaching kids about money on feedthepig.org; a public service campaign of the American Institute of CPAs (AICPA.) Online calculators at www.feedthepig.org include goal setting, money management, paying off credit cards, student loans, mortgages and more.

View Your Social Security Benefits

As a starting point, if you haven't done this recently, visit the Social Security Administration website at: www.ssa.gov. For many years, Social Security would mail everyone an annual statement around three months prior to your birthday. This is no longer mailed, but statements are available on the website after signing up.

[2] Employee Benefit Research Institute EBRI.org
2014 Retirement Confidence Survey

Invest it Right

This will show if you've earned enough credits to receive Social Security benefits, along with amounts:

- **Monthly benefit if disabled.**
- **Monthly benefit at retirement age 62.**
- **Monthly benefit at your full retirement age.**

It's suggested you verify the Earnings Record reported over the years for accuracy in order to correct if required. Waiting years later may make correcting more difficult, especially if an employer goes out of business. Social Security is meant to be a backstop if needed in the event of disability, and to help in retirement. It was not intended to be an individual's only retirement income. Bear in mind the estimated monthly benefit amounts are in today's dollars, which may not go as far 20 years from now. To grow and maximize additional retirement savings consider: Grow More Money in Tax Advantaged Accounts

Employer Match: If your employer matches retirement money that you contribute take advantage of the match, it's free money and fewer employers are offering.

Traditional IRA: By investing through an IRA the investment is made with pretax money up to annual limits. Meaning instead of getting a paycheck that has all the taxes taken out, and then investing with money you've paid tax on, the investment is made before taxes and grows tax deferred. When the money is taken out either in retirement when tax bracket may be lower or for other qualifying reason taxes are then paid. Your contributions may be tax deductible depending on income, and other requirements. If you aren't contributing to an IRA see how doing so will impact your tax bill. At tax time, calculate your taxes, and then see the impact contributing to an IRA will have. Your tax bill should reduce, or refund amount will increase. That savings is money that can be contributed to retirement and savings. You normally have until April 15 to contribute to the previous years' IRA, making it worth checking out.

Roth IRA: Similar in some ways to the traditional IRA, but contributions to the Roth IRA are not tax deductible. Because taxes are paid on the money when it is earned, money then grows and qualified distributions when your money is withdrawn in retirement is then tax free. By growing your money in tax advantaged investments there will be a dramatically larger amount of money when needed in retirement. There are many online calculators to plug numbers in, including from Bankrate.com:
http://www.bankrate.com/calculators/retirement/tax-advantaged-investment-calculator-tool.aspx

Tax Advantaged College Savings Plans

Investment into college savings plans like **529 Plans** and **Coverdell Education Savings Accounts** are done with after tax money - meaning from the money received in your net paycheck. Earnings then grow without being taxed if used for qualified education expenses. 529 College Savings allows money to be saved for college tuition, room & board and other related expenses. Coverdell is similar (with lower limits) and also includes primary and secondary schools.

Beneficiaries may be able to be changed, and some make the case that even if it doesn't get used for higher education and the gain ends up being taxed you may be better off than if it were in traditional taxable investments all along. Since the gain isn't taxed every year it can accumulate more money. The earnings aren't subject to federal and many states' taxes. Above are a few, very brief and simplified ways to invest. There are many additional options, and requirements to meet tax regulations. Review your details with advisor and choose what's best for you. To **grow your money**, find tax advantaged ways instead of trying to save using money that has been taxed, and paying taxes on the interest earned each year.

"A little money, invested over a long period of time, equals a lot of money. "

The magic of compounding to grow your money

Compounding is what happens when you save money and the interest earned keeps earning interest, year after year, so it grows like pushing a snowball to make a snowman. By starting to save early and often the effects of compounding can create significant savings. A little bit of money, invested over long period of time, equals a lot of money. In an example of compounding from www.feedthepig.org:

"A 21 year old who saves $3,000 per year until age 65 at 8% growth will have $1,156,517, while someone who waits until age 28 to save the same amount will only have $657,948, even though the first person only put away $21,000 more. Don't wait to start saving!" Don't miss out on the benefits of compound interest. The earlier you start investing, the more you can benefit from compounding. That's why you need to get going as soon as possible. Ask anyone who's retired if they wished they had saved more over the years and most will say yes. **Before buying a lot of Stuff** you probably don't really need ask yourself the following questions:

Financial Plan: Do I have a long term plan in place?

Budget: Do I have a budget in place for each month before the month begins?

Consumer Debt: Are all credit cards and consumer loans paid off, with 0 balance?

Emergency Fund: Before allowing unnecessary spending, do I have 6 months (ideally up to 12 months) of readily available money in the bank as an emergency fund? This is necessary in the event of being laid off work, disabled, or for unexpected emergency expenses. Keep in mind that if out of work a variety of factors play a role in how long it may take to find a new job, including level of education, skills, and the unemployment rate in your area. Adjust your emergency fund accordingly.

College Savings: Am I fully on track with college savings should I have children?

Invest it Right

Insurance Needs: Have I reviewed my insurance needs including life and disability insurance to make certain I am leaving nothing to chance?

Retirement Savings: Am I on track with funding my retirement? Maximizing any employer matching contributions and/or funding IRA Individual retirement Account? Often businesses that offer retirement plans may have an annual staff meeting to discuss the plan and investment options. An employee that's 21 years old may not want to choose the same investment choices as a 57 year old nearing retirement. Each has a different time horizon and objective for the investments.

> **"Every person's combination of income, obligations and net worth is unique – so no formula of investing is universally applicable."** The Consumer Reports Money Book

If your employer gives you shares of their own company stock, or the option to buy company stock weigh carefully whether or not you want to keep all of your money in your company stock. Having "all your eggs in one basket" can either help if it all increases in value as in a Microsoft, or devastate you financially if the company goes under. Enron is an often cited example of a company that went bankrupt leaving all the workers that were relying on its stock for retirement to lose all. Often you may be able to move some stock away from the company stock as it gradually over time becomes unrestricted and is allowed to be moved to other investments. Make it a point to have a meeting with a good financial advisor for a consultation and set up a plan that you monitor and review each year. Most advisors will begin the process by doing a review, some in great detail looking at all income and expenses. Relate it to a Doctor trying to diagnose an illness over the phone. By getting all the facts, your advisor is able to make suggestions based on your needs and goals. Be sure you fully understand any products discussed – never buy something that you don't 100% understand, and don't be afraid to keep on asking questions until you do. If the advisor you are working with is not able to spend the time explaining the features, benefits, and potential risks of an investment find someone who will. It is *your* money.

Keep in mind the compensation method of the advisor you work with:

FEE-ONLY ADVISOR: Develops a comprehensive plan for how you can reach your financial goals, but leaves the execution of the plan up to you. This type of advisor doesn't sell any products or services except the plan itself.

FEE AND COMMISSION OR PERCENTAGE OF ASSETS: The fee (which may be lower than for a fee only advisor) covers the cost of creating a plan and the commissions paid to them for products purchased covers executing the plan. A variation of this arrangement would have an annual fee based on a percentage of the portfolio they manage for you.

COMMISSION BASED: The advisor earns compensation based on the type of product they sell that you invest in. The criticism of commission based, though a common practice in the industry is to ensure the product you're being told to invest in is right for you. Not simply the product that pays the largest sales commission, bonus, trip to a sales conference, or is the flavor of the month a home office is pushing.

"If it looks too good to be true"

Keep in mind that all through history there have been con artists praying on victims. Recently we've seen the likes of people like Bernard "Bernie" Madoff who *made off* with $18 billion of his clients' money. Madoff was convicted in a Ponzi scheme and sentenced to the maximum 150 years in prison. On paper with fabricated gains the accounts lost $65 billion. There are Ponzi schemes occurring frequently, where fraudsters take money claiming to invest, and replace with new victims moneys until the scheme collapses. Additionally, there are many well intentioned financial advisors that are enticed to sell highly risky or unregulated financial products promising higher returns. Often these advisors invest their own and family investments, sometimes losing all. In the case of Bernie Madoff, those he swindled include a who's who of celebrities, pension funds, church and nonprofit organizations, often investing because of the high returns someone they know has been receiving in the Ponzi scheme.

Helpful Financial Terminology

Diversify: Your financial plan may include a variety of investment products. By not putting "all your eggs in one basket" you may avoid risking all your assets.

Dollar Cost Averaging: With share prices of investments fluctuating up and down, dollar cost averaging is buying on a regular schedule regardless of share price. By doing so, more shares are purchased when prices are low, and fewer shares purchased when prices are high.

Breakpoint Discounts:

When investing with mutual funds, those that charge front-end sales loads will often reduce those fees for larger investments. A consideration in decisions regarding how much and where to invest is that of breakpoint discounts. Sometimes increasing the amount invested with one mutual fund company can reduces the overall fees charged. Many are entitled to receive these breakpoints but are unaware. Often investments are with the same mutual fund company but with different advisors. Review all investments carefully to see if entitled to sizeable ongoing savings. We normally know that buying in bulk can save money. The same principle applies to buying mutual fund shares. Some mutual funds that charge front-end sales loads will reduce those fees for larger investments. For example, a fund might charge a 5% front-end sales load for investments up to $25,000, but reduce that to a 4% load for investments between $25,000 and $50,000, and 3% for investments exceeding $50,000. The investment levels required to obtain a reduced sales load – in this case, $25,000 and $50,000 – are commonly referred to as "breakpoints." Funds are not required to offer breakpoint discounts and those that do may set them at their discretion."

Invest it Right

This from the Securities and Exchange Commission (SEC) website: www.sec.gov/answers/breakpt.htm

FINRA (Financial Industry Regulatory Authority) website offers a broker search to check the background of an investment professional: www.finra.org From their page: *Learn About Different Types of Investment Professionals:* www.finra.org/Investors/SmartInvesting/GettingStarted/SelectingInvestmentProfessional/P117278

"Your next step should be to understand which products and services each different type of professional can and cannot provide. Sorting it all out may be complicated by the fact that some individuals and the firms where they work may wear multiple hats, depending on the licenses they hold and the training they have. For example, an insurance agent may be qualified to sell you both life insurance and variable annuities. A broker may also be a financial planner.

Certified Financial Planner (CFP) website includes a page for types of financial planners: http://www.letsmakeaplan.org/cfp-pros-their-expertise/TypesofFinancialAdvisors

Mutual Fund: A pool of funds collected from many investors and operated by money managers. Funds are invested in stocks, bonds, and money market instruments and sold by prospectus which outlines the investment objectives. To explain the contrast of investing in a mutual fund to investing in an individual stock; think of buying individual stock as holding one pencil and snapping it in half. Then, consider investing in mutual funds as a stack of pencils which held together are more difficult to break. One stock dropping in value would be felt less than if all your money were invested in that stock.

Rebalancing: With a review of an investor's tolerance for risk having been done, rebalancing is the process of buying and selling assets in a portfolio to maintain the original asset allocation. Without rebalancing, funds may increase and decrease over time, moving larger percentages of investments into aggressive or conservative investments than originally planned.

The Way to *Begin* Investing *is to Begin.*

If you haven't done much of buying stocks and investing so far don't feel it's something only large investors do. It's best to get trusted, qualified and professional advice; and the way to begin investing…is to begin. Start paying attention to investment news. There are a number of online companies that allow you to buy and sell stock online. Some have a demo where you can practice buying and selling.

Websites like www.sharebuilder.com which is now part of CapitalOneInvesting.com allow you to purchase even partial shares of stocks, for example a $100 gift to your child can be invested in 2 stocks that may each cost more than $50, by setting dollar amount to invest in each. Investments that go into stocks and stock mutual funds can go up and down in value. As do mutual funds that invest in many bonds. If the economy were in a recession, or the stock market were at a low point, and you were laid off work or disabled you may not want to pull a lot of your money out while the investments are all low. By having your 6 to 12 month emergency fund available in a low risk savings or money market type account you're able to hold off withdrawing until the market picks up in value, without having to sell while the market is low.

Trying to jump in and out of the stock market is called market timing. Normally doing this doesn't work. By the time a person hears that stocks are going up, they've missed the train. It's Time in the Market - how long you stay invested as opposed to timing - trying to time when the market will increase or drop. The saying slow and steady wins may apply here. If you contribute the same amount of money each month to your investments – whether the market is up or down, then when the market is down, and stock prices are low you are able to buy more shares. This is called Dollar Cost Averaging. The average price per share you are paying is lower because you continue to buy when the market is down. There are some age based mutual funds that are set up to automatically move the funds. Say a college fund, where initially the investments have more in equities (stocks) that can go up and down, and less in bonds that typically don't fluctuate as much (but do also increase and decrease in value.) As time goes on the money moves to where, just before the college years the money is out of the stocks and into bonds which may not go up and down as much. You would not want to be at the point where money is needed for tuition at the same time that the investments all dropped lower had they been in stocks.

Invest it Right

We've discussed striving as a goal to live debt free except for your home mortgage, and then work on getting rid of the mortgage. By saving and investing, delaying the gratification of buying something until it can be purchased in full with cash and having no loans in the long run is a much more stress free way of life, and creates more substantial wealth. Next, in **Chapter 5** we help better understand the type of mortgage interest rate you have and watch for options to refinance to lower the payment, and ways to save when it's time to drop the expense of private mortgage insurance if you have. We'll also look to avoid possible concerns with tax and insurance escrow if included with your monthly payment.

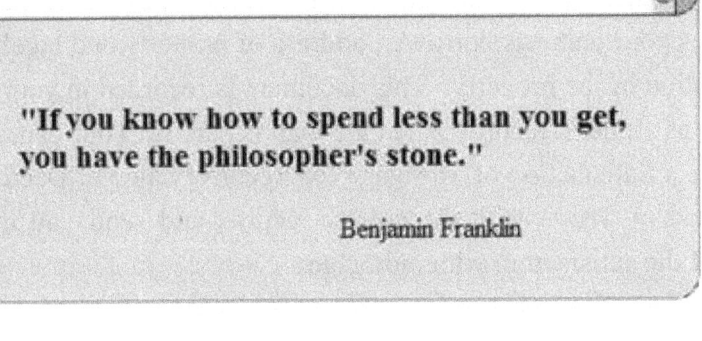

"If you know how to spend less than you get, you have the philosopher's stone."

Benjamin Franklin

Chapter 5

Mortgage, Property Taxes & Assessment

With all the work that goes into finding a home, buying and closing - it's a busy time. As a homeowner (or soon to be homeowner!) if you're not familiar with details of your mortgage it's good to know the basics. When the mortgage is taken out to buy your home two documents are signed. The first is the mortgage, which is sometimes called deed of trust, and a promissory note to go along with it.

Mortgage (or Deed of Trust) Provides security for the loan that's evidenced by the promissory note. The mortgage includes your name as borrower, address of property and legal description of the property. This document is recorded in your county as a public record. When the loan is paid off your bank will file a Satisfaction of Mortgage (or Reconveyance of Deed for Deed of Trust) with the county records and send you a copy of the satisfaction with mortgage.

Promissory Note Is the IOU that includes the promise to repay your loan. This outlines details of the loan including your name and address as borrower, property address, interest rate, term of years, and how late charges are applied. The promissory note is normally not recorded in your county records.

Mortgage, Property Taxes & Assessment

Mortgage Company Name Address Address Phone	
Loan Officer Name Phone	
Loan #	
Mortgage Amount	
Mortgage Type (Conventional/FHA/VA:	
Years: Interest Rate:	
Loan Servicing Phone #	
2nd Mortgage Company Name Address Address Phone	
Loan Officer Name Phone	
Loan #	
Mortgage Amount	
Mortgage Type (Conventional/FHA/VA:	
Years: Interest Rate:	
Loan Servicing Phone #	

Things to know about your mortgage:

1) Is your mortgage **Fixed Rate** or **Adjustable Rate Mortgage** (ARM)? _____
2) What is the **Interest Rate?** _____%
3) **How many years** is your current rate locked in for? ___
4) Is there a **penalty to prepay** the loan if you refinance to a new loan? Yes___ No___

Mortgage, Property Taxes & Assessment

Prepayment penalties are either a flat penalty or percent of the mortgage amount as a penalty should the mortgage be paid off early. Penalties often decrease each year. Understand if there is a penalty, and when it drops off. It'd be good to know this if in the future delaying a refinance or sale closing until after a certain date will save payment of a penalty. Some banks may put a penalty on to reimburse them for a special promotion, where they may have you pay back say the $500 they paid for title insurance if paid off early. Loans that are fixed for a period of time, like five years then reset to a new rate may have the prepayment penalty also reset for the next 5 years. For example, in year one there may be a penalty of 5%, in year two 4%, 3% in year three, 2% in year four, and 1% in year five. But then in some cases resetting at the new rate being set in five years to 5,4,3,2,1 starting the penalty over again. Know what you have or will be getting.

5) What's included in your monthly mortgage payment, PITI?
- **P**rincipal & **I**nterest on the mortgage
- **T**axes
- **I**nsurance
- Is there also **PMI**, Private Mortgage Insurance?

Are both property taxes and insurance included in an escrow payment or do you pay either of these yourself? Your Mortgage Principal and Interest payment could be either one of these types of loans, or a variation:

Fixed Interest Rate: Which should not change for the period your rate is locked in.

Mortgage, Property Taxes & Assessment

Adjustable Rate: To adjust at intervals according to your mortgage note. Say 1, 3, 5, 7, 10 years or otherwise based on index it's tied to - prime rate, treasury indexes, or a number of others. Know which index your rate is tied to, and when it is scheduled to change. A rate that is scheduled to change every three years according to an index, that all news reports say is raising may make you want to pay attention. If your rate will change in one more year, is it time to refinance? Or, to be careful not take on a higher car payment in advance of a possible increase?

Negative Interest: Some loans are written with negative interest. This is where a loan is taken out, but the payment due each month is for less than the interest due. Someone can borrow $500,000 today, and end up owing $510,000 in a few years. This allows for a smaller payment now, with the hope that the home will appreciate when time to sell, or you'll be able to increase monthly payment to pay down the loan.

Interest Rate

Look at your mortgage interest rate. Are you getting best rates available? What are current rates? How long will it take to begin to realize any savings if refinancing. Know milestone of when you may qualify for a better rate, such as when credit concerns may drop off report, or number of years on new job makes you qualify for a better rate. When shopping for a new rate compare all major expenses along with the rate itself: Any closing costs, application fee, mortgage points (each equals 1% of the mortgage,) title, attorney fee, etc. Compare rate shopped with a side by side list. Often, a locally owned community

Mortgage, Property Taxes & Assessment

oriented bank or local credit union offers good rates with reasonable closing costs.

Watch the Ads: Banks often run promotions where they pay closing costs to refinance, though on occasion will throw a prepayment on the new loan. Be careful if plans may include selling or paying off the loan.

For those with a 30 year mortgage, as time passes and you consider refinancing, calculate whether a 15 year mortgage can be within your budget to pay the loan off sooner. Other loans such as car loans or student loans may be paid off, and interest rates on a 15 year loan are normally lower than 20 or 30 years.

Calculate Refi Payback: When considering whether to refinance, look at all closing costs for a new mortgage, and calculate the payback it will take to realize a savings.

Pay off in 15 Years if in the Budget: If closing costs for a new mortgage make it not cost effective to refinance, discuss the option of paying the mortgage off based on a 15 year payment schedule. This, if your finances permit, having an emergency fund in place and on track funding retirement savings.

Are you leaving a job? Consider if you have a need to refinance first while your employment history is continuous. Many banks are looking for 2 years of W2 income as an employee, or 3 years tax returns if self-employed. Changing employment status can affect qualifying for a new loan.

Mortgage, Property Taxes & Assessment

Reverse Mortgages: If you're 62 or older and looking for money to finance a home improvement, pay off your current mortgage, supplement retirement income, or pay for healthcare expenses an option may be a reverse mortgage. A reverse mortgage allows you to convert part of the equity in your home into cash without having to sell your home or pay additional monthly bills. Some reverse mortgage companies are more reputable than others. It's important to research and work with a reputable bank, possibly a long established local bank in your area may offer. The Federal Trade Commission (FTC), is a good source of information to understand how reverse mortgages work, types of reverse mortgages available, and how to get the best deal.

www.consumer.ftc.gov/articles/0192-reverse-mortgages

In a "regular" mortgage, you make monthly payments to the lender. In a "reverse" mortgage, you receive money from the lender, and generally don't have to pay it back for as long as you live in your home. The loan is repaid when you die, sell your home, or when your home is no longer your primary residence. The proceeds of a reverse mortgage generally are tax-free, and many reverse mortgages have no income restrictions.

Private Mortgage Insurance (PMI): Many homebuyers lacking 20% or more down payment have PMI included in their mortgage payment. Prior to PMI, on a $100,000 house $20,000 was required to be saved as a down payment. With PMI, a buyer could put down less; say 5% or $5,000. With such a small down payment a slight drop in the home value makes the loan more than the house value. Often in a

Mortgage, Property Taxes & Assessment

foreclosure the home may be vacant and neglected causing an auction to bring in less in proceeds than the bank loaned. Often misunderstood, the purpose of PMI is so that in the event you default on your mortgage the bank is covered for potential losses, guaranteeing the loan.

Can You Save by Dropping the PMI Payment? As the mortgage is paid down, improvements are done, or the home has appreciated in value, your equity in the home may then exceed 20%. This is as though you put 20% down payment, as the banks' mortgage is then 80% or less of its value. Check with your bank for the process required to drop the sizeable monthly expense of PMI in your mortgage payment.

Property Taxes and Assessment

Property Taxes: Municipalities around the country raise money through various methods including through property taxes, as well as through their share of state income and sales tax. School Districts may raise money through property taxes or, in the example of a city like New York City, through income tax.

Review your tax bill carefully each year and understand all details fully. If you have any questions call or stop by the assessor's office or tax collector. Their website may answer questions as well. Understand taxes and structure, discounts, and exemptions. Know what exemptions are offered, if you qualify, and deadlines to apply. Applications may be needed to be applied for each tax separately, and some counties and states require reapplying annually. Some need proof of income submitted.

Mortgage, Property Taxes & Assessment

Assessed Value: Properties in most municipalities countrywide are taxed based on what the assessor believes its market value is. This isn't always correct, and the property may be over assessed causing taxes to be too high. Most towns have booklets explaining how to challenge an assessment and when Grievance Day is. Even if at first glance the assessed value appears correct it is always worth researching to fully understand. What appears to be a fair assessment and your true market value may still have you over assessed in comparison to your neighbor's assessment, and paying taxes that are too high.

An example would be where ten homes on a street are similar and each assessed for $100,000. A new buyer pays and is now assessed for $250,000. This home should be assessed at $100,000 or all the similar homes should be assessed equally at $250,000 by the town doing a revaluation. Taxing the one owner at the higher $250,000 was struck down by courts in what was termed "welcome stranger." Welcome to town – you're taxed higher than others now being the new guy on the block. Taxes are required to be fair and equitable. It's often best to arrange to meet with assessor first to resolve if possible before filing grievance. Review the assessor's records in case of any errors that you are being taxed on. For example, an outbuilding that was demolished years ago may still be on record, or an extra bath you don't have.

Homestead Exemption: Often, especially if property taxes are being escrowed by a bank, opportunities are ignored to find errors on the tax bill that could save hundreds or thousands annually. Many taxing authorities offer a homestead exemption on the primary residence, in some case on a land tax, other cases on school tax if collected - or on all taxes. This exemption is not automatic and must be applied for. If a deadline is missed normally applying later means not receiving the exemption for an entire year. Some states have unique requirements to qualify for a homestead exemption, especially where "snowbirds" from the north own second homes for the winter months. Proof may be needed by showing a car is registered in the state, or state income taxes paid as a resident. In addition, with a primary and secondary or rental property in the same state proof needs to be submitted to get the homestead exemption on your primary residence. Many states have been digging deeper to weed out property owners receiving homestead exemption on more than one property.

Other Tax Exemptions & Discounts: Aside from a homestead exemption, know all other exemptions and discounts that are offered by your taxing authorities such as senior and veteran's exemptions. Read requirements to qualify. For example, some municipalities allow un-remarried surviving spouse of a veteran to qualify for exemption, and some that assisted in civilian capacity during WWII may also qualify for exemption.

Tax Status Day and Valuation Day: Planning a home improvement, or getting a Certificate of Occupancy (C/O) for a project? Many towns have a tax status day, where they value the home on this day as the value it would have been worth as of a certain date. For example: Tax status day may be March 1, with the valuation day being July 1 of the previous year. The assessment is based on the value of the property on valuation date, and based on the property condition and ownership as of taxable status date.

Mortgage, Property Taxes & Assessment

The lag between the tax roll date and valuation date allows assessors and taxpayers to use all available sales before and after valuation date to estimate property value. It may be worth clarifying key dates your taxing authorities use, keeping in mind when starting improvements and/or demolishing structures to complete to avoid being taxed on their value an additional year.

Grievance Day: Many taxing authorities allow you to challenge the assessment on your property, and have booklets that explain "How to Challenge Your Assessment." If meeting with the assessor did not correct what may be an unfair assessment you would present the details to a Board of Assessment Review – or "Grievance Board." This can often be done on your own, or by paying a company to represent you. There are companies that specialize in challenging assessments, some taking no money up front, but sharing in a portion of your tax savings.

1. Review the assessor's records in case any errors that you are being taxed on. For example, an outbuilding that was demolished years ago may still be on record, or an extra bath you don't have.
2. Find other similar homes in your town and note their assessment. As a starting point consider if you'd rather own the other home or yours, and why? An application for grievance is completed, and often a cover letter can be attached to summarize. My home is assessed for $Dollars, These two homes are assessed for $$. My home has (pick out negative factors – wet basement,

Mortgage, Property Taxes & Assessment

etc.) Based on this my assessment should be $XX Dollars.

Escrow Payment

If your monthly mortgage payment includes escrow, what's included in this calculation?

When a mortgage includes an escrow payment, normally it's set up from the outset at the closing. It's important to know if you have an escrow account, and what's being paid through it. Some mortgages don't require escrow, some escrow taxes only, others require home insurance be escrowed too.

In a simplified explanation, you may have paid a full years property taxes and a full year's insurance by the time you closed. Then, each of the next 12 months you pay 1/12 of this amount monthly so when the bills come due a year from now your bank will have the money in your escrow account to pay the amount due.

In actual practice, the one year's taxes paid at closing may have reimbursed the seller for taxes he paid for the time period from closing day on, which you are responsible for. The amount calculated for the escrow payment is so that as each of the bills is due throughout the next year at various intervals there is sufficient money in your escrow to pay. Normally it's calculated with a 1 ½ to 2 month cushion because taxes and insurance amounts often increase.

There may be a number of taxes due at different times of the year, Town or City General/Land Tax, Village Tax, School District Tax (if your district if funded through property tax, for example New York City funds instead through an income tax.) There may be other miscellaneous bills you receive that aren't included in the escrow. For example, again in New York City the property tax bill may be paid through the escrow, but within the bill there may be water, sewer, frontage bills, and special assessments that the owner pays and aren't part of escrow.

Once a year the escrow account is analyzed based on payments made and expected in the next year, the monthly payment is adjusted up, down, or a surplus check may be mailed back to you.

Often when taxes are escrowed and paid by the bank the owner doesn't get the tax bill. Obtain copies of each from the tax office or online if available and review all details, exemptions and assessed value.

Normally escrow accounts work like clockwork, but it pays to understand details. Trust it will work as set up – but verify. If you have more than one parcel that's supposed to be escrowed verify taxes are paid on all. Some properties straddle more than one tax district complicating further with additional tax bills. Verify all are paid correctly. A bill due shortly after closing may get mailed to the previous owner, if the title company didn't have details at closing time to collect payment. With many banks outsourcing the servicing of loans and escrow payments to third party providers errors can occur. Payments may be made to a tax office in bulk for dozens, even hundreds of parcels. A mistype of one digit in a lot number can create an unpaid bill, making it best to follow the process closely.

Shorting an Escrow Payment: Don't let an escrow portion of your payment that changed by even a small amount make your

Mortgage, Property Taxes & Assessment

payment late and affect your good credit rating. Banks may need to refigure the escrow portion of payment annually to allow for changes in property tax and insurance if escrowed. A change that you neglect to adjust in the payment you send in can cause the entire mortgage payment to be considered late. It's important to understand what your monthly payment includes. Know the amount of payment due each month, and watch for any changes.

Your bank may be sweeping a payment out of your bank account, in which case as an amount due changes, they would normally adjust and take the new amount out of your account. Those with an automatic monthly ACH payment set up to *deduct* monthly payment from their checking may lose track of changes in payment amount due. Pay attention to any notice of payment change to be certain you have the funds available.

Bill Pay Services: With more people using bill pay services - if you are the one who set up a bill pay service at your bank to have a payment *sent* to pay your mortgage watch for monthly changes in amount due. For example, if your payment due each month is $1,000, you may set up a schedule to have the $1,000 sent for the next 12 months to pay the mortgage. If the payment amount due changes to $1,015 monthly you'll have to change the monthly amount scheduled to be sent. The payment amount due on some mortgages can change due to rate change, escrow payment change, or other factors. Sometimes it may change only by dollars, other times by hundreds of dollars. Not adjusting to pay the correct amount due can cause a late pay to be reported to the credit bureaus for as simple as not realizing the escrow payment amount due changed by $15.

Mortgage, Property Taxes & Assessment

Home Insurance & Mortgage Escrow

Home insurance can be included in the escrow, or some mortgages do not include insurance in an escrow payment in which case you'll pay the bill yourself. If not escrowed, your bank as mortgagee would receive notices of changes and non-payment. If changing insurance companies at the last minute on a policy's cancellation or non-renewal it may be good to let your bank know so they don't issue more expensive force placed insurance as explained below. If insurance is being escrowed, and you have more than one type of insurance policy understand which the escrow will pay, and which you are responsible to pay. Is there flood insurance, a separate jewelry floater, earthquake policy?

Force Placed Insurance: When banks require home or other types of insurance as a condition for making the loan, you are required to maintain this insurance. When the bank is notified that the insurance is cancelling, they will write what is known as force placed insurance to protect their interest. Key points to know about force placed insurance:

1. This insurance protects only the bank's mortgage.
2. If the bank is owed $100,000 and the cost to rebuild the home is $500,000 it will only pay off the bank's $100,000 loan in the event of a claim.
3. It will not pay for your contents.
4. Will not cover you if a liability lawsuit.
5. Due to the nature of force placed insurance it is much more expensive than having your own policy. It's quickly placed, not knowing the condition of the home,

Mortgage, Property Taxes & Assessment

if vacant or occupied, and without details of the occupants. Force placed insurance has been in the news recently, with banks that owned insurance agencies accused of overcharging and profiting at the expense of homeowners. The concern was that these homeowners, who may have been having financial difficulties already and can least afford it had large expense of force placed insurance added to their monthly escrow payment.

Mortgage Life Insurance: Is Life insurance that pays the mortgage off in the event of the death of insured. When this type of life insurance is written through the lender it does just that – pays the mortgage, which may be all that you want it to do. Having a policy that you own and ear mark to pay off the mortgage may be a better option. It's often less expensive to have a policy not tied to the mortgage, and if you sell the house or refinance it will remain in force. A change in health may make you pay more or not qualify for a new policy to cover a new mortgage. See discussion on this in Home and Family Insurance.

Unpaid Tax, Water, Sewer and Other Lien Sales

Losing your home for not paying a $496 Sewer Bill: When a property owner falls behind on their property taxes, water, sewer and other levies it can be very difficult to get caught up. Municipalities add hefty late charges, interest, advertising expense, and legal fees. Municipalities, school districts, counties and states have different methods of handling unpaid levies. For example, an unpaid school tax may get sent to the county to pay, who then adds penalty and interest to have the

Mortgage, Property Taxes & Assessment

property owner pay or be sold at lien sale. Sometimes, as delinquent years pile up municipalities follow their own unique process for redemption. As an example, a property owner may be required to pay the current year taxes before being able to redeem a three year old delinquency to avoid an auction of their property for back taxes.

Today more than ever, cash strapped municipalities are looking for ways to collect delinquent payments sooner. Each has their own process for collection, at times changing from year to year. Some will wait until arrears are three years past due then hold an auction for delinquent properties. Some sell the liens shortly after becoming delinquent. Many municipalities will sell liens in bulk to investors hoping to cash in on others troubles. For example, in Rhode Island, the Madeline Walker Act of 2006 was named after an 81 year old woman was evicted from her home in December 2005 because she had failed pay a sewer bill of $496. Under the new Rhode Island law, effective January 1, 2007, cities, towns, and other taxing authorities are required to notify Rhode Island Housing of delinquent liens well in advance of tax sales.

You may notice advertisements including pop up web ads to invest in property tax liens, promising substantial returns. Many of these companies pool money to buy large blocks of unpaid liens. Some are law firms buying liens across the country and adding a slew of additional fees to the arrears, including their legal fees in order for you to redeem. If an owner can't pay many offer their prepared financing plan with payment arrangements at high rates of interest.

Mortgage, Property Taxes & Assessment

In some cities and towns, these unpaid liens actually jump ahead of a bank's mortgage, putting them at risk of losing their collateral for your loan. The "lien loan sharks" in some cases may then own the property free and clear without a mortgage.

The AARP Bulletin April, 2014 addresses the topic of this predatory practice of buying unpaid liens. http://www.aarp.org/money/taxes/info-2014/tax-liens-target-homeowners.html and it uses a number of examples in addition to the above mentioned Madeline Walker case including:

In Syracuse, N.Y., Calvin James, 61: Now renting the two-bedroom bungalow he once owned after it was foreclosed on for back taxes. He had paid the city $9,877 in back taxes over but still had a $936 lien in place from 2011.

In District of Columbia: Melvin and Steven Phillips owed $8,000 in back taxes. The tax lien was sold to Elm Capital LLC of Jericho, N.Y., a debt-collection operation that sometimes snapped up more than 100 liens at a time at the D.C. Tax auction. Elm Capital had moved to seize the Phillips' home through foreclosure. The attorney for Elm Capital approached him and asked, "Are you prepared to pay $15,000 today?"

The AARP article states: "In some communities, it's not just property taxes that cause problems. Unpaid water, sewer and municipal fees lead to liens, which in turn can trigger foreclosures. And some municipalities add other fees, from "nuisance abatements" (when a city crew cuts weeds or mows overgrown grass, for example) to annual storm water assessments, to property tax bills."

"Some cities even off-load their tax debts to private firms for cash. Last August, for example, the city of New Britain, Conn., agreed to sell all of its delinquent water, sewer and property taxes in a lump-sum deal with American Tax Funding Servicing, which paid the city with a wire transfer of $6.6 million. In November 2013, a federal grand jury in Newark, N.J., indicted several individuals for conspiring, over more than a decade, to rig the bidding at municipal tax-lien auctions in the state by agreeing in advance which liens each of them would bid on, by flipping coins, drawing numbers out of a hat or drawing from a deck of cards. The long-running scheme forced many property owners to pay higher interest rates than if their tax liens had been purchased "in open and honest competition," prosecutors alleged."

With these previous examples in mind:

1. Stay current on property taxes, and all other levies including water, sewer and other assessments.
2. Monitor that all payments are made, receipts received and records show as paid.
3. Verify all answers received from municipalities regarding delinquencies are correct and have written correspondence received from municipalities clarifying answers.
4. If no other options to pay arrears, see if your bank can assist. They may be able to set up an escrow account and build this into your mortgage or a second mortgage payment.

The Insurance Leg of the 3 Legged Stool

Getting back to protecting homeownership and our 3 legged stool analogy, Chapters 6 through 12 look at protecting homeownership with the right insurance. In **Chapter 6** we look to understand the basics of family insurance from your standpoint now as a homeowner. The goal is to balance keeping costs reasonable in order to protect homeownership, with the need for proper insurance protection should a concern arise in the many areas of your life that may need insurance.

Chapter 6

Household View of Insurance Needs

"Insurance is the one thing you buy when you don't need, because when you need it you can't buy it."

As a homeowner your insurance needs have changed. If not a homeowner prior to now you may have had auto insurance and renters insurance, among other policies. As a homeowner there are now many additional risks we face. As with all insurance, the decision is made to either assume some risks yourself, or have someone else assume the risk...an insurance company. Paying for insurance may seem like a bottomless pit to throw money into. With all the types of insurance to pay for it may feel as though you're living to pay for insurance. Some may use the phrase that they're "insurance poor" due to all they pay year after year. Yet the term insurance poor can also mean having a claim arise that you have no insurance in force to cover, or defend you in a lawsuit. Insurance is the one thing you buy when you don't need, because when you need it you can't buy. When an event occurs that causes an insurance claim think of it like taking two pictures. The first of the claim, say a tree that just fell, or a car accident scene. The second picture a snapshot of your insurance policy. That's what will dictate the coverage (if any) you'll have to repair your house, car, pay medical bills or help defend you for a potential lawsuit. You can't call your

Household View of Insurance Needs

agent to add coverage or write a policy to cover something that happened yesterday.

Paraphrasing an insurance ad campaign: "The time to think about life insurance isn't when you're doing a 360 on the freeway." The reasonable solution to feeling insurance poor is to self-insure for as much as you can afford to pay out of pocket yourself, by having higher deductibles to lower insurance expense. Having large deductibles on auto and home insurance over the course of 10 to 20 years saves a lot of money. Then, insure for those risks you cannot or do not want to pay for, like perhaps a million dollar lawsuit. To take your insurance money and spread it around to cover areas that pose a potential claim that could devastate you financially.

We're looking mainly at home insurance and will explain differences in policies in the next chapter. The discussion though should include reviewing all your household insurance expenses and protection needs to protect your assets and find opportunities for savings. By getting all the available discounts including an auto/home discount when available helps protect homeownership; and taking some of that savings to buy life insurance to pay the mortgage in the event of the unthinkable is protecting homeownership. Having adequate liability insurance in place in the event of an auto accident - to avoid a lawsuit resulting in garnishing your income also helps protect homeowners. Additionally, from our discussion later on home insurance if it appears you have a need for higher liability insurance to protect your income and assets you may want to insure to the same level on auto and other insurances.

Household View of Insurance Needs

Take the Biggest Deductible You Can Afford

When a larger deductible saves enough to justify, consider the benefits. If you had to pay money out of pocket for an insurance claim would you rather get stuck paying $250 yourself or $700,000? Would you lose more sleep over having to pay an extra $250 to fix your home after a claim, or if your dog bit someone and you received a knock on the door with a subpoena for a $1 million lawsuit? Ask anyone who's ever been sued if a million dollar lawsuit dragging on for years in the courts caused some sleepless nights. We'll discuss insurance coverage further, but if you're not familiar with it, the liability portion of insurance is what pays if you're found to be legally liability for a mishap. If your home insurance policy were the exact same price to have a $250 deductible for your claims, with $300,000 liability coverage, as a policy with $500 deductible and $1 million of liability coverage which would you prefer? Now what if the policy with $1 million liability may actually cost less which would you prefer? The point here is to not make you pay more for insurance, but to self-insure for the small stuff, and insure for the things that could devastate you financially.

    Discuss with your insurance agent the savings of raising deductibles on cars with collision, home, and other policies. Consider even dropping collision on older cars with no bank loan, possibly keeping comprehensive coverage for other claims and glass coverage. Then estimate the number of years it takes to pay itself back. You may be surprised at how much you can save. If by raising your auto collision deductible on all cars from $250 to $500 you were to save $100 per year, you'd be paying $250 additional for a dent, but saving $100 every

Household View of Insurance Needs

year. If you bought a TV set for $250 would you pay $100 per year to insure it? That would be expensive insurance. The downside is if there were an accident right away you didn't have a chance to save. If in the winter climates now, perhaps raise deductible after the winter in case of icy road accidents. Add up ongoing savings in year two, year three and so forth, and the savings really multiply. Also, if you were to invest that $100 savings per year in some good growth investments you may see a sizeable amount in 20 years.

Could this money be put to better use someplace else? Life insurance to help pay off the mortgage, disability insurance? Or, it can be saved as additional money towards your emergency fund to have cash on hand. The goal here is not to make you pay more money for insurance, but to spread your insurance dollar around to cover a variety of risks you may face, at home as well as in all areas of your life. If a concern arises where you are sued for something that you have no insurance coverage for, have you spent a lot of money for insurance that could have been better allocated to cover the risks in your life? The other benefit to keeping deductibles higher is it discourages putting in small insurance claims.

Since you never know what the next three years will bring why put a claim for a little ding backing into your lamp post? Incidents where there are other parties involved, injuries and a potential for lawsuit claims need to be reported to your insurer. Review auto insurance policies and understand all the coverage's and premiums being paid. Items such as car rental coverage in the event of a claim may not be cost effective, and is an example of small items you may want to self-insure for. A policy with say 2 to 4 cars all paying to get a rental may cost

Household View of Insurance Needs

more over the course of a few years than the benefit received. If someone damages your car, and they have insurance that accepts liability they'll have to reimburse you for a car rental. Normally, on your policy the most you would receive is 30 days of a rental, but most only use a few days while their car is in the shop. If your policy has $30 a day rental coverage the most you would receive is $900 of benefit if an accident with one car happens once in the year. Can you self-insure or share cars if needed to save this annual cost?

Less than 10% to Insure Rule of Thumb: If it costs more than 10 % of the value of an item to insure it for damage may not pay. 10% of a $500 TV is $50.00. If it cost $25 to insure it may pay. $50 or more to insure may not be cost effective. To say, take a deductible that's $500 larger on a home insurance policy and only save $25 a year may not be cost effective. A deductible raised from $500 to $1,000 would mean paying an additional $500 for a claim. $500 divided by $25 means it would take 20 years to save the extra $500 you'd have to pay for a claim. This 10% may be applicable to physical damage and theft to an item, but not for liability. A motorcycle that's only worth $250 pays to have liability insurance at a cost or $100 or $250 a year - but probably is not cost effective to pay additional for coverage for damage to the motorcycle.

Avoid Getting Non Renewed

An added reason to avoid filing smaller insurance claims is to keep a clean record with your insurance company. When insurers are profitable in your state they want to keep you as a premium paying customer. Should they begin to see

Household View of Insurance Needs

unprofitable loss ratios in the state (losses divided by premiums) they may look to reduce potentially unprofitable business. Companies may send notices of non-renewal to homeowners with say one claim in the past three years, or two claims in five. Also, if a homeowner who has had a few claims sell their home and look to buy another it may be more difficult to get new insurance. This, especially if the home to be insured is in a higher risk area of the country, or if there is a blemish on a person's credit. Insurance companies create a list of their underwriting guidelines. For example, they may say: "We'll write homeowners insurance on this side of Highway 1, closer to the ocean only for homeowners with no claims in 3 years or two claims in five years, and credit tier 1 & 2." Inability to obtain home insurance in a preferred market may cause a homeowner to get insurance through a non-preferred market such as the FAIR plan, essentially an assigned risk of home insurance that's much more expensive and not as easy to deal with.

The 15 minutes could save you 15% concern

A good detailed review of your insurance needs takes more than 15 minutes. In the conversation risks may be uncovered that will help you choose and set up the insurance program that you feel best protects your home and family based on your budget and needs. To do this, it's best to look at the entire picture. Marketing campaigns such as "15 minutes could save 15%" do not say *will* save 15% but it gets the companies phone to ring. The 15% savings is touted as due to cutting out an insurance broker as the middleman. In reality though, these companies while saving the 10-15% agents and brokers may earn have their own often much larger expenses of massive advertising campaigns to reach customers. In addition, their employees in call center cubicles have pay packages and benefits that are the expense of the middleman shifted to their payroll. There may be niches at times as with all insurance companies where these direct writers may be less expensive, but as a rule they aren't always. Understand any benefits and concerns; then get quotes and write insurance that's best for you. Often, to save a few dollars someone will call to "save 15%," and change insurance companies, only to realize they may have reduced coverage's they could have done with their present company.

With auto insurance being many insurance companies lead line, often when a home is purchased homebuyers will have the same company write the home insurance just as hastily. There is no comparison in the knowledge and skill set an experienced insurance broker brings to the table. Advanced insurance designation such as Certified Insurance Counselor (CIC) designations among other professional programs involve reading and understanding the small print in insurance policies along with an array of additional coverage's that are available. All insurance policies are not the same, and having the discussion may help uncover needs you may want to insure such as a home based or daycare business. In addition, local insurance agencies normally play a vital role in supporting your community, and are a resource you can walk in to and discuss needs and concerns as they arise. Insurance brokers may also provide guidance at claim time which can help with the process, especially when situations arise that need additional guidance.

Household View of Insurance Needs

How *can* so many auto insurance companies say the average savings switching to them is over $500?

Commercial after commercial, ads and billboards claim the average saving switching auto insurance is over $400 to $500. That doesn't say that everyone that calls will see a savings; they can receive 1,000 calls, and save one person $500. Most of the 999 others will not switch without a savings unless they have to because their present insurance is being dropped. They can then advertise that the average savings *of those who switched* was $500. One reason for initial savings is that there are many drivers who have tickets and accidents that their present insurance company is surcharging for, and a new company will also surcharge for. If the surcharge period is over, perhaps on the next 6 month or year renewal it will drop off on the present policy. By calling for a quote today there may be an initial savings as the surcharge is off. It's possible though that when the current insurance company removed the surcharge on the next renewal it may have been less premium than the bargain no agent company that was switched to.

Credit History and Other Rating Factors

In addition to your driving record, insurance companies may include a number of factors that can affect the price you pay. These include your age, marital status, garaging location, education and credit score. Where years ago insurers priced without using credit score, today most all do. If your credit is better than most you may see quotes lower than your present premium for home and auto insurance. If credit is worse than average pricing will be higher. In this case seek out an insurer that doesn't price based on credit score. Someone with excellent credit that has had the same auto or home insurance for decades may see a savings with a new insurance company, but may want to weigh the savings with the loss of tenure having had the same insurer brings. There may even be the option of writing a new policy with your same insurance company, if new tiering makes the policy less expensive.

The Value of a Good Broker

Taking a household view and looking at the big picture of having one broker who knows and understands all your insurance needs helps. A knowledgeable insurance broker can discuss the many variables to help you chose an insurance program that's right for you. Being in contact over the years with annual reviews may proactively suggest the need to adjust insurance. An auto policy that for example, grows to four cars and four drivers may benefit by moving one or more drivers on to their own policy. Homeowners with students away at school may want to make sure home insurance will extend coverage for their contents and liability insurance.

Own vacant land? Verify if liability coverage from your home insurance would cover a claim should someone be injured. Often also, when owning a second home liability coverage from your primary home insurance may be able to extend without paying for the coverage twice. Find an agent who will spend the time reviewing needs to write your home insurance. Then review your needs annually and as needed. Most agents will want to work with you, explain options and help you protect home and family.

Household View of Insurance Needs

Auto and Home Insurance with the Same Carrier

Though not always possible, there are benefits to having the same insurance company insure both your home and autos, along with other needs. There are cases though where one company isn't able, for example with some unique properties, or in higher risk areas of the country. When the same insurance company does insure home and auto a **multi policy discount** may be received on both policies. Both policies see that you have a second supporting line. If there were an increase in the amount of claims on the auto or home policy the insurer may retain your policies, and not non-renew due to the existence of supporting lines.

Personal Umbrella Policy (PUP)

Jury awards for negligence lawsuits have increased tremendously over the past few decades. Headlines often read of settlements in the millions when there is injury or death. When these settlements are for an amount over and above the amount of liability insurance on a home, auto, or other policy the insured's assets are at risk. Income may also be garnished to satisfy the jury award, putting all an individual has worked for in jeopardy.

Household View of Insurance Needs

Personal Umbrella Policies (also known as **PUP** policies) and **Excess Liability** Insurance increase the amount of liability coverage available in the event of a lawsuit. Normally, an insured is required to maintain a certain amount of *Required Underlying Insurance* in order to have the umbrella or excess liability insurance, which then kicks in if the underlying insurance is exhausted. The amount of required underlying insurance is normally stated in the policy itself, and should be understood at the outset to be insured correctly. For example, the policy may state that the home and any boat insurance must have $300,000 liability insurance, and the auto must have say $250,000 per person, $500,000 per accident. If these required minimum limits aren't maintained the insured may have a gap in coverage of several hundred thousand dollars. In the event of a liability claim for over these amounts the umbrella policy would provide another $1 million, and up to $10 million coverage may be available. Most insurers will readily write the $1 million policies, but may require financials to show a need as the coverage is raised to $2 to $10 million.

The names PUP policy and excess liability insurance are often used interchangeably, though they are actually different. An excess liability policy normally follows the same coverage as the underlying home or auto policy, without broadening the coverage. Historically, an umbrella policy provided broader insurance coverage than the underlying insurance itself, think of a large umbrella covering over your home, auto, and recreational vehicles insurance, giving more protection. Many Personal Umbrella Policies have offered more coverage than the underlying home policy in the area of libel and slander in

Household View of Insurance Needs

particular. There are companies though that use the term Personal Umbrella Policy without broadened coverage.

Self-Insured Retention (SIR): When an underlying insurance policy does not cover a claim and an excess liability or PUP policy does, the policy may require the insured to pay a retained limit. This may be a different amount than the actual deductible may have been on the underlying policy.

 PUP policies aren't that expensive, considering the amount of coverage and peace of mind they offer. As discussed previously, it may be worth considering raising deductibles when possible and taking some of the savings to include a personal umbrella policy. Keep in mind though that your insurance dollars should be spent wisely. It's good to have high liability coverage such as the umbrella policy, but consider the entire picture. If there is no life insurance in place there is a gap in that area. It may be worth considering putting money towards getting life insurance in place if budgeting doesn't allow for both. The liability limits on the home, auto and recreational policies may also be raised higher than minimum, without the larger expense of the umbrella policy. Some insurers will offer auto and home liability insurance as high as $500,000 to $1 million.

Changing Insurance Companies

When deciding to change insurance policies weigh whether the new policy should take effect immediately, or for a future date, say on the renewal. While waiting for a renewal is often cleaner to keep billing and a mortgage escrow account on track, it isn't always best. Consider which policy you'd be better off having in the event of a claim. If the newer policy saves money and or gives better coverage for a claim it may pay to start now. If your present company is cancelling, and the new policy is charging more for the same coverage start the new insurance effective the day and time the old policy stops to start the new coverage.

Verify Refund is Prorated: If changing insurance on a date other than the renewal it may be worth checking first to see if the old insurance company will cancel pro-rata, and refund per day to the day the new policy starts. If the old policy wasn't paid in full for the year, the final bill is better prorated to the day new policy starts. Most personal lines insurance policies will cancel prorated, but some will cancel with a short rate penalty, costing more per day.

Insurance Cost Needs to be within your Budget

We've discussed the importance of having enough of the right insurance coverage and to have higher liability limits in case of a lawsuit. Keep in mind also that the insurance must fit your needs, budget and insure as many, if not all of the risks you face. The insurance should also protect the level of assets and income you've worked hard to build. It's great to have to have $1 million liability insurance on the home and auto, but if it's unaffordable and the insurance lapses for nonpayment would it have been better to have lower coverage that you could afford to keep? To have high liability but ride an ATV without any insurance in effect for it is taking a big chance if there's an injury and lawsuit.

Household View of Insurance Needs

With an understanding of the basics of household insurance in mind, **Chapter 7** explains the different types of home insurance. Keep in mind that home insurance isn't one size fits all by any means; there are a number of different types of policies. Some will not cover items like a tree falling on the roof or pipes in the house freezing. Making getting the right insurance policy even more difficult is that often the new agent or call center employee doesn't even know the difference in types of home insurance policies.

Notes

Chapter 7

Types of Home Insurance

"All home insurance policies are not the same."

Most people don't read their insurance policy until a claim is denied, which is too late. Many insurance policies are written in legalese which is difficult for the average person, and many new insurance people to understand. It'd be helpful if there were a plain English summary of the major types of coverage with every policy as all home insurance policies are not the same. For example:

- Some home insurance policies only cover **10** types of claims, some cover **16** types of claims, and a better policy covers **all** types of claims except only those they list as excluded.
- Some policies will not fully repair or rebuild a home after a claim.
- Some will not cover a tree hitting your house, weight of snow causing a roof collapse, or pipes freezing.
- Some policies will only pay the used value for all your contents. What are a 5 year old TV and all your used clothing worth? Instead of being able to replace all with new.

Types of Home Insurance

It's important to understand what type of home insurance you have, and make sure it meets your needs and budget. Adjusting coverage and priorities does not always mean paying more. What follows is a brief overview of home insurance, which in no way can be a substitute for reviewing insurance in detail with a knowledgeable broker. Commercials often make light of insurance, yet having a serious claim without the right insurance in place can be very costly.

Homeowners insurance provides financial protection from disasters. The insurance is designed to cover sudden and direct losses. Sudden, meaning a fire, a frozen pipe, a slip and fall, or a dog bite. The right home insurance would cover a pipe bursting that creates water damage, but would not cover damage caused by water dripping under the sink for the past year causing a rotted floor. The water drip is a maintenance issue. Home insurance is not designed for maintenance, and isn't a home warranty to cover a broken appliance. Again, think "sudden and direct" losses.

Package policies: Most homeowner's insurance policies written today are package policies. It covers both damage to your property as well as legal liability for any injuries and property damage you or your family cause to other people. Damage caused by most disasters is usually covered, with the exceptions of flood and earthquake. Separate policies must be purchased for these. There are policies though that can be written to cover only fires, or only liability claims. Home insurance policies are not created equal. To compare policies

Types of Home Insurance

solely on the basis of the annual premium cannot be done. There are many variations of policies and coverage's for the house itself, how the contents are covered, and what types of claims are covered.

Choice of insurance company: The claims paying ability and level of service provided by the insurance company on an ongoing basis, and especially at claim time are also important considerations when comparing policies. Insurance companies receive ratings of financial strength by ratings companies such as Standard & Poor's and AM Best. Banks will normally set requirements that home insurance be with an insurer of a certain minimum rating.

Differences to look for in Homeowners Insurance

Of the many variations in home insurance policies, areas of greatest difference in what claims are covered and how much of the claim is paid are listed below; we'll discuss what these terms mean in more detail. Your insurance broker should be able to explain what type of policy you have. A concern though is where homeowners buy insurance from websites and shopping only by annual cost of the policy. Often, insurance buyers have no understanding of various insurance options, getting very little help online or through the newly hired call center staff. If you do prefer to get insurance by the do it yourself way, be sure to read all the coverage options. As a start, what we are looking for is to know if your home insurance policy has:

Types of Home Insurance

On the Dwelling and Detached Structures:
　__Actual Cash Value (ACV) or__Replacement Cost
　__Named Peril Coverage　　or__Open Peril

Contents:
　__Actual Cash Value (ACV) or__Replacement Cost
　__Named Peril Coverage (more common) or__Open Peril

Home Insurance, as well as Condominium and Renters Insurance offers 3 methods of settling claims:

Actual cash value: Pays to replace your home or contents based on a calculation of the replacement value, less a deduction for depreciation. This type of settlement normally will not pay enough to replace with new construction or items.

Replacement cost: Pays the cost of rebuilding or repairing your home or replacing your contents without deducting depreciation. This will normally pay more, and can even reimburse for more than the amount originally paid once rebuilt or purchased.

Guaranteed or Extended Replacement Cost: Pays the replacement cost to rebuild your home, even if it exceeds the policy limit. This gives protection against increases in construction costs due to a shortage of building materials after a widespread disaster. Extended replacement cost will pay a percentage over the dwelling limit, say 10, 20 or 25% above. Guaranteed replacement cost coverage offers the highest level of protection, though has been replaced by most companies with extended replacement cost. There is normally an added cost for this coverage.

Types of Home Insurance

Building Codes, or Ordinance of Law: Insurance policies will look to rebuild your home based on how it was before the claim. It won't cover the cost of upgrading the house to comply with current, possibly more stringent building codes. Adding an endorsement called Building Codes, or Ordinance of Law will pay these additional costs. For example if a wall has one outlet, and the new code requires two. Additionally, when there is damage to a certain percent of a home, towns may require the entire home be brought up to meet the new code.

To help understand the explanation of insurance policies that will follow consider the following example:

$100,000 House, Cost to Build New $750,000

Say you bought a home somewhere in small town America for $100,000 and took out an $80,000 mortgage. The home is a large 100 year old Victorian that needs work, in a less expensive neighborhood. It has high ceilings, many high pitched roof lines, and details inside and very ornate details in and out. There's also a large wraparound porch. If you got a price to rebuild the home new its replacement would cost $750,000.

Which insurance policy would you want to buy for this house?

A) Policy A has $100,000 dwelling coverage and costs $750.00 per year. Satisfies your bank mortgage and the $20,000 down payment you invested. If there were a loss you wouldn't want to rebuild the home anyway. You may take the money and buy a house down the street if one similar were available. Plus you still have the land value.

Types of Home Insurance

B) Policy B for $750,000 replacement coverage for $1,500 per year. This would satisfy the bank and rebuild the home even if the cost may exceed $750,000.

Policy A is written for Actual Cash Value "ACV" and is less expensive. ACV is calculated as the replacement cost less depreciation. The ACV policy isn't normally half the price because many of the homes written are older and have concerns, and policies still offer liability and other coverage's. In this case, if there were a fire that damaged the kitchen, it doesn't mean that since the policy has $100,000 of coverage that can all be used to rebuild the kitchen. We can't pick which half the house the $100,000 was insuring. All claims are settled based on the ACV, depreciated value of the kitchen. Meaning, the walls and cabinets are a certain age, and a settlement is made for less than the replacement cost to rebuild. This policy uses modern day materials like drywall instead of replacing plaster, and will not replicate ornate detail.

The replacement cost policy (B) is a better policy, and in this case costs more. If the home has been in the family for generations, someone may want the replacement cost policy to ensure being able to rebuild as it was. Replacement cost policies look to replace what was there, including plaster walls and ornate trim work. Some companies will not offer replacement cost coverage on older homes. Years ago replacement policies may have paid like a blank check, an unlimited amount to rebuild a home. Many insurers were losing their shirts with claims. Insurance companies found that often policies weren't updated with increased cost of construction. Today, most replacement cost policies state that you have to insure to the true replacement cost. This dwelling limit is then adjusted annually as the cost of construction increases. Then, if rebuilding due to a claim the policy may pay an additional 10%, or 25% or with guaranteed replacement costs possibly more if the costs came in higher. This say 25% is a good cushion for an isolated home claim. At times of catastrophe though where entire towns are rebuilding all costs for labor and materials tend to rise; and a 25% cushion may not be as much of a cushion as expected. It's important to insure to the correct replacement value all along to ensure the ability to rebuild.

Coinsurance: Many policies include a "coinsurance clause." that can impact coverage. If a damaged home were insured to 80% or more of the replacement cost value a replacement cost settlement will be used on a replacement cost policy. If the home were underinsured at less than 80% of replacement value the loss is settled on the Actual Cash Value (ACV.) We discuss this in more detail when we get to dwelling coverage.

Now, a last point to make on the example: If both of the above two policies were the same annual premium, which would you choose? Policy A may be a policy with a $100 or $250 deductible. It's possible that Policy B could be similar in premium by having a $500, $1,000 or $2,000 deductible if the bank allows higher. If we are looking at self-insuring for small things, and avoiding having many small claims in our claim history might it make sense to choose Policy B to insure the entire home better?

Types of Home Insurance

Lenders Unreasonable Requirement for Dwelling Coverage

Insurance needs arise with situations that are somewhat reversed than the previous example; such as where a small home is purchased in an expensive area. An example would be if a home were purchased for $500,000 in Westchester County, in the suburbs north of New York City, with the buyer taking out a mortgage for $400,000. If the home only had a $100,000 cost to rebuild the bank could not require $400,000 of insurance. Yet, often the bank will incorrectly require the borrower to get home insurance to cover the amount of their mortgage. On occasion, a bank employee will incorrectly insist that the amount of insurance has to equal or exceed the amount of the mortgage. It may require discussing further with a supervisor. Normally, banks can only require enough insurance to either A) Cover the mortgage, or B) To be able to rebuild the structures after a claim. The land has value, especially in this location. Homeowners with unusually high dwelling limits may want to review more closely and get estimates of the true cost to rebuild, and consider insuring to replacement cost. When in doubt, it's better to have additional coverage instead of being underinsured. The price paid for a house should have little bearing on the amount of insurance coverage on the dwelling. What's important is the cost to fully rebuild to protect the bank's collateral.

Types of Home Insurance

Property Damage Settlement:
Replacement Cost or Actual Cash Value

As the example above points out, there is a difference in settlement for property damage claims with replacement cost coverage versus ACV coverage on the dwelling. Replacement cost looks to replace at today's cost to rebuild.

Replacement Cost Calculator: Should be used to estimate the cost to rebuild the home, with adjustments made annually to avoid finding that 20 years later the home is grossly underinsured. Most brokers will estimate this value based on a series of questions about the home. The more detailed the calculator, the more accurate the replacement cost should be. A home can be built with inexpensive kitchen and counter tops, or high quality with granite tops, and upgrades throughout the house.

Contents: When used with contents coverage, replacement cost will replace your contents at today's cost. A television purchased 2 years ago for $1,000 that say has an actual cash value of $300 would be replaced with a brand new set. Even if a new like kind TV cost $1,200.

What's Covered?? Is your Home Insurance
Named Peril *or* Open Peril formerly "All Risk"?

The HO-0 through HO-8 Policies: Insurance policy types can differ in what perils they'll cover in paying claims. Perils are the various causes of loss that can occur. Many insurance companies will use somewhat standardized Insurance Services

Types of Home Insurance

Office (ISO) http://www.iso.com/ policy forms numbered HO-0 through HO-8 as a template, with many having variations of these. Additionally, some states have their own requirements. Aside from the HO-0 used for bank force placed insurance and H0-1 which is mostly discontinued, there are 6 of these policy forms currently in use. Some insurance companies and certain states will name the type of policy, such as Standard or Deluxe form. Below is a general overview of the coverage in each. Your actual policy should be reviewed for specific coverage's.

Named Peril Insurance

Named peril insurance policies will list each and every peril covered in your policy. If something happens to your home or contents and **the peril isn't listed in your insurance policy, it's not covered.** If the policy wording states: "you are insured for the following perils" then it is normally a named peril policy. Other perils can be added at additional premium.

If not able to read ask your broker to explain and show you if you have **Named Peril,** or **Open Peril Insurance**, which the latter covers more types of claims.

HO-0 | Dwelling Fire Form, is a Named Peril Policy: insures against perils of fire, smoke, windstorm, hail, lightning, explosion, vehicles and civil unrest. These perils only cover the structure. There is no coverage for contents, personal liability, or medical expenses. This is the type of policy a bank may place as force placed coverage when a borrowers' insurance lapses to protect the banks collateral.

Types of Home Insurance

HO-1 | Basic Form, is a Named Peril Policy: Has very limited coverage, has been discontinued in most states. Insures for **10** Perils: Fire or Lightning, Windstorm or Hail, Explosion, Riot or Civil Commotion, Aircraft, Vehicles (unless driven by the insured,) Smoke, Vandalism (limited) or Malicious Mischief, Theft (normally $1,000 limit,) and Volcanic Eruption.

HO-2 | Broad Form, is a Named Peril Policy: Insures for **16** perils. The 10 Perils just named, and adds: Falling Objects; Weight of Ice, Sleet or Snow; Accidental Discharge or Overflow of Water or Steam; Cracking, Burning or Bulging of Heating System or Air Conditioner or Hot Water Heater; Sudden & Accidental Damage from Artificially-Generated Electrical Current; Freezing. Includes personal liability and medical payments to others coverage.

Mobile Homes often use a version of the **HO-2**

HO-8 | Modified Coverage Form Basic is a Named Peril Policy: Insures for **10** Perils: Fire or Lightening, Windstorm or Hail, Explosion, Riot or Civil Commotion, Aircraft, vehicles, smoke, Vandalism (limited,) and Volcanic eruption. **HO-8 is the most limited of the coverage forms that is currently in use.** This is used primarily for homes that are older and lower in value, where the market value is much lower than the replacement cost to rebuild the home. The policy also rebuilds based on modern day materials and methods, without restoration of original materials and workmanship. Many companies do not offer full replacement cost policies on older

Types of Home Insurance

homes. Includes personal liability and medical payments to others coverage.

Open Perils Insurance (Formerly "All Risk")

Open Peril insurance policies are worded in the reverse of named peril insurance. Instead of listing the items that are covered, open peril policies state that you are covered for all risks, except those specifically excluded. Open Peril **then lists only the perils not insured for.** Open Peril policies were previously called "All Risk" Insurance, but changed by most insurers after many lawsuits claimed the name implied all risks were covered.

HO-3 | Special Form, Open Peril Policy: Normally covers everything *except what is excluded*, such as: Earth Movement, Water Damage, Power Failure, Neglect, War, Nuclear Hazard, Intentional Loss, and Loss Caused by government Action. The Open Peril Policy then lists a dozen or so additional exclusions to clarify coverage such as: Wear & Tear, Pipe Freeze due to not taking precautions to maintain heat or drain pipes, Birds, Vermin, Rodents or Insects. HO-3 Policy is the most common and includes personal liability and medical payments to others coverage. It is often also used for owners that live in a multi-family and rent to others by adding an endorsement.

HO-5 | Comprehensive Form, Open Peril Policy: Normally covers what the HO-3 includes - everything except what is excluded, such as: Earth Movement, Water Damage, Power Failure, Neglect, War, Nuclear Hazard, Intentional Loss, and Loss Caused by government Action. Then lists a dozen or so

Types of Home Insurance

additional exclusions to clarify coverage like: Wear & Tear, Pipe Freeze due to not taking precautions to maintain heat or drain pipes, Birds, Vermin, Rodents or Insects. This is the broadest of homeowner's forms, with open perils coverage for the dwelling, other structures and contents. The primary addition is the personal property/contents being insured for open perils, where other forms cover contents based on named perils claim settlement.

Additional Policy Forms

HO-4 | Contents Broad Form (Renters Insurance): Are most commonly Named Peril Policies for contents: Used for renters insurance, including personal liability and medical payments to others. This policy insures similar to the HO-2, without

Coverage A Dwelling coverage as in a homeowner's policy. There is an option to add coverage for alterations, improvements and betterments to resemble coverage A in a dwelling policy. The newer policy form since the year 2000 has the option to add open peril coverage by endorsement.

HO-6 | Named Peril Policy: Condominiums: Is commonly referred to as the condominium form as this is its most often use. Provides coverage for contents, and the structural parts of the unit owned by you can be insured. Many policies will insure contents, and start by including 10% of contents for unit improvements. So a policy with $100,000 contents coverage may start with $10,000 for improvements. Always verify the amount of coverage for improvements will replace all items

Types of Home Insurance

you are responsible for. This normally requires reviewing the homeowner's association bylaws and master insurance policy. Some master insurance policies will provide a summary of what their insurance covers and what each unit owner is responsible to insure. Some master policies insure only to the studs, and some insure drywall and all kitchen and bath fixtures as originally built. Unit owners own the airspace inside their specific unit, and an undivided interest along with all other unit owners in the common elements. Unit owners will want to insure for all upgrades not insured by the master insurance policy to rebuild as they have improved. Includes personal liability and medical payments to others coverage.

Co-ops: Cooperatives can be insured with either the HO-4 Tenants insurance if they do not own any of the structure; or the HO-6 if portions of structure are owned such as kitchen and bath. Owners of cooperatives own a share in the structure or corporation giving the right to occupy and sell the share (sometimes with board approval.) Owners do not own any part of the structure or land.

HO-7 Policy was left open by the Insurance Services Office because it is company specific.

Endorsements: There are also **over 100 endorsements** that can be added to home insurance policies to insure various needs, such as:

- Home Daycare
- Business Pursuits
- Rented to others, when renting out part of your home.
- Permitted Incidental Occupancy

Types of Home Insurance

- Property Rented to Others
- Personal Injury (to broaden coverage)
- Watercraft
- Backup of water and sewer
- Building Codes/Ordinance of Law, to meet new codes
- Loss Assessments: For those with homeowners associations, condo & townhouses.

Lipstick on a Pig

Having a basic understanding of the types of homeowners insurance we next review your individual policy coverage in **Chapter 8**. Keep in mind that with all the variations of home insurance policies, names can be deceiving. An XYZ "Deluxe" policy may be only a *Deluxe* version of the company's' most basic policy, meaning it adds some coverage's over and above their basic policy. Akin to putting lipstick on a pig, is *still* a pig. This policy may possibly be the most suited home insurance based on the situation and the insured's budget. The insured though should understand the type of insurance they have since there are many types of insurance to meet individual needs. When shopping and comparing insurance policies be sure to compare apples with apples. Two policies may be close in price, but one may give much better replacement cost coverage, the other a depreciated ACV claim settlement and no coverage for events such as frozen pipes or a tree hitting the roof.

Types of Home Insurance

Home Insurance Review Notes

Chapter 8

Review *Your* Insurance Policy

There are usually a few pages that are typed just for you called the **declaration pages**. This has who the named insured is, the insured premises, and details of the limits of coverage and deductibles. There are also many additional pages sent to policyholders that are "boilerplate" for different types of policies. When a new policy is written a full policy is received on issuance. Then, in many states annual renewals are received with only the declaration page and reduced information. Every 3 years a full policy is then received. In New York for example, many major policy changes or non-renewals must occur on the 3 year renewal cycle.

Look for the coverage that says **Dwelling,** and see how much your house is insured for. The first question is, if there were a total loss – would the policy pay a penny more than your dwelling limit? If written as a replacement cost policy with extended limits as discussed earlier the answer would be yes.

Some points to consider as you review your insurance

Named Insured: Being listed as a named insured on the insurance policy declaration page gives broader coverage.

Review *Your* Insurance Policy

Resident relatives are insured's, but if they move out of the household they are no longer resident relatives, and coverage normally ceases. Spouses and owners of the property are best listed as named insured's which may extend some coverage in the event of a separation where one named insured no longer resides in the residence. The concern arises when a mortgage may be in only one spouse's name, and the bank only wants their borrower listed as named insured to avoid the event of a claim check issued to both spouses.

Mailing Address: Verify mailing address is listed correctly, and be aware that notifying your insurance company of a change of address due to a move often triggers a review to see if a vacant house may be insured. (See **Occupancy** below)

Property Address: Verify the insured property address is the correct physical address and clarify if needed. If your home fronts on two streets with a second structure like a garage on contiguous land list it to be clear if coverage is intended. Property Address can be listed as 123 Main Street to 11 Smith Street, Yourtown. Verify with underwriter that all is worded correct and insured as intended.

Town Class Errors: The Insurance Service Office (ISO) assigns town class 1 -10 to 47,000 US fire protection districts. The lower the town class number the better the fire protection and lower your premium. Often your responding department may be listed on the policy wrong, especially when PO Boxes and mail address doesn't match correct fire department. Check to see what fire department town class is listed on your policy.

Review *Your* Insurance Policy

Policy Type: Verify your insurance is the correct policy type. Was it a rental house that you now moved in to, that requires changing Landlord Insurance to Homeowners? Is it a condo that is also rented to others? Homeowners that become "Accidental Landlords" are becoming a growing concern. Job transfers out of the area, and households combining may change a home to become a rental. More insurance companies are denying claims on homeowner's policies that failed to change to landlord insurance, and courts are upholding the decision. This especially where many renewals of the home insurance policy are taken without rewriting to the landlord policy.

Occupancy: Homes are either **occupied, unoccupied**, meaning you live there but may be away, or **Vacant**. Vacant homes become a larger risk that may cause your insurance company to reduce or deny coverage. More insurers are including inserts with policies reminding of the need to notify them of material changes to the risk. If a home is recently purchased but not moved in to, or the old residence hasn't sold it may be best to keep both homes occupied with electric and heat on. Have a spouse or family member occupy, and keep curtains in the windows. Vacant homes generate larger and more frequent claims for insurers. A broken pipe isn't noticed as quickly, and fires may be unattended. If a vacant home policy is required to be written while a home is being sold, they are normally much more expensive, and may limit coverage.

Review *Your* Insurance Policy

Bank/Mortgagee: Is your bank name and address listed correct as lien holder? Are there additional banks listed that should be removed? Your bank will want to receive copy of insurance policy and renewals or they may issue force placed insurance. Additionally, having the wrong bank listed may cause a claim check to get issued jointly to you and the wrong bank causing a delay. Requesting a correction is easy, and the few weeks it may take now to have processed is much easier than waiting for a new corrected check to be issued at claim time.

Differences in Insurance Policies and a Cure for Insomnia

Take some time to read your insurance policy, and read or at least skim endorsements insurance companies sometimes attach to the policy to know what they're changing. If you have difficulty sleeping, reading an insurance policy may just do the trick. As insurance companies adopt different versions of their or ISO policy forms you may receive changes in your renewal. Reading and understanding your home insurance may trigger a concern you may need to address within you insurance. An example of a **huge** change many insurance companies slipped into their policies years back makes the difference in possibly tens of thousands of dollars in claim settlements to some long time insured's that may still be unaware. Some 15 to 20 years back home insurance policies that had guaranteed replacement cost insurance would receive whatever amount it would take to rebuild a home to the same pre loss condition. Rebuilding the home would be like a

Review *Your* Insurance Policy

blank check to ensure it was replaced as was. Insurance companies began including endorsements with policy renewals, with a heading "This Changes Your Insurance, Read it Carefully." Most probably just tossed the notice in the trash; leaving them unaware that the revised policy will only pay 10 to 25% more than their coverage amount *if* they are insured to the correct replacement cost amount at time of loss.

Nuances in Insurance - Life Happens: Some direct writers of insurance will make a policy appear to be something that can be pulled off the shelf at Walmart in a box - a commodity. Insurance though isn't always one size fits all and life happens. Policies need to be updated to cover new needs. ISO policy forms will get updated from time to time, and insurance companies may change to new terms. For example:

- Policies years ago didn't address differences between a personal portable item being stolen from your car like a navigation system that may straddle the line between being considered a claim on homeowners insurance or auto, depending how installed or used.

- A year 2000 revision in the ISO policy clarified who is considered an insured. A full time student under age 24 away at school in the dorm may be insured, but if they got their own apartment first for a while, then chose to go back to school they may not be insured under your policy. A laptop stolen, contents fire claim, or liability issue could be uninsured events. A golf game accidentally hitting someone with a misdirected drive,

Review *Your* Insurance Policy

or a malfunctioning small appliance starting a student residence building fire could create a very large self-insured payout.

With over 100 endorsements available to clarify insurance coverage when needed it's important to keep on top of life changes by reviewing with your broker. If going the self-insured - do it yourself route, don't just click and buy. Read all the available information and insure correctly. Everyone dislikes the cost of insurance, **until we need it.**

No Coverage Letter: Insurance companies are happy to collect premium payments, often unaware that you may have the wrong coverage in place. When a claim event happens though, and details are gathered if the policy doesn't provide coverage the insurer will send a letter that there was no coverage for the claim.

Home Insurance Notes

Review *Your* Insurance Policy

Major coverage's of homeowner's insurance policies

Home Insurance Policy at a Glance

Coverage Type	Description and Notes
Coverage A Dwelling	Covers damage to your house. Can be written for replacement cost (better) or the depreciated actual cash value (ACV)
Coverage B Other Structures	Covers damage to other structures, like a detached garage, barn, shed or fencing. Normally 10% of the dwelling limits automatically included whether you have outbuildings or not. Increased if the cost to replace all is higher.
Coverage C Contents	Covers damage to, or loss of your personal property. There are limits for certain types of property listed in the policy. For example jewelry may be $1,000, business property $1,500. Review and increase as needed. Often replacement cost coverage amount will equal 70-75% of dwelling limits standard. ACV coverage will include 50% of dwelling limits for contents limit.
Coverage D Additional Living Expense	Pays additional living expense necessary to maintain same standard of living when house cannot be occupied due to covered loss. May include cost to rent similar home and other miscellaneous expenses.
Coverage E Personal Liability	Protects you against claims arising from accidents, except auto and boating. Follows you wherever you go.
Coverage F Medical Payments	Pays medical expenses regardless of liability. Coverage limited to an amount per person & per accident caused by you, family member, or pet.

Review *Your* Insurance Policy

Dwelling | Coverage A: As discussed, the home can be insured for either the actual cash value (ACV) which would settle claims deducting for depreciation or its replacement cost. When replacement cost coverage is written a cost of construction estimator is used to generate an accurate cost to rebuild. These programs such as by Marshall & Swift www.marshallswift.com (part of CoreLogic) and others use detailed home information to generate cost to rebuild by location. Brokers may each have their own programs. All of the home features are compiled to generate an amount that it is estimated will cost to build new. Bear in mind that many older homes were built with larger wood, deeper window and door jambs and ornate trim raising the cost per square foot to build.

Are you underinsured? Over 2/3 of US homes are underinsured by an average of 18%. According to a survey by insurance services firm MSB, reported on MSN Money: "That means someone whose house cost $200,000 to replace would be short by $36,000." After many of the countries natural disasters such as Hurricane Katrina, tornadoes, and wildfires the media runs stories of how many homes were uninsured. Marshall & Swift ad on their website states "Is Your Home Properly Insured?" Then charging a homeowner $7.95 for a report to find out. A survey by United Policyholders, a consumer advocacy group states that where rebuilding costs are high the problem is worse - with 75% of the California homeowners affected by the 2007 wildfires underinsured by an average of $240,000.

Replacement Cost Coverage: It's important to insure as close as possible to the true replacement cost. Once a replacement cost policy is written, insurance companies will adjust the amount of dwelling coverage annually as the cost of construction increases, based on costs of labor and materials. If this were not done gradually, a homeowner may find themselves drastically underinsured 20 years later.

The "Coinsurance Penalty" concern: Most insurance policies state that a home with replacement cost coverage must be insured to at least 80% of the cost to rebuild to be considered fully insured. If not, it allows the insurer to underpay for partial claims. So a home with $100,000 cost to rebuild has to have been insured for at least 80% or $80,000. A home with $500,000 cost to build must be insured to $400,000. If insured for less the insurance company will treat you as coinsuring the house. If you were only insured for $200,000 you'd be only 50% insured, thus a kitchen fire with $40,000 damage would generate a $20,000 claim settlement. The rest is your coinsurance.

Other Structures | Coverage B: Following the same coverage chosen on the dwelling, detached structures would be insured for either the actual cash value (ACV) or replacement cost. Most insurance policies automatically include other structures coverage in the amount of 10% of the dwelling limit. So a home insured for $100,000 would have $10,000 of other structures coverage whether you have other structures there or not. This would cover also fences or sheds you install. If a tree were to hit a fence, the other structures portion of insurance is what would pay. If a house has a detached garage,

Review *Your* Insurance Policy

which later becomes attached by building a breezeway, the dwelling coverage should then be increased as it becomes part of the dwelling. If the cost to build your other structures exceeds the 10%, the coverage must be raised to an amount that would replace all detached structures. Homes with several large barns need to have the other structures coverage increased substantially for the cost to rebuild the structures.

Contents | Coverage C: When ACV coverage is selected, the amount of contents insurance is normally listed as 50% of dwelling limit. So a policy that has $100,000 of dwelling coverage would reflect contents coverage of $50,000. Dwelling coverage of $500,000 would have $250,000 contents coverage. At first glance, seeing $250,000 contents insurance a person may think they have more than enough coverage. The concern though is that any settlement would be at the lower actual cash value. A TV that new costs $1,000.00 would be settled for the used value, less deductible. When contents are insured for Replacement Cost most insurance policies will list contents at either 70 to 75% of the dwelling limit. A $100,000 home would reflect contents coverage of $70,000 to $75,000. This would give "new for old coverage" to give all new contents, without deduction for depreciation. The TV that cost $1,000 would be replaced with new, even if it cost $1,200 today.

Combined limits: Some insurance companies write their policies with combined limits, including both dwelling and contents in one larger total. This, to allow use of the money anyway needed. Verify the type and amount of coverage meets your needs.

Review *Your* Insurance Policy

Home Inventory

As discussed earlier, and worth repeating here, take a household inventory with support of photos/video of all your furniture, fixtures and belongings as you settle in. Many insurance agents have inventory booklets, and there are many online and as easy to use apps such as:

www.knowyourstuff.org
By the Insurance Information Institute
www.insureuonline.org
By the National Association of Insurance Commissioners:

Upload pictures and update as needed. Include make, model and serial numbers if possible. If not web based, store the inventory in your fireproof box, or off premises in the event of a fire.

It's easier to take an hour or two for an inventory now, than to have to sift through ashes in the unthinkable event of a fire or break-in and have to remember what was in the home.

Special Limits for Certain Personal Property: Homeowners policies normally have limits on 8 to 11 categories of personal property. Without listing each due to variations it's important to review the page in our policy.

Review *Your* Insurance Policy

There are limits of varying dollar amounts set by the insurer. Pay attention especially that **jewelry limits** meet your needs.

    $ 200 for money, bank notes, bullion, gold....
    $1,500 for securities, notes, tickets, stamps.....
    $1,500 for watercraft....
    $1,500 for jewelry, watches, furs, precious stones...
    $2,500 theft of firearms
    $2,500 business property while on the premises
    $ 500 business property away from premises.

Some of the limits apply only to theft. Review your coverage's and needs, then discuss with your agent.

Many limits can be raised by endorsement for added premium. **Jewelry** limits can be increased or scheduled with floater, to be discussed shortly. **Collectibles, Hummel Figurines, Sports and Memorabilia** should be reviewed and discussed with underwriter to confirm correct coverage.

A rule of thumb is that whatever should be insured on its own policy needs to be insured on its own policy. For example:

Boat: A homeowners' policy gives limited coverage for a small boat as personal property, but a larger boat with more horsepower needs its own policy.
An ATV needs its own policy, unless possibly only to service the property as a lawn tractor may.

Homeowner's policies aren't designed for a business. A business with $5,000 worth of samples needs to increase business property. Professional photographers or carpenters with tens of thousands invested in business equipment need to get business insurance.

Additional Living Expense - Loss of Use | Coverage D:
After a covered loss, additional living expense pays the additional expenses necessary to maintain your standard of living. This may include a hotel stay, or rental house. Often many miscellaneous expenses such as restaurant dinners, extra mileage due to longer work commute and cell phone expense may be approved. Expenses you would normally have without the claim such as property taxes are not covered.

Fair Rental Value: May be reimbursed for rental income lost due to the claim.

Civil Authority Prohibits Use: May pay for the above expenses for up to 2 weeks if authorities prohibit use of your premises due to a covered loss of a neighboring property, such as a wildfire.

Personal Liability | Coverage E:
Liability coverage is similar in most policies. It protects you against claims arising from accidents and follows you wherever you go. Most policies start with $100,000 liability coverage and most people write policies with at least $300,000 coverage. Additional personal liability coverage can be purchased inexpensively that gives a lot of protection and peace of mind. Most people looking to protect assets need to have at minimum $500,000 to $1 million liability limit as no one sues for "only" $250,000 today, and jury awards are often high. The cost

Review *Your* Insurance Policy

though needs to be within your budget as discussed later in the chapter.

What's not covered: With the concept of whatever needs to be insured on its own policy - needs its own policy, homeowners liability is not designed or priced to include certain exposures. The policy will list exclusions it will not cover such as liability claims involving Business Activities, Motor Vehicle, Aircraft, Hovercraft, and Watercraft Liability.

Trampolines: Some insurers will not write home insurance when a trampoline is present. Additionally, over the years many insurers have slipped "trampoline exclusions" into renewal policies. It's important to check to see if your insurer will cover liability claims for trampolines prior to buying a trampoline or switching insurance if you have one.

Medical Payments to Others | Coverage F: Is a no-fault type of coverage that pays medical expenses regardless of legal obligation. Coverage is limited to an amount per person & per accident caused by you, a family member, or your pet. Medical payments pays if someone is hurt, say in your home, yard or other insured location within 3 years of the accident, along with funeral expenses if necessary. It could even be a case of someone tripping over their own feet, with no negligence on the part of you as insured. Think of this as the Band-Aid or arm in the sling to avoid someone needing to sue you.

The "to others" of medical payments means it will not pay for injuries to you or other resident of the household unless they were a residence employee.

Review *Your* Insurance Policy

Floaters, Endorsements and Scheduled Personal Property (SPP): As discussed, home insurance put limits on categories of personal property such as jewelry. Some will put a per item and total limit such as Jewelry $1,500 maximum value per item which may be very low for some jewelry, and $3,000 total. These limits can be raised in increments per item and total, or individual items can be scheduled. It costs less to raise the limits on a policy, but coverage is not as broad as insuring through a Scheduled Personal Property (SPP) rider. Items that can be insured more broadly through an SPP rider are:

1. Jewelry
2. Fur
3. Cameras
4. Musical Instruments (nonprofessional)
5. Silverware
6. Golf Equipment
7. Fine Art
8. Stamps and Coins

To do this an appraisal of value from an expert should be obtained (otherwise how would it be valued when it's stolen, or destroyed in a fire?) **Benefits of SPP Riders:**

Replacement Cost loss settlement without deduction for depreciation. **Open Perils coverage** as opposed to most policies having named peril coverage for contents. More types of claims are normally covered, such as losing an item like an earring, or a diamond lost after coming loose from its setting, accidentally dropping a ring down the drain or leaving in a hotel room. **Deductible** can be set higher than home or as low as 0.

Review *Your* Insurance Policy

Cancelling prior insurance: When writing new insurance policies to replace a present policy it may be wise to discuss with your broker not cancelling the old policy until after the new inspection is complete. This, to verify there are no concerns and policy is issued as written. Normally then, the old policy can be then cancelled for the same day and time the new policy started. Why burn your bridges on the old policy should the new insurer decline writing due to an overhanging tree or other concern.

Home Insurance Property Inspection: When writing a new home insurance most all insurance companies today will do a property inspection. Some inspectors are employees of the company, while others are independent companies they hire. During the home inspection most will measure the home and detached buildings to verify square footage insured. They'll also look for potential claim exposures such as an aging roof, missing or loose railings and unfenced pools. Most non high value home inspections do not include the interior.

High value homes are often inspected more thoroughly, may include interior due to the larger exposure if a claim.

In **Chapter 9**, flood insurance is explained. Keep in mind that to be considered a flood for flood insurance claim purposes the water has to meet certain criteria. Having a gutter drain pipe kicked off when cutting the lawn, causing a wet basement normally isn't considered a flood insurance claim.

Chapter 9

Flood & Earthquake Insurance

> "One out of every four flood claims comes from areas that are not considered flood risks."
>
> FEMA

More Natural Disasters: Without getting into a political debate of whether or not climate change is happening, the fact is the frequency and severity of natural disasters is increasing. Flood and earthquake are not covered by standard home insurance policies, as many homeowners have learned the hard way. These are typically standard exclusions and to be insured for these risks separate policies must be written. For example, as claims progressed from Hurricane Katrina in New Orleans there were many lawsuits over whether the flood itself or the hurricane force wind damaged homes. Many insurers argued that the flood caused damage and was not an insured claim.

Earthquake Insurance: As stated, standard home insurance does not cover earthquake damage. An earthquake endorsement must be added to the homeowner's policy or a separate policy must be purchased. Premiums for this insurance are highest in states with higher risk of earthquakes such as California, Washington and Oregon. Higher risk states

Flood & Earthquake Insurance

also base their pricing with higher deductibles, such as 15% of the dwelling coverage. Some insurers have options to lower deductibles to 10% or as low as 2% in non-high risk states. The National Association of Insurance Commissioners (NAIC) has a Consumer Guide to Earthquake Insurance, along with additional on their Insurance U website:
http://www.insurance.insureuonline.org/consumer_guide_earthquake.pdf

Insurance and wet basements: Many homes at some point have problems with damp, wet or flooded basements. Water can cause a multitude of problems ranging from mold in the home, to dry rot of the wood, to health concerns provoking allergies and asthma. Families have ended up in a hotel for a year while mold remediation was done in their home. Many people are surprised to learn that most home insurance policies don't cover water that seeps in to the home. Some policies may cover a pipe that bursts and floods water, or if a tree hits the home causing water to enter. But gradual seepage and flooded basements are almost always not covered. There are many older, over 100 year old homes that were built with stacked stone foundations, with a little mortar in the joints. These homes *were not built* to have waterproof basements. Even some newer homes are built that end up with water seeping in for various reasons.

What's a Flood? Flood Insurance can be purchased to cover floods, but may not cover your wet basement if the damage doesn't meet the Federal Emergency Management Agency (FEMA) definition of a flood which is:

Flood & Earthquake Insurance

"A flood is a general and temporary condition where two or more acres of normally dry land or two or more properties are inundated by water or mudflow. Many conditions can result in a flood: hurricanes, overtopped levees, outdated or clogged drainage systems and rapid accumulation of rainfall."

Is it a Flood? Note that a flood is defined as **two acres or more of land**, or **two or more properties flooded, one being yours**. If your gutter clogs, and the resulting seepage causes your basement to flood, in most cases home insurance, and flood insurance (if you have) will not pay. This can be a gap in coverage.

FEMA's National Flood Insurance Program website at **www.floodsmart.gov/floodsmart** has excellent resources, videos, and calculators. They also make available an online interactive tool to show how much flooding can cost.

Consider your need for Flood Insurance: Talk to your agent and get a quote for flood insurance. If you are in a high risk area and got bank financing for the mortgage it may have been required.

Exception to Flood Insurance Requirement: If your mortgage required flood insurance by the flood map area your home is located in, but you feel your particular parcel of land is higher and will not flood, you are allowed to file for a waiver with an elevation certificate from a surveyor. This may drop the banks requirement for the flood insurance, lower your cost for the policy should you keep, and possibly a buyer's requirement to have if you someday sell.

Flood & Earthquake Insurance

Preferred Risk Flood Policy is not that expensive if you are not in a high risk area. Additionally, if the bank allows, you can consider only having a policy to cover the mortgage amount, or with a higher deductible. It may not rebuild the home fully, or pay for all of your contents, but it is a way to self-insure for some items if you want to spread your insurance money into other needs, and assume more of the flood risk yourself.

Notes

Chapter 10

Condominiums and Co-ops

Insuring condominiums, co-ops and townhouses is often misunderstood. Adding to the concern is that often the information being given out by some members of homeowners associations may be incorrect. This results in many unit owners unknowingly having the wrong coverage.

If you own or are buying with a bank mortgage your bank would require insurance to be in force for the closing to protect their investment in your home. Some banks may only want to see proof of the Homeowners Association insurance being in force for the building, and some banks may also want proof of the owners insurance for the unit too. Even though your bank may not have required you to have your own condo policy it is still essential to have. The association master policies normally cover the building structure including roof, halls, elevators, walkways, parking areas, and common areas such as pool, and tennis for liability claims and property damage. The association policy may also cover some items the unit owner owns. **The bylaws determine insurance responsibilities.**

Step 1 – What's the Association Insuring?

See it in writing: Review the bylaws to see what the association insures. Also, try to receive something in writing from the association insurance to clarify what they insure and what you need to insure. If in doubt start with more building coverage as discussed later, it can be reduced once clarification is received. There are also some townhouses without a master policy to cover the structure, each owner insures their own.

To the studs, drywall, or fixtures? Finding out what the association insurance covers should be easy, as every unit owner needs this information. Yet, in some complexes it's more difficult to find out. Many of the insurance companies that insure associations will provide a summary to distribute to owners explaining what the association policy covers and what items the individual owners need to insure. The association bylaws or proprietary lease that applies to your unit will tell the story. There isn't one uniform procedure that applies to condos throughout the country, and there are various practices regionally.

Does the association insure as originally built? Do the bylaws state that the association insurance will cover all that was originally built? As an example, picture a builder buying a piece of land and building 100 condo units ready to be sold. Each finished with kitchen and baths. The builder would have needed insurance for these buildings. If this is what the association policy covers then if there were a claim this may be exactly the amount of what is covered. Any improvements over the years beyond what was originally spec'd out by builder is not insured by the master policy.

Condominiums and Co-ops

Bare walls, floor and ceiling: Does the association policy cover none of the kitchen and bath fixtures? If this is the case your insurance needs to include this portion of building improvement coverage to rebuild the kitchen and baths along with all other improvements beyond the bare walls. The interior partitions may also be the responsibility of the unit owner.

Studs Only: Were the units sold with the studs visible? Perhaps as vacant loft space with bare brick walls allowing each owner to build out with their own kitchen and baths? Whether this is the case, or if built with all fixtures the association bylaws may have been written requiring the association insure only to the studs and each unit owner insuring the finished drywall and all fixtures.

By the association having one company insure the entire building in a master policy as they do, makes it much easier at time of claim. Can you imagine the delays settling claims that can ensue if there were a building fire, with every unit owner having a different insurance company?

Step 2 – Insure *Your* Risks.

Once you know what the association is insuring, insure for your risks. Normally condos are insured with the HO-6 type of policy form as it allows for some building improvement coverage. Co-ops can be insured with an HO-4 policy as in renters if there is no building or improvement coverage needed, or with the HO-6 for condos. If the association insurance will rebuild only as originally built then you may

Condominiums and Co-ops

want to insure for all alterations and upgrades that have been done since it was built. This would include improvements that may have been done prior to you owning.

- **Upgraded kitchen**
- **Upgraded baths**
- **Hardwood floors**
- **Built-ins and chair rails**
- **All other upgrades**

If upgraded kitchen and bath was done by the original owner, verify if the association insurance will replace. If the kitchen as insured by the association would cost $50,000 to replace, and you tore it out and installed a new kitchen at a cost of $75,000 you may only need to insure the additional $25,000 of improvement, verify with the association insurer.

Unit Owners Condo or Co-Op Policy Insures

Contents Coverage: A base condominium policy will insure the contents of the unit, normally starting with a room estimator to calculate the cost to furnish based on economy, average or upper end value furnishings. Replacement coverage is better than ACV as discussed previously. This dollar amount can be adjusted to meet the appropriate amount of coverage, in this example, contents of say $100,000.

Building Improvements Coverage: Many condo insurance policies then include an automatic 10% of the contents coverage for the building improvements. In this case 10% of the $100,000 contents equal $10,000 for building improvements. Many policies seem to leave this coverage at the 10% limit. This coverage should be increased to the replacement cost necessary to rebuild the unit as improved. If in doubt as to what the association master policy covers, it may be best to err on the side of additional building coverage until clarified.

Liability Insurance: Protects you against claims arising from accidents and follows you wherever you go, with most policies worldwide. Most policies start with $100,000 liability coverage and most people write policies with at least $300,000 coverage but can inexpensively be raised to $500,000 to $1 million, with Personal Umbrella or Excess Liability policies available higher. Having other units above, below or next door makes liability insurance all the more important.

Common liability claims examples are a tub overflowing and pouring water to a unit below, say damaging the walls below and a computer. Or a BBQ grill on the patio, small appliance or candle fire in your unit causes a building fire.

Additional Living Expense Coverage: Even if nothing happens in your unit, if a claim occurs in your building for a covered loss this will provide money to maintain your standard of living. This can include a hotel stay, miscellaneous expenses, or renting a similar condo if needed. Often, an entire building is posted as unfit for occupancy due to a fire in a different unit.

Condominiums and Co-ops

Add Endorsements & Floater as Needed

Loss (or Unit) Assessments: This important endorsement is often missing on condo policies. Normally not too costly, and will reimburse for share of assessment levied against each unit owner due to a covered loss. Note: Some loss assessment endorsements will pay a claim based on the date the loss is assessed to the unit owner – not on the date of the actual claim.

Back Up of Water & Sewer: Covers a limited amount of damage, normally written for $5,000 coverage or less should a sewer or drain back up into the unit.

Scheduled Personal Property (SPP) for jewelry and other valuables.

Endorsements: Discuss with your broker other coverage's needed such as for business, daycare, etc.

Rented to Others: Many condo owners will rent their unit out yearound or seasonally. Check with your broker to verify how much you are allowed if at all to rent, and add endorsement if needed.

Flood and Earthquake: Coverage is normally not part of a condo or co-op policy, and must be written separately or endorsed.

Condo Discounts

Verify you receive all available qualifying discounts. These may include the normal multi policy discount for having auto insurance and retired discount, but also discounts or better rating factors if the building has sprinkler, is masonry/fire resistant, or has 24 hr. monitored fire and security alarms among others.

With Condos…Don't Go Without

Just because your bank may not have required a condo policy on your individual unit, is not reason to go without insurance. As stressed previously, the time to buy insurance is when you don't need it, because when you need it you can't buy it. All too frequently claims occur in condos and co-ops that cause the owner to scramble to buy coverage that same day in the hopes of having coverage, but then becomes an investigated red flag having a policy start same day as a claim. In which case the date and time bound will play a role. At minimum, if you don't want the additional expense of your own condo policy, get the barest bones policy to at least have liability protection in your life. If you're satisfied with the amount of coverage the association policy will pay for the structure, minimize contents to the lowest, with ACV used value, and take the highest deductible. Have liability and loss assessments coverage to protect your assets. If you maintain auto insurance, you may find the amount of multi policy savings on the auto pays the cost of the condo policy.

Whether you own a condo or a house, the reason for insurance is to protect you (and your mortgage holder) in the event of a claim. In **Chapter 11** we next discuss dealing with claims.

Notes

Chapter 11

Dealing with Insurance Claims
And Neighborly Tree Advice

We've discussed the suggestion of considering the benefits of maintaining higher deductibles among your insurance policies. This, where the amount of years it takes to save the deductible makes it cost effective; then taking the savings to buy higher liability insurance. To self-insure for the small things, and insure for the risks you can't afford to pay out of pocket for. This also encourages you to avoid submitting claims for small things. Benefits are that it keeps a cleaner record with your insurance company, a claim free discount if they offer, and makes it easier to get new insurance policies if needed; especially in higher risk areas around the country. Additionally, if an insurance company sees larger losses in your state or nationally, they often will look to non-renew policyholders that have more claims. They may say for example that they are non-renewing insured's with one claim in 3 years, or two claims in 5 years. Not knowing what may happen in the next three years, why put a claim in to get a check for only a few hundred dollars?

No Agent??

Often, having insurance with a direct writer of insurance leaves no opportunity to have a discussion regarding reporting a claim. The business model is to either discuss buying insurance through a sales department, or report a claim to the claim department. The decision to submit the claim isn't always black and white, and requires a review of the entire picture including where you are at in relation to claims, and your insurance companies underwriting guidelines.

An example may be where an insurance company gives claim free discounts. If a previous claim from a few years back is just getting old enough to give a substantial discount, a new claim may lose the discount for another 3 to 5 years. Receiving a claim check for $400 may help today, but may cost more in the long run and may make it more difficult to insure another home or vacation home you may consider buying.

High Risk Home Insurance: Homeowners that have filed too many claims may find their insurance company non-renewing their policy. New insurance may be written that is high risk, excess lines or in what is known as the FAIR plan, an assigned risk for homeowners that have had too many claims. If the only reason this is required was due to having had say 3 homeowner claims four years ago, there may be an option to write a less expensive preferred policy when claims become older. Every company has their own individual guidelines, discuss with your agent. Should it happen that a home (or in cases auto) policy is written with a higher risk carrier it's good to know at the outset, and make note of the soonest day you may be able to qualify for a less expensive policy to know when to shop for new with your broker. Most brokers tend to

Dealing with Insurance Claims

review insurance policies on each renewal and requote to see if the premium can be reduced.

When a claim does occur, read your insurance policy to understand both your obligations and the insurers, and discuss with your agent or broker.

Ten Steps in Insurance Claims

1. Report to Fire Department/Emergency Services, or if a crime to the police. If the claim were for a serious fire it may go without saying that you would have notified the fire department and emergency services may have been at the scene. For a small fire that caused damage but was put out on your own the fire department may not have been notified. See if there is a requirement to notify, and understand that reporting may trigger compliance inspections and requirements to upgrade to current codes. If the crime caused you to be a victim of a theft, vandalism, burglary, or property damage accident report the incident to the police. Request a copy of the police report and log the names of those you speak to.

Public Adjusters: Often, independent public adjusters that may be in the area may arrive at the scene to introduce themselves and to assist in the claim. Some may hear of a fire or incident through police and fire scanners (See number 7.)

2. Temporary Repairs/Minimize Additional Damage Insurance policies specify the responsibilities of both the insurance company, *and* of you. One of your responsibilities is to take steps to protect your property and minimize further damage as soon as possible after claim. Most insurance

Dealing with Insurance Claims

policies will reimburse you for the reasonable and necessary expense to protect from further damage; with some policies putting a maximum dollar amount for this expense. If time permits and the claim is open it may be good to advise your insurance company for preapproval, and see if company doing work, such as board up is able to bill the insurance company directly. Save all receipts and submit them to the insurance company for reimbursement. Also, make notes of conversations, dates, times and who you spoke to.

3. Report the claim to your insurance or not report?
Decide if this is a claim you should report to your insurance company or if in your better interest to not claim and treat as self-insuring. Is there another responsible party you can submit the claim to their insurance? This may avoid having a claim against your insurance; such as in the case of a car driving on your property causing property damage, or a neighbors tree falling on your house.

According to David Shaffer, insurance agency owner who has been part of United Policyholders as reported on their website uphelp.org "In an ideal world, my advice would be that every time an insured event under your home insurance policy occurs, you should be able to simply turn it in. Unfortunately, over the years I have heard an earful from my clients who have faced having their home insurance coverage canceled due to claim activity. My message is that consumers need to proactively prevent small losses from happening since they are going to cover them if they do occur, pocket the savings over all of the years they will own a home, and truly view one's home insurance policy as a consumer product to cover major losses." There is further discussion on the topic in

Dealing with Insurance Claims

the article titled *To Claim or Not to Claim...That is the question* by David Shaffer on the website.

4. Report claim to your Agent, or Insurer
If there are injuries, or substantial property damage above your deductible to warrant submitting a claim you may either submit the claim to your insurance companies claim department, or to your agent/broker. There may be a time limit to notify of a claim. As mentioned, your insurance policy outlines responsibilities and procedures your insurance company and you must follow during the claims process. If timing allows you to discuss with your agent the conversation can include if the claim is too small to report, or if it may be the type of claim to submit to another party's insurance company such as in the case of someone else's auto or tree causing property damage. After a brief conversation with your agent, they may either take the claims information from you for them to report, or they may direct you to the insurance companies claims office to report the claim on your own further. The claims office will need to get your statement anyway, giving all the pertinent facts to them directly will save having to go through all the details twice (or more.) Your insurance company will send claims form paperwork to complete and return by a specified date (many states require specific claims handling deadlines.) Having a broker to discuss the claim with helps. For example, in a case where there may be a small amount of damage that is near or below your deductible and no injuries you may choose not to submit a claim. When you have no agent and are working only with a call center the initial conversation may be logged in as a claim either way.

Dealing with Insurance Claims

Read all information received carefully and act upon to avoid delays.

Duty to Report a Claim, and Late Notice
Even though the amount of damage may make the claim not worth submitting as an insurance claim there may still be reasons to report it. If there is the possibility of an injury involved, or that a small payout may grow to a large one due to unforeseen damage it may be best to have the claim filed. Many insurance companies will seek to deny a claim for failure to report an incident that wasn't submitted promptly. This is where it is necessary to use your judgment in deciding whether or not to submit an insurance claim. Should you decide to discuss with your insurance agent keep in mind that many agents know there is a duty to report. If you discuss with your agent, and the agent does not report the claim there may be concern should the claim need to be reported weeks, or months later.

5. Hotel Stay/Dinner Out, Additional Living Expense
News stories in local papers after a household fire will often say the family was relocated to a shelter, or the Red Cross provided hotel accommodations. Normally, under home insurance, additional living expense "ALE" coverage will pay for hotel, car rental, and miscellaneous expenses such as reasonable restaurant expense for loss of use if your home isn't habitable. It's best to get preapproval if possible as the claim is opened up. If time does not permit to get advance authorization you may have to pay, save receipts, and hope you will get reimbursed. There should be no need to stay in a shelter. Over the next few weeks and months your additional

living expense coverage should reimburse you for the expense of a similar rental to your home and miscellaneous expenses to provide as close as possible to the same quality of life as before claim. Some insurance will give the option to locate a temporary mobile home on site if your town's ordinance allows. Additional Living Expense coverage normally either has a dollar amount limit or a time deadline such as up to one year. These payments should be made directly to you, and not your lender.

6. Insurance Company Assigns Adjuster(s)

Your insurance company will assign an adjuster to your claim. Depending on details from the first report of claim made, they may assign more than one adjuster based on claims payments expected. For each adjuster assigned, companies will either have an individual adjuster or may use a team approach. For example the structure may be handled by their "blue team.' By using a team approach anyone on the team can assist to avoid a delay while an adjuster is out of the office.

Structure Adjuster: Handles settling the claim on house and detached structures.
Contents Adjuster: Handles personal property.
Medical Adjuster: Handles medical expenses.
Liability Adjuster: Handles liability claims, and those that may develop into a lawsuit.
A Field Adjuster may be sent to inspect the damage. This can either be an employee of the insurance company or may be an adjustment company that your insurance company hires.

Dealing with Insurance Claims

With small insurance claims, many insurance companies will simply have you submit paperwork, and reimburse to expedite the claim settlement.

Advance Check: Often, insurers will pay a first check as an advance against the total settlement. Once they verify an insurance policy is in force, and a claim isn't ruled suspicious they know a larger payment will be made. This advance payment isn't normally the final payment.

Claim Payments may be made separately for structure, contents and additional living expenses.

7. Public Adjuster As mentioned in Item 1, often at the claim scene or shortly after an independent public adjuster may reach out to you, especially if a larger fire. Your insurance company has their own adjusters (either their employee, or a subcontractor) provided at no charge to you. The Independent Public Adjuster is looking to be hired by you to assist in the claim. Most are reputable, but as in any industry there may be some that aren't. In the confusion of the moment of the claim some homeowners sign agreements without considering options, researching the credentials, background and references of the public adjuster. Some may offer helpful advice, and work with you to make a decision in hiring them - at a cost of up to 15% of the claim. This money normally is paid out of your insurance claim money. Some may allow you to seek out the highest and best settlement from your insurance company, and take a percentage of any additional money they are able to realize over and above the insurers settlement. Weigh benefits and drawbacks of working with your own public adjuster, and understand that signing with the wrong one may further delay settling a claim. Check the adjusters' record with the Better Business Bureau, and State Insurance Department, which may also set a cap on the rate charged. Submitting receipts for reimbursement to your own public adjuster may have you wondering after two weeks where a payment is, to find out the paperwork is on a middleman's desk while away on vacation. A good public adjuster may more than earn their fee by thoroughly reading your policy, and maximizing your settlement. There is more on this topic on the National Association of Independent Insurance Adjusters website **www.naiia.com.**

8. Get Estimates to repair damages. Your insurance company may have you submit the estimates for reimbursement. To be more thorough, securing three estimates will generate a more precise estimate; and may uncover better methods to repair. The insurer may on their own estimate damages and cut a check to you. By having your own estimates, if their estimate is less than yours you can use your estimates to agree to costs.

9. Inventory of Destroyed & Damaged Items: To substantiate your loss prepare an inventory list for your insurer, and avoid throwing out damaged items until the insurance companies adjuster has inspected damages and allows removal.

Photograph and/or videotape the damages. If you don't have an inventory that was created prior to the loss look for old pictures, seek receipts where possible, and keep copies of all documents submitted. Remember to seek reimbursement for all property, from basement to attic.

10. Replacement cost. If you have replacement cost contents coverage shop around to replace items with similar quality. Not IKEA build it yourself furniture if you have better quality. Normally, the insurance company will pay you the depreciated lower Actual Cash Value (ACV) settlement and have you submit receipt to get difference of replacement cost once the item has been purchased. Ask your insurer how many months you will be allowed to purchase new items and submit receipts to be reimbursed the remainder of the replacement cost.

Check Payable to Insured(s) and Bank: Depending on the dollar amount of the claim the check for repairs will either be made payable to the named insured(s) on the declaration page only, or will include the bank's name if there is a mortgage. As a condition of the mortgage lenders require they are named and are a party to insurance payments. It is important to have both the named insured and bank correct at all times, and to review prior to checks being issued. If an insured no longer owns the home jointly, or is now (sadly) deceased, discuss with your broker and consider reason name should be continued on the policy or removed. If a bank changed or second mortgage paid off update the insurance policy promptly. Banks normally put the check in an escrow account and release payments as work is completed. They may inspect the property prior to final payment being made. If the check is made payable to you, there may be an option to repair some work yourself, or to get the work done for less to bring the work in for less. Check laws in your state if allowed.

Dealing with Insurance Claims

Additional Claims Considerations

Many States have laws requiring insurance companies to process claims promptly.

For any questions about claim filing laws in your state, check with your insurance broker or state insurance department.

Don't cash checks marked full/final settlement or similar wording without checking with your attorney.

Be careful not to sign a release of future payments. Seek attorney or legal services advice.

Trees, Insurance, Claims and Neighborly Advice

Well positioned trees can lower utility bills, and increase the value of your home. The other side of the coin is that trees can also cause injuries and property damage. To avoid concerns it's best to trim and prune trees as needed to keep them safe.

Tree Roots can also cause damage to foundations, raise sidewalks and driveways, and wreak havoc with sewer lines. Since insurance is to cover sudden and direct losses most insurance policies will not pay for damage caused by tree roots. This can be a gray area, as open peril insurance policies (the type that pay all claims except those excluded) don't have an exclusion for "tree roots' specifically. If roots that cause a blockage in a sewer line create damage from say a toilet overflow, the subsequent damage may be a covered loss. Roots that raised a sidewalk wouldn't be a covered loss in order to repair the sidewalk, but if someone tripped and sued for injuries the liability portion of your insurance would provide coverage due to your negligence in not repairing the sidewalk. While most policies wouldn't cover root damage it is an area that some insurance companies have extended coverage, especially for long time insured's as a courtesy.

Trees and Branches Falling: In itself, a tree or branch falling isn't normally a covered home insurance loss. It's when the tree or limb hits a structure on your property that most home insurance covers; unless the policy is written without falling objects coverage, and many secondary homeowner policies. The payment is not necessarily to cover the tree, but to allow it to be removed in order to repair your structure. Standard home insurance normally allows $500 to $1,000 coverage depending on the insurer and policy purchased to remove the portion of the tree that hit the structure. To put this in perspective, there are homes that sit on a small lot, and there are homes that sit on acres of land. For a home that has 100 acres of woodland there will be trees constantly falling in the woods. Home insurance is not designed to pay to cut up every tree that falls on the property, in essence paying for debris removal to lumber property. The insurance kicks in only when a tree or limb damages an insured structure such as your home, detached garage, shed, barn or even fence. This is to repair the structure and the contents in it based on type of policy. Some insurers may pay to remove the tree if it falls and blocks a driveway or ramps designed to assist the handicapped.

Dealing with Insurance Claims

A Neighbors Tree Damages Your Property

When a neighbors' tree falls and damages one of your structures three scenarios can occur:

1. **Your home insurance** would pay the $500 to $1,000 to remove the tree to repair your structure as a claim on your insurance. A long as your policy covers trees falling, the policy would respond, and you would pay the deductible. Your policy doesn't differentiate where the branch came from, as in the case of strong hurricane force winds making branches fly from anywhere.

When the Neighbors Tree was Hazardous or Dead: When a neighbors' tree is hazardous or dead then your neighbors' liability insurance may be the place to look to pay for the damages. This would be similar say, to if your neighbor were in his backyard with a chain saw cutting the tree and goofed, causing it to fall on your structure. They would be legally liable for the damage they caused. When a neighbor has a hazardous or dead tree they are responsible to make it safe. This requires inspecting their trees, and trimming or removing as needed. If the tree or branch that falls on your structure is dead, then they may be legally liable to pay for 100% of your damages - without you paying your deductible. This would be done to make you whole again as was the case before the loss. For example, if a homeowner had tree cutting companies in and was advised that trees were dangerous, but did not act they may be more liable if a tree limb fell. Along the same line, though a touchy subject - if a tree is visibly dangerous and a neighbor refuses to make it safe you can put them on notice. A certified

Dealing with Insurance Claims

letter stating you are concerned that the tree is a hazard and requesting they rectify puts them on notice. Doing this may strain a neighborly relationship though, and you may want to seek an attorneys' opinion based on your state laws.

Your neighbors insurance can be sought to pay for damages to your property in one of the next two ways:

2. **Go through your own insurance**, and pay your deductible to get the damages repaired. Your insurance company would then go after reimbursement from your neighbors insurance in a process called subrogation. They would look to get both the money they paid, as well as your deductible back if they can prove the tree was hazardous and the neighbor was legally responsible.

3. **Submit the claim to your neighbors insurance.** If they accept liability, they will pay for damages without your needing to pay the deductible.

Tree negligence often applies in other situations. If a car is hit by a falling branch and it appears the branch was dead, a claim can be made to the tree owner's insurer to avoid putting a claim on your insurance and paying a deductible. The property owner may look to provide a statement that they regularly inspect and maintain trees to avoid being held liable. Whether a tree is dead can at times be a gray area. In rare occasions insurance companies have been known to pay to trim and cut trees as a preventative measure, to avoid a larger claim. This may be the case when they see a very long term customer without much claim history.

Widow Maker Branches: While we're on the topic of trees, keep a lookout for dangling and dangerous branches on your property. These widow maker branches earned the name for causing unexpected injuries and fatalities.

Tax Deductions for Unreimbursed Losses

The IRS tax code allows unreimbursed property and casualty losses to be included with itemized deductions. Explained in Publication 547: www.irs.gov/publications/p547/ar02.html
If your home, car or boat is damaged or destroyed and it was not entirely covered by your insurance, you may be able to deduct a portion of the loss on your federal income tax return. The publication discusses loss requirements, as well as a 2%, 10% and $100 rule that applies. To qualify for the deduction, these losses usually need to be substantial. If you were significantly underinsured or had a large catastrophe deductible, you may have a sizable unreimbursed casualty loss. An unreimbursed loss can be deducted to the extent it exceeds 10 percent of a homeowner's adjusted gross income. To determine whether you qualify for the deduction, you will first need to substantiate your property loss. Be sure to collect all receipts, insurance statements and any available police reports and documentation to present to your tax preparer.

Notes

Chapter 12

Protecting the "What if"

Life & Disability Insurance

Primary reasons many homeowners are faced with foreclosure includes the death or disability of a bread winner. It stands to reason that if a person's income was counted in to qualify for a mortgage to buy a home, no longer having the income makes it difficult to pay the mortgage and other expenses. Many commercial mortgages require the borrowers have life insurance in place - with the bank as beneficiary in order to get a loan. While home mortgages don't normally require life insurance, it is a cornerstone in building financial security and isn't that expensive.

While life insurance is a crucial cornerstone to a financial plan, many people do not realize that the chance of disability is actually even greater. Balance the need for these policies with your budget and need to also establish an emergency fund. The following is an overview, with links to additional reading.

Life Insurance

Having life insurance in force to provide for loved ones in your absence is one of the most caring things we can do. Though a sensitive subject - we all hope and plan for a long life, but the reality is that many homes are lost due to premature death. Consider that for every 1,000 thirty year old males there are about 1.5 deaths annually. Using our lottery analogy - if the chance of winning the lottery were 1.5 in 1000 you'd probably pick up a lottery ticket thinking the odds of winning were great. Below shows deaths per thousand at each decade, increasing to 140 deaths per thousand for males at age 85. Females death rates are lower, which explains why nursing homes have so many more women residents.

Age	Male Chance of Death Per Thousand People	Female Chance of Death Per Thousand People
15-24	1.16	.42
25-34	1.44	.64
35-44	2.32	1.37
45-54	5.30	3.15
55-64	11.01	6.70
65-74	24.57	16.33
75-84	60.38	43.04
85 +	140.06	124.42

Source: US Center for Disease Control
http://www.cdc.gov/nchs/data/hus/2010/029.pdf

"Buy life insurance when you don't need it. Because when you need it you can't buy it."

The Short Answer: If the next few pages discussing life insurance seems too complicated, make sure you have life insurance in force that at minimum will pay funeral and final expenses to not stick someone else with the bills. Ideally, a

Protecting the "What if"

policy to replace 5 to 10 times your income if you have others relying on your income to pay the mortgage. Term insurance with the option to convert to a permanent policy will allow you time to decide if you want to convert all or some of it to a permanent policy. If you do want permanent insurance the longer you wait, the older you will be and more expensive the insurance. Life insurance is needed now because:

Accidents can happen suddenly; meaning the time to think about life insurance is not when the pilot announces "we're having mechanical difficulties."

Medical Diagnosis and MIB - No, not *Men in Black* as in the movie. MIB is what the life insurance industry calls the *Medical Information Bureau*. If not a sudden accident, when a person receives a diagnosis of what may be a serious health concern it may be reported to the Medical Information Bureau. Many may be unaware of this, but similar to a credit report or motor vehicle record, the MIB reports health diagnosis that life insurance underwriters will look at before issuing life insurance policies. In order to get life insurance, the application asks very specific questions about health issues. Additionally, most policies will require a physical or will seek information from your physician, depending on face amount of policy applied for. When a health concern arises, people will go to the doctor's office before making an application for life insurance. Once the medical records reflect an issue, life insurance applications will either be denied, or will receive table ratings making the premium more expensive based on the possibly shorter life expectancy. If the diagnosis isn't picked up and the life insurance policy is issued, most policies have what may be a 2 year contestability period where if a person passes away, the insurance company may investigate the application for fraud before paying the death benefit.

Concern with Work & Group Life Insurance: Consider group and work life insurance as good to have, adding to the death benefit available; but *be careful not to rely solely* on this as your only life insurance. The concern arises where an employer may drop this coverage, or where a person leaves the job and the policy stops. There are many cases where a person works and has group life insurance and stops working due to a terminal illness. The policy then may stop due to no longer being an employee just when it's needed. It's important to have life insurance that you own.

Having life insurance in force to pay off the mortgage and support family needs is important.

Receiving news of a terminal illness is devastating in itself. As a family tries to cope personally and get things in order financially it is very sad to know there is no life insurance in place and a policy cannot be obtained.

5 to 10 Times Income: It's usually recommended that you have life insurance to replace between 5 and 10 times your income. Do a "needs analysis" with a financial advisor or on one of the many online calculators to see how much life insurance you really need. Include items such as the amount

Protecting the "What if"

of mortgage, age of children if any, the cost of raising and fulfilling college funding plans. If a person makes $50,000 a year income and has ten times this amount in life insurance, would be $500,000 in life insurance. Should they pass away, the $500,000 could be invested. If it earned a 10% return, they would receive $50,000 a year earnings to replace the lost income. 10% return isn't always achievable, plug in a number that is realistic based on how you would invest and your expected budget.

There is a need for life insurance even in the case of a stay at home spouse, especially if they are taking care of kids. Should they pass away prematurely there is a cost of having to add daycare or other expenses.

Aiming for kids to go to public or private colleges? What good is setting up a college funding account if there's a premature death and the money isn't fully funded yet? Life insurance allows you to fulfill college funding plans even though you aren't able to.

Life insurance pays a death benefit that's tax free (as of this writing) to the beneficiary right at the time it is needed.

There are different types of life insurance, with most falling into one of two areas: **Term insurance** is less expensive, but does not build cash value and will stop at some point in the future.

Permanent insurance builds cash value, and *if funded correctly* will take you into old age and eventually will pay a

Protecting the "What if"

death benefit (can't escape death and taxes.) The only question is when, we hope later not sooner.

Term Life Insurance is actually as the name implies. It is life insurance for a term of time, or for a temporary period. You can buy term type of insurance for the "term" of one airline flight, or for a set time period such as one year term, 5, 10, 15, 20 and 30 year periods. The longer the term, the more expensive the policy is annually. The reason term life insurance is less expensive is that most people do not die during the term. The coverage is designed to end before death, and pays nothing if the insured lives past the end of the coverage period.

There are many variations of term insurance, more than the scope of this book allows. Keep in mind some policies are *Renewable* with options to renew the policy for additional years, and some with a *Conversion Option* allow the policy to be converted into a permanent policy without having to reapply and take a new physical.

Don't always buy the least expensive policy. Some at first glance may appear a little less expensive, but may not be with a financially higher rated company. Also some policies may not be renewable or convertible. It would be sad to see someone 9 years into a 10 year policy, develop a serious illness. Knowing the policy cannot be renewed or converted to a permanent policy, and they may then be uninsurable.

Term Mortgage Life Insurance: If your mortgage (or other loans also) includes mortgage life insurance written by the lender compare prices by getting price for your own policy that is not tied to the loan. Policies tied to the loan:

Protecting the "What if"

- Are often more expensive.
- Decrease the death benefit along with the pay down of the loan. A 20 year mortgage with 20 year mortgage life insurance will have the life death benefit decrease to 0 at 20 years.
- With good health, your own policy, in the example above for the full death benefit would have the same death benefit at 20 years as in year 1.
- With bank mortgage life, it pays the mortgage. Your beneficiary may prefer to keep a mortgage that may have a low rate, and use the death benefit for other needs.

If you pay off the mortgage to refinance with a different bank, or to buy another house the bank mortgage life policy is cancelled with the mortgage. If health has changed and older age it may cost more to buy new policy; or a person may now be uninsurable.

Before cancelling mortgage life make sure new policy is in force and all rules regarding replacement of the old policy are followed for your protection.

Permanent Life Insurance normally costs more than permanent life insurance because it builds cash value, and if funded correctly will stay in force your entire life. Most common types of permanent policies include:

Whole Life is the simplest and most basic type of permanent, cash value life insurance with level premiums. The life insurance pays a stated death benefit. The investment component builds cash value in a savings account where dividends or interest builds up tax deferred.

Protecting the "What if"

Universal Life (UL) is life insurance where investment is based on interest rates. When interest rates are high it earns more, and when rates are low the earnings are low. The payments can be flexible and adjusted up and down based on life circumstances.

Universal life insurance was created to provide more flexibility than whole life insurance, and the ability to earn higher, rising interest rates. Annual statements should be reviewed to ensure they are properly funded. For example, if a policy was written and funded based on interest rates that were earning 8%, with the assumption that rates will continue to average 8% the policy may be underfunded with extended periods of low rates. Verify through an inforce projection that there is sufficient cash value to fund the policy as required.

Variable Universal Life (VUL) is similar to universal life except instead of solely earning based on interest rates, investments are in funds that mirror mutual funds. The investment portion goes in a separate account to invest in a portfolio of stocks, bonds, equity funds, and money markets. These are securities contracts and sold by prospectus.

Whole Life policies are normally written more as a set it and forget it policy. The payments are outlined for the entire contract; payments are made with a consistent - though conservative rate of return. Review statements and verify properly funded. Universal and Variable Life policies were created when interest rates and earnings in other investments were higher than whole life. As mentioned, it's important to review policies at minimum annually to ensure they are properly funded. If not, the insured may find that a large payment is needed to continue the policy or it will lapse.

Protecting the "What if"

Term vs. Permanent Life Insurance Debate

Do you buy term life or permanent? Most beneficiaries receiving a $500,000 death benefit will not ask if the policy was term or permanent. At a time when grieving over the loss of a loved one is hard enough, having life insurance come through at the moment needed avoids having financial strain compound the problem. Some advisors suggest only buying permanent policies, with term insurance being a waste of money as it has no cash value build up. Others suggest buying only term insurance, and take the difference that would have gone into a permanent insurance policy and investing it yourself ("buy term and invest the difference.") The concern here is if you don't invest the difference, will there be money available if you pass away after the term insurance stops? To help decide what's best for you, consider:

- If a needs analysis calls for having say $750,000 of life insurance today to cover the mortgage, raising a family and college funding - will you still want the same $750,000 when the mortgage is paid off and kids are all grown? Some will say no. Others may still want the death benefit as a way to pass money on to the next generation. A person can spend every cent they have in retirement, die with $0 and have the life insurance money there to create an inheritance.
- If there is not a needed for the same say $750,000 of life insurance when the family is raised, a term policy may be appropriate, having it stop when he mortgage is paid and family is raised.
- Many of us though, have seen instances where a person passes away and with no money for funeral expenses - in some

cases leaving the family to chip in to pay the bill. There may be a home owned, but until sold may not have cash available.
- You can combine the policies: If your needs analysis determines a need for $750,000 of life insurance now, you can write a $250,000 permanent policy that goes into old age and eventually pays a death benefit to your beneficiary, with a $500,000 **Term Rider.** The term portion may be written for a number of years, scheduled to drop off when kids are out of school, or the mortgage is paid off, to have a death benefit in the event of a *premature death.*
- **An option also is to have a smaller permanent policy** for funeral expenses, to know it will be there, along with a larger term policy. Companies often have ratios of the amount of term rider allowed on a permanent policy. If not all on one policy, having a permanent policy to ensure final expenses are covered, for example $50,000 of permanent life along with larger $750,000 term insurance raises a family but ensures if you "invested the difference" but if spent there will be some money available to pay final expenses. Your needs analysis can determine what's right for you.
- **Emergency Fund:** Before funding a permanent, cash value life insurance policy, do you have an emergency fund to cover 6 to 12 months household expenses?
- **Permanent, cash value building life insurance** has been around for years, and allows money to grow tax deferred. Years ago life insurance was a place additional money could be paid into to grow without paying taxes on the earnings. There are now many areas to grow money without paying taxes on earnings annually. Before over funding permanent insurance are you taking advantage of employer matches in retirement

Protecting the "What if"

plans? Are you getting income tax deductions for contributing to an IRA annually? Consider along with your need for permanent insurance.

- **Life Insurance and Estate Taxes:** Large estates and those with businesses should have estate planning done with an attorney and CPA. Consider if using life insurance death benefit to pay estate taxes may be appropriate. There have been many cases of celebrities whose family heirlooms had to be sold off to satisfy estate taxes.

Musical Chairs: Over the years, you may end up changing and having different life insurance policies for various reasons. Keep in mind that starting new policies may have new policy fees. With people living longer, often life insurance rates will decrease; or you may find less expensive policies. A concern though when changing insurance is that new 2 year contestability period and suicide clauses start over. In any event, to use an analogy, as in the game musical chairs, when the music stops everyone jumps in a chair. If your health changes with a diagnosis, or if a premature death what you have in place for life insurance is what you have as a death benefit and have to live with if no longer insurable. The person who with no life insurance is like the person with no chair.

Smokers: When applying for life insurance smokers pay more, often a lot more. Applications ask if you smoke, and have you smoked in the past say two, five years, or ever - with varying premium rates. Most will test for nicotine during the physical, or with a swab in the mouth. These will pick up nicotine in the system, some in the past 3 or so months. Even just one

Protecting the "What if"

celebratory cigar at a wedding can make you have a smoker rate. Some insurers will issue as nonsmoker rate if the one cigar was disclosed on the application.

Benefits of Life Insurance

Named Beneficiary: With life insurance, a beneficiary (one or more) is named to receive the death benefit. Where money in the bank and investments becomes part of an estate and disbursed based on a will, life insurance is paid on passing. We all may have heard of cases of a will being contested, but life insurance pays the beneficiary you name. If a child is to become a beneficiary or "contingent' beneficiary if the first beneficiary predeceases, it's best to name the person who will raise or a trustee. Minor child may not be able to access funds until of age.

Advance Death Benefit: Some life policies have a feature that will advance up to half the death benefit now if diagnosed with a terminal illness, with the remainder on passing. This is a helpful living benefit of life insurance that allows getting things in order and paying bills if out of work with a terminal illness.

Life Settlement | Sell your life insurance: Before dropping or cashing out life insurance, there are companies in the business of buying life insurance policies that may pay you more than the cash value sitting in the policy. The amount they will pay is based on the insured's age, health and life expectancy. This is becoming a debated issue as it puts life insurance in a different perspective, where someone else owns the policy that has no insurable interest - a stranger. The concern with stranger owned life insurance (STOLI) is that someone other than a loved one benefits from you not living. Rather than one individual, there are investment pools that also buy life settlements.

Remember, the time to buy life insurance is when you don't need it. Normally, if a health concern arises a person sees their doctor before they talk to their life insurance agent.

Disability Insurance

Just over 1 in 4 of today's twenty year olds will become disabled before reaching age 67.
www.ssa.gov/news/press/basicfact.html

Disability of a breadwinner is a major cause of home foreclosure. Having an emergency fund will help for a while, but may not last. The answer may be a combination of savings and *Disability Insurance.* There are many options for length of coverage and waiting periods before coverage begins. For example, you could write a policy with a one week waiting period, or a policy with a 3 month wait. The 3 month wait will lower your cost for the policy, and would require you to dip into savings for the first 3 months. Many people have no disability insurance coverage at all. The point was made earlier that it is important to spread your insurance money to cover as many risks as possible that you may face. You may never need disability insurance and may have paid for years on it. Having a policy that covers from your first week on may be appropriate if you are really living paycheck to paycheck. It means weighing the cost of the policy, along with other savings, retirement, and insurance needs. When someone is disabled their income is greatly reduced. If your state has disability benefits it usually pays minimal amounts, not

Protecting the "What if"

normally enough to cover all household expenses and your mortgage. Additionally, most policies will not be allowed to be written to replace 100% of your income, as there would be no incentive to return to work. Most are written to replace 60% to 70% of your pretax income.

Other sources of income after a disability are:

State Disability: If your state requires, state disability pays for injuries or illness **off the job**. The payments though are small though in relation to a normal paycheck. This could be paid if say you had an injury home on a ladder or due to a car accident even though not on the job.

Workers Compensation Insurance if injury occurred **on the job;** has notoriously long delays before receiving monthly or lump sum payments. Since Workers Compensation insurance pays more that State Disability, it happens that Monday's were always the day more workers comp claims were filed. Possibly from the weekend warrior getting injured at home, then dragging themselves to work Monday where they get "hurt" to claim on the job workers comp benefits.

- **Dip into savings account or other funds**
- **Borrow from friends, relatives, or the bank**
- **Sell Home or Other Assets**
- **Live off credit cards** until they're maxed out.

Disability Insurance can be written as **short term** disability coverage (normally under 2 years) or **long term** disability coverage up to age 65.

Social Security but there is a 5 month waiting period before benefits begin (a good reason for having an emergency fund) The disability must last, or be expected to last 12 months or result in death. The disabled person cannot do any work, and only 30% of those that apply are approved. It is very difficult to get social security disability approved, and there are many law offices that specialize is assisting in the process.

The Social Security Administrations Definition of Disability is...

"The inability to engage in any gainful activity by reason of any medically determinable physical or mental impairment which has lasted or is expected to last for a continuous period of 12 months or result in death. The impairment must be so severe that the individual is unable to engage in substantial gainful work that exists in the national economy regardless of whether or not such work exists in the immediate area in which the applicant lives."

Disability Insurance (DI) policies have many options are riders. More than the scope of this book allows. Policies can be written with different benefit amounts, and your occupation plays a role in whether or not you can obtain a policy. There are many variations of policies, along with riders for cost of living increases. Some policies also coordinate the benefits with money you may receive from workers compensation insurance, state disability, social security, and some state's no fault auto insurance. *AnyOcc* policies define a disability as you being disabled because of an accident or sickness if you cannot do the main duties of **any** occupation. *OwnOcc* policies say

Protecting the "What if"

you are totally disabled if because of an accident or sickness you cannot do the main duties of **your** occupation. If considering disability insurance be sure to understand all of the policies terms and conditions.

Protecting Your Home, Third Leg of the 3 Legged Stool

We discussed the financial and insurances needs of protecting homeownership. The third leg in the sturdy 3 legged stool is protecting the physical home itself. Protecting your home includes the need for ongoing maintenance, following in **Chapter 13**.

Scheduled Maintenance Record

Chapter 13

Home Maintenance

House and Home

Owning a *house* is owning an asset. It's an asset on your personal balance sheet. You can own a dozen houses, and rent them out. The difference between these houses and your home is that where a person lives is their *home*. As paint colors and wallpapers are chosen, the house is furnished, decorations and paintings hung the impersonal house becomes your home. It's a part of you. Your home is an extension of your personality. As with anything you own, it's important to maintain your home to keep from incurring major expenses in the future due to neglect, and for personal health and safety.

There will be some home improvements you may want to do because this *is* your home and for no other reason. The improvement is for your personal enjoyment. Keep in mind though that your choice of these improvements will play a role in your home's value, and in the marketability of your home should you decide to sell. Should you suddenly decide to sell it may take a while longer to find a buyer that appreciates an unusual addition or paint colors.

Home Maintenance

A home needs maintenance, and preventive maintenance to keep it running smoothly. The thought here is – are you going to have an "if it ain't broke don't fix it" mindset and wait until everything breaks before fixing, or be proactive to avoid bigger, more expensive problems? A radio commercial once made the point of how $3 could save you $10,000. The tagline was that it was a commercial for a tube of caulk. If the tub area is not properly caulked, water is able to get in the walls where wood can be damaged and a mold problem created, which may cost far in excess of $10,000 to correct. There are different types of molds that can develop in a home, some of which can cause very serious illness or in rare cases be fatal.

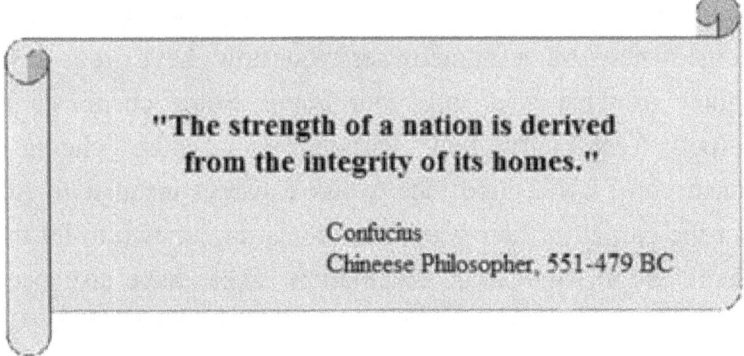

"The strength of a nation is derived from the integrity of its homes."

Confucius
Chineese Philosopher, 551-479 BC

Don't Let Your Home Make You Sick

Florence Nightingale once said that "The connection between the health and the dwelling of the population is one of the most important that exists." The book **Why Your House**

Home Maintenance

May Endanger Your Health written by Dr. Alfred V. Zamm in 1982 is often quoted in today's books that address the issue of how your living environment can affect your health. Dr. Zamm, then a clinical ecologist in Kingston, NY made the point that indoor air in industrialized nations is of poorer quality than breathing the air outdoors. An example is used of a person who is sick, goes in the hospital and gets better. Then goes back home and feels ill again. Getting ill when home can be caused by something as simple as the drain tray under the refrigerator having water with mold, which the fan motor blows in the home. Dr. Zamm pointed out that many homes with gas pipes or stoves with even a slight gas leak have been known to cause a multitude of health concerns, including depression. He recommended that all homes with gas have pipes and joints checked with a meter. There are many areas of a home that can create health concerns. This would be true whether you rented, or now as a homeowner. As a homeowner you now have your own choice of what goes into your home. Some chemicals in carpets (especially new carpets) can cause chemical sensitivity. It's a good idea to ask a carpet installer to roll out the carpet in their warehouse for a day or two to let the chemicals air out before installation. There have also been concerns with glues used in certain types of paneling. Pay attention to both your home and to your health. If a concern arises at the home, say a roof leak, tub area tile loose, or dripping pipe, tend to the item as soon as possible or a little concern may become a major one. If you're trying to figure out why you don't feel well, don't overlook recent changes around your home while you are trying to diagnose yourself.

Are you getting migraine headaches and constantly popping pain relievers? Think outside the box to see if something in the home is making you or a family member ill. Could it be the new carpet? Or, perhaps it's the beautiful lilac bush in full bloom just outside your open bedroom window causing the concern. Getting a coughing spell every night at bedtime? It just may be your wife's powder puff by an open window. Sometimes it takes a little detective work.

Water, Foundation and Wet Basements

We all know the importance of water to our survival, yet water if not directed properly can cause serious and often very expensive damage to home and property. To make the point on a larger – *much larger* scale, look at the creation of the Grand Canyon through water and erosion. By paying attention to your home and grounds when it's raining you may note concerns that if corrected can avoid water eroding your land, damaging your home's foundation and entering the home. Water in the home causes wood to dry rot and moisture creates mold causing asthma and other respiratory conditions.

To Avoid Water in a Basement, Start with the Gutters, Land and Grounds

Improper drainage can direct water towards your house and foundation, as well as wash out garden areas.

What to Do: Check gutters and downspouts: Make sure connected properly and direct water away from house. Best to make permanent solutions that will work whether or not you are home, but you may need to include solutions to put in **place**

during unusual expected storms. For example, downspouts can extend away from foundation at least 5 feet, better 8 feet into landscaped areas, But, if heavy rain is expected an additional 8 foot drain pipe can be easily inserted to get the volume of rain away from the house.

Clean gutters to ensure all water flows into gutters and drains properly. Stay within your skill level based on the height of roofs and utilize proper ladders for the job. If beyond your skill level a company can be hired to clean. Wire "baskets" can be installed in the gutters where water drains into downspouts to avoid leaves clogging. Home centers sell screens that can be inserted in gutters to avoid leaves clogging. There are also many companies that install various gutter protection systems such as:

- **GutterBrush**   www.gutterbrush.com
- **GutterGuard**   www.gutterguard.com
- **GutterHelmet**   www.gutterhelmet.com

Does the rainwater flow ***towards*** the house or ***away*** as it should? **Soil** around the house and foundation needs to slope away by at minimum a 6 inch drop for 10 feet away from the house. The soil should be against the cement, not as high as the sill plate wood and siding. Years of water pitching towards the house can cause foundation cracks, settling, and dry rot of wood and sill plate. All of which are very expensive items to rectify.

Get creative to get the problem solved: If needed, get professionals opinion on the drainage. Items such as digging

Home Maintenance

a French drain to avoid water running towards the house can help. Putting a trench at the far end of a patio and filling with gravel topped with decorative white gravel will provide a place for the water to drain into – and away from the house.

Driveway, walkways and patios should pitch away from the house.

Go out in the rain (sing if you want) with an umbrella or raincoat on, note flow of water around the house. Is it creating a deep puddle against the foundation? Do the gutters handle all the water, or does it run down the roof and pour over the edge of gutter to damage the foundation? Without needing to getting wet, looking out windows noting runoff over gutters during heavy downpours may tip off improper or clogged gutters as leaves accumulate.

Water in Basement

Is often simply the result of improper drainage towards the house as discussed above. Homeowners that need to worry about wet basements during every rainstorm need to be proactive. The thought of "insanity is doing the same thing over and over again, expecting a different result," may come to mind. By solving properly, many years of wet basements needing to be pumped and subsequent moisture and damage to the home will be avoided. When water does enter in the home and cause a wet basement try to *locate the cause.* As soon as the rain starts, pay attention. If necessary use a flashlight or spotlight in a basement or crawlspace and watch the foundation walls. You may find that water is entering from one particular area like an outside corner, or by the front steps draining improperly towards the house instead of away.

If the water isn't coming in from surface water seeping in, you may find there may be a high water table all around the house, with water even coming up from the floor. Seek professional advice, and get quotes to rectify from basement waterproofing companies. There are many independent and franchised throughout the country.

Sump Pump

If you go the route of installing a sump pump to pump water from inside the house out, bear in mind future power outages in planning the installation. During a storm with torrential rain, when there is the highest risk of flooding will often be when the power may go out for an extended time. That is exactly the time you may need the pump to be working. If you don't have a generator, you may want to consider a battery backup unit for the pump. Additionally, the motor in the pumps can burn out as they're working hard during a storm. In homes prone to wet basements consider a second backup pump. Pumps often are installed with a small pit type hole so that it catches the water below floor level. A submersible pump sits right in the water and pumps, and other type pumps have the motor mounted up high out of the water itself. There are also different horsepower motors, depending on how much work it will be doing, and how high and far it will have to pump the water. Once you make a sump hole and install a pump it may actually become a spot more water needs pumping from, and pumps that work hard will cause a spike in your utility bills. If there is a way to solve a water problem without installing a sump pump an additional benefit is avoiding a concern potential future homebuyer's express when they see a sump pump. Again, if possible try to rectify the problem to avoid the need for a sump pump. Test pumps as needed to verify operational.

Household Humidity

The concern: Too much moisture in air can cause damage to your home as well as allergic reactions and respiratory problems like asthma. While it's impossible to eliminate all moisture in the air inside your home steps can be taken to reduce.

Solution: Humidity should be 30 to 60% inside the home to avoid excessive moisture. The EPA, United States Environmental Protection Agency offers tips at http://www.epa.gov/mold/moldresources.html

A **De-Humidifier** can be run to reduce moisture in the air, setting the humidity level to between 30 and 60. The lower the number, the more it will run which will raise the electric bill.

Home Maintenance

De-Humidifiers require emptying water, or install unit that can drain to laundry sink or direct to plumbing.

Vent bathrooms, dryers and other moisture generating sources to the outside. Let the bath exhaust fan run at least 15 minutes after a steamy shower to avoid moisture build up.

"Listen to Your Home"

Literally and figuratively: As you're living in your home a while you'll get to know it well. Pay attention to any changes that may occur. If pipes never rattled, and lately when flushing the toilet a rattle is heard determine why. This new rattle could eventually loosen a joint and cause a more serious water damage concern at an inconvenient time with an emergency repair. The rattle may have been due to an easily tightened loose clamp. If an area of the floor develops a new squeak it may be normal settling or a concern brewing. Perhaps the weight of a large fish tank, waterbed or heavy marble bench caused a floor beam to begin a crack. Cracks appearing in the walls or doors that used to close easily but now have the frames slightly askew may be signs of concern. Concerns such as water from a downspout washing out a corner of the foundation can cause a house to gradually drop in the corner.

Household Maintenance Suggestions

Caulk Exterior: Old caulk may become brittle and gaps are created, causing drafts as well as water leaking in. Siding and trim may conceal the damage escalating inside. Seal air leaks and prevent water from seeping in the home causing mold damage inexpensively with caulk. Pick up a caulking gun and tubes of exterior caulk (most common is white but some colors are also available) and caulk as needed around windows and doors.

Caulk Interior: Check caulking around bath tub, tile, and sinks. Caulk as needed to avoid water seepage causing wood to rot and mold issues behind the walls and in the floors.

Driveway Blacktop/Cement: When blacktop or cement work is needed stopping to talk to companies doing work in the neighborhood can often score a good deal since trucks and workers are in the neighborhood already. Always check references.

Lighting: Many injuries are caused by walking in to dark rooms, or dark areas around the home. Where appropriate having lights on three way switches allows you to turn the light on as the room is entered, and off when exiting.

Use exterior motion detector lights: Many look like any other decorative lighting fixtures, provide safe lighting for you as you are outdoors, and security in the event of unwanted prowlers on the property.

Electrical

Homes that were built 50 to 100 plus years ago were never wired for the demands of today's energy uses. There were no computers, microwaves, blow dryers, and the list goes on and on. The wiring thickness or gauge wasn't designed to have excessive flow of current, which can overheat. In addition many of the electrical boxes weren't large enough to hold the addition of many circuits that get added over the years. The newer the home the more the building codes have been updated.

Never work beyond the scope of your expertise: Consult a professional as needed. Even "simple" electrical items can cause a danger for you, and a potential fire hazard if done improperly. Something as easy as hanging a new light fixture can be complicated once old wiring is disturbed. In addition, many of the very old electrical boxes were not meant to accommodate the weight of some new fixtures.

When doing wiring on your own be sure to turn the electric off at the electric box: Merely turning off the light switch may still leave live "hot" wires in the box that the switch interrupts. Occasionally, even with the one breaker off at the box, there may be times where there is still a junction of other hot wires in the same box, running off another circuit.

Extension cords: Do not overload, and do not run under carpet or heavy furniture as it will become overheated. Use only for temporary needs. Install permanent outlets.

Never overload electrical outlets: An octopus of plugs creates a fire hazard.

Close fuse box door: To avoid accidentally tripping breakers. **Circuit Breakers Trip often/Fuses Blow:** Does your home have older screw in fuses that trip? Could be that there is too much demand on the circuit creating an overload. Do not install a larger amp fuse (unless it is what the panel called for initially.) An electrician should be called to determine the cause and correct. An old "trick" was to stick a penny in the fuse to avoid having to replace. This is extremely dangerous. If your panel has a penny or other bypass to avoid fuses tripping this is a hazard; fuses are supposed to trip to avoid overheating a circuit and causing fire.

Light switches work inconsistently: Does it seem an older switch has to be wiggled to make it work, or it feels and sounds odd? Older plugs and outlets, as well as some newer that have defects may end up with loose wires. The concern is a loose wire causes the electricity to arch from one side to the other and becomes a fire hazard.

Fireplace/Woodstove

The warmth and charm of a glowing fire is one more item that can make a *house* feel like a *home*. Having an open flame inside your home also comes with responsibility for you and your family's safety. Glowing embers can jump out and cause a house fire. A wood burning seminar once pointed out that household heat loss occurs when the fire is beginning to die out, but is not fully out. You may be off to bed as the fire slowly fades away, but your household heat is also escaping. Glass doors may help on fireplaces, and woodstoves can be closed.

Inspect chimney, flue and/or stovepipe before each season: Clean annually or as needed. Chimney fires are serious business and happen frequently. Burning wood causes creosote buildup which becomes flammable. There are creosote logs to burn and help clean, along with professional chimney sweeps.

Open the flue: Before starting a fire, and be certain there was no insulation stuffed up the chimney.

Home Maintenance

Keep the flue closed: When not in use so as not to lose household heat up the chimney.

Have your Fire Department inspect woodstove hookups: To be certain all safety regulations and clearances are being met. You may be told you cannot use the stove, but better safe.

Pest Control

The first steps to keep from paying pest control costs is also the safest; avoiding dangerous animals, rodents and insects, as well as the need for chemical treatment.

- Keep the home sealed with no gaps in wood, siding, and around the home from foundation to eaves and roof. This is easier, safer and less expensive than needing to exterminate.
- Keep trash cans sealed, and house, floors and counters clean of any food and crumbs to avoid attracting pests.
- Use natural pest control methods.

Many pest control issues can be solved inexpensively with simple do it yourself solutions from the local hardware or home center.

Ants: Often found near sources of food and moisture in the kitchen or are attracted to crumbs around the home. Keep food areas clear and food storage sealed to avoid attracting ants. Carpenter Ants are often found near sources of moisture at foundation areas, and near leaks in plumbing in kitchen and bath. These destructive ants eat the wood, and cause structural damage if not remedied. Bait traps attract the ants, who then bring the deadly food back to the queen.

Home Maintenance

Plumbing & Heating

Pay attention to unusual noises: Pipes rattle? Washing machine bounces around? Many items that seem minor tend to develop into other more serious concerns. The washing machine bouncing around may cause the hoses feeding the water to scrape an edge and split, causing a flood. When there is a noise, or something seems wrong it's best to take care of it sooner than later.

Heating System: Have cleaned and serviced annually. Having a service contract that is priced fairly can be important. Call around and compare plans with various companies, what the plans cover, along with the cost of fuel.

Pool

Water Filter Timer: Save money by putting the pool filter on a timer. If your utility has lower off peak rates run the filter at these times.

Dye for Leaks: If water needs to be added to the pool more frequently than usual try using small squeeze bottle of food coloring. Without the filter running, try squeezing a little at various points in the pool water. Dye will stream towards and leaks.

Baking Soda: Raise alkalinity in the pool by using baking soda, which is sodium bicarbonate to save money. Arm and Hammer sells a 12 lb. bag for pools for $7.57, which is .63 cents a pound. A brand of Alkalinity Plus is $29.97 for three 5 lb. containers, about $2.00 a pound.

Liquid Chlorine: In bulk 5 gallon containers saves on chlorine expense, though be careful not to cause discoloration with a splash or spill. Many pool supply stores use returnable containers with deposit.

Pool Cover: Or solar blanket reduces water loss through evaporation, can save energy and the need for chemicals.

Roof

Be careful to remain within your skill level: With proper ladders or scaffolding as needed; when appropriate use qualified roofing contractors to avoid injury.

Inspect Roof: Look for any worn or raised shingles. Sometimes a simple repair can avoid larger expenses.

Flashing: Check that all flashing around chimneys and vents are sealed and protecting as designed; roofing tar is available in tubes for caulking guns. Squeeze roofing tar into holes in the tar around chimney, and vents as needed.

Shampoo: Often a roof that may appear to need replacing due to acid rain streaks or moss growth only needs a shampoo. If not stopped, moss can dig deep into shingles which is both unsightly and a cause of leaks. There are professional roof shampoo companies. Depending on the pitch of roof and your level of handyman skills, it can be washed with a scrub brush, soap, water and possibly bleach on white shingles. Some use a stiff brush to brush the moss off a dry roof.

Overhanging Trees: Keep branches trimmed away from the roof to avoid damage from falling, as well as to allow sunlight and avoid moss build up.

Repair: Small holes caused in the roof by moss that was removed or otherwise can be repaired to avoid water damage inside the home. Until ready for your new roof, you or a roofer could replace a shingle, though it may not match the others.

Small Hole Fix: Check gutter, as often the colored shingle granules collect as they are washed off the roof. Press roofing tar in hole with a small putty knife and smooth even. Cover the tar with shingle granules. Use a small roller to roll the granules into the tar until blends in and not noticeable.

Get a Snow Rake: In snow regions, avoid the cost of roofers needing to assist with snow removal and fixing roof leaks by keeping a snow rake on hand. These are normally in short supply when a snowstorm hits. The snow rakes normally have a flat solid plastic braced end along with a long pole, often in 3 sections depending on the length needed to pull snow off the roof. Snow is removed while safely on the ground to avoid the extra weight, and freezing of snow along the edge and gutters. Not removed, this snow causes ice damming and water leaking in the house and walls.

Wildlife Control

When animals find their way to your property or nest inside the home it may be necessary to locate a wildlife control expert. Keep the home sealed from below grade to roof top to avoid points of entry. Wildlife control experts know the habits of animals, and many trap then release in faraway woods to avoid their return.

Septic/Cesspools

Know whether your home has municipal sewers or uses a septic or cesspool on your own property for sewage disposal.

Home Maintenance

With municipal sewers you may receive a sewer bill monthly or quarterly, possibly as part of a water bill. Whereas with a septic or cesspool the tank and field is normally on your property and no bill is received. Not having this bill though, the system may have expenses over the years to maintain or replace. It's always a good idea to avoid flushing bulky items down the drain and toilet, but even more so if your property has its own septic or cesspool. This is where the sewage and drain water goes out into a tank buried on your property, and the liquids leach out underground; possibly in a drain field of pipes with holes.

Add Yeast to Avoid Expense of Pumping: To reduce septic maintenance expense in the long run add either baker's yeast, RidX brand, or other type of product once a month by flushing down the toilet. Many stores offer generics. This creates microbial action in the tank to promote the breakdown of solids through the use of active bacteria and enzymes and avoids expense of pumping tank or backhoe needing to dig. A box of this type of product left in a warm moist area will begin to show signs of life. You may want to buy amount needed for one month treatment and buy as needed instead of bulk supply.

Buy Safe for Septic Toilet Tissue: to avoid costly septic repairs. Many toilet tissues don't break down as easily in the tank. Buy products labeled "Safe for Septic" that are designed to break down quicker in the tank.

Buy Low Phosphorus or Phosphorus Free Soaps and detergents for the laundry and dishwasher; as soaps can slow down the breakdown of solids in the tank. Phosphorus is a major water pollutant and acts like a fertilizer causing algal blooms to grow.

Home Maintenance

Consider Installing a Greywater Tank: If land area and regulations permit, installing a greywater tank to catch water from some or all sinks, showers, washing machine or dishwasher will reduce the amount of fluids going into the septic tank. Soaps harm the breakdown of solids in tank.

Deal with Now…on Your Schedule, or Later?

Taking some time for home maintenance will help you see problems sooner, avoid problems from happening at unexpected (and inconvenient) times, and prevent more expensive repairs later.

To keep organized, checklists follow for ongoing and seasonal home maintenance. Include additional items as needed.

Home Maintenance

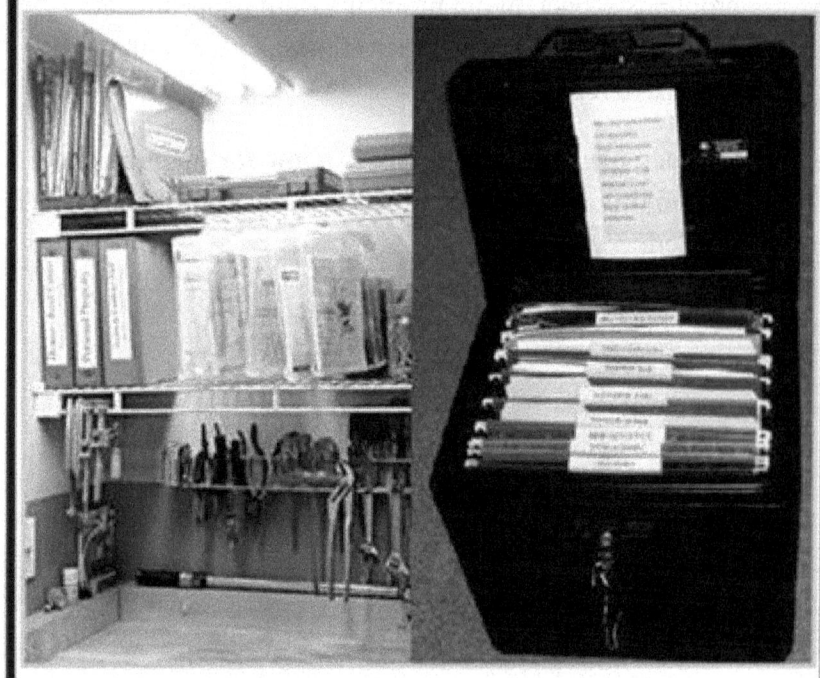

Home Maintenance

	Ongoing Home Maintenance Checklist
	Smoke detectors: Test weekly, or per manufacturer's instructions.
	Security system: Test per company guidelines. Often they have you call to plan a test with them on the line and your permission/pass codes.
	Clothes dryer: Clean/vacuum lint filter, check and vacuum in and around ductwork.
	Washing machine hoses: Inspect regularly, replace with new rubber or braided metal hoses before they crack/burst.
	Drainage: Verify that leaders, gutters, and drains are installed and working properly. Clean out leaves and debris frequently, especially in the Fall, prior to first snow and before Spring rains.
	Heating/A/C: Follow recommended service schedules of your heating, ventilation and air conditioner units. Annual preventative maintenance service will avoid breakdowns at inconvenient times.
	Mold: Check, empty and clean water pan under refrigerator, and any rarely used, stagnant drains to avoid mold buildup.
	Check GFI plugs: Ground Fault Circuit Interrupter Plugs are installed where the deadly combination of water and electricity mix. They should be in any outlets near sinks or tub in the kitchen and bath, laundry, garage and exterior. Some outlets do not have, but may be on a GFI circuit in the electric panel. If your home was built prior to code it may not be required to have, but still should. Outlets have "test" and "reset" buttons. Test at minimum monthly or per manufacturers guidelines.
	House numbers: Must always be visible in case of emergency.

Home Maintenance

	Ongoing Home Maintenance Checklist

Home Maintenance

Spring Home Maintenance Checklist
Drains and gutters: Before the first sign of spring rains verify that gutters are clear, all drainage is working properly, and extended away from house and foundation. Between snow melt and rains spring is a time that many homes experience flooding nationally.
If gutters are safely reachable: Acid rain black streaks are easily wiped off before they permanently discolor. Spray 409, generic cleaner, or soap and water on a rag to wipe gutters clean to keep them looking new.
Screens: Change out the storm windows for screens as needed.
Lawn: Check for winter damage, and pick up branches, rake out winter debris especially curbside before lawn grows and first cutting. Rocks and pebbles can cause injury and property damage if projected by mower.
Air conditioners: Install, uncover, or prep central A/C with new filters before the first hot day.
Outdoor: Repair and paint fences, trellises, etc.
Potting: Prep or establish planters.
Swimming pool: Inspect and begin to prep for opening day per operating manual.
Clean dirty windows: Spring is a good time to open the house up to air out, and clean windows and sills of accumulated winter grime.
Check for leaks: In harsh winter climates, check the house before and *during* spring rains for leaks caused over the winter. Look in basement, crawl areas and all areas including the attic.
Moisture: Keep to a minimum in the home, especially in the south. Excessive moisture damages homes, causes mold, and makes the heat *feel* hotter. Consider using a dehumidifier in the warm months.

Home Maintenance

	Spring Home Maintenance Checklist
	Ant traps: Before ant activity increases in warmer weather, place traps in safe locations around the home, under sinks; away from kids and pets.
	Lawn mower: Prep, change oil and service to ready for the season.
	Clocks Change: Spring ahead 1 hour.
	Ceiling Fans: If reversible, change switch for the warm months. Rotation should be opposite of the clock change. Instead of "Spring ahead" as though the clock dial is changing. Fans change to counterclockwise. See Chapter 14, Energy Savings.

Home Maintenance

Summer Home Maintenance Checklist
Filters: Inspect and change A/C filters monthly or as needed.
Seal coat driveway if blacktop: Patch if cement to fill in holes/pores. This avoids water ice freezing and damage. Too late into fall, the sun isn't as warm to spread seal coat, dropping leaves make difficult.
Power wash home: Clean exterior as needed.
Moisture: Should be kept to a minimum in the home, especially in the south. Excessive moisture damages homes, causes mold, and makes the heat *feel* hotter. Consider using a dehumidifier in the warm months.
Lawn and Garden: Water as needed.
Gutters and Downspouts: Check and clean as needed to make sure water flows freely, and away from the home.
Run Dehumidifier: To avoid moisture buildup in the home, and to make more comfortable.
Pool: Clean and service as needed.

Home Maintenance

	Fall Home Maintenance Checklist
	Smoke detectors: October is Fire Safety Month, change batteries, test all detectors and replace per manufacturers requirements. Detectors have a useful life and must be replaced.
	Check all gutters: For leaf buildup as needed based on number of nearby trees.
	Heating system: Serviced, fuel scheduled for deliveries (if oil, propane, etc.) Clean and vacuum baseboard, ducts, change filters. Consider starting furnace before the first cold day to verify all works, and if necessary open windows to allow fresh air as the initial startup odors vent.
	Vents and returns: Should have no obstructions to ensure maximum efficiency.
	Fireplace or woodstove: Inspect hookups and have flue cleaned at minimum annually. Make sure all flues and dampers are working.
	Close unused damper: If fireplace will not be used, close and seal damper to reduce heat loss. Be sure to indicate as a warning in case the fireplace is then used.
	Burning wood: create stockpile.
	Complete any paint, sealing and caulking projects: before temperature drops below 50 degrees, including night time temperature to allow for drying time. If temperature is cooling off, consider some of the low temperature paints that allow painting down to 40 degrees.
	Seal up: Any areas where mice and other rodents may try to enter the home as temperature begins to drop.
	Install storm door windows: Switch from screens and verify storm windows are in place all around.

Home Maintenance

	Fall Home Maintenance Checklist (continued)
☐	**Check weather stripping:** On all doors. Add insulation where needed.
☐	**Cover any delicate shrubs:** That may be affected by weight of snow if climate dictates.
☐	**Air conditioners:** Window style put away or cover.
☐	**Close and seal air conditioning vents:** To avoid heat loss.
☐	**Lawn furniture and decorations:** Clean and store away.
☐	**Rake or mulch leaves:** Compost as needed. Letting too many leaves accumulate can smother the lawn, prevents sunlight for reaching the grass and may increase lawn disease. Using a mulching mower can turn the mowed over mulched leaves into nutrients for the lawn. Balance raking out bulk of leaves to spread around lawn, mulching, and creating compost with leaves mixed with green clippings to create rich topsoil for next season.
☐	**Planters/flower beds:** Trim back as plant needs dictate.
☐	**If in deer climate:** Consider wrapping shrubs that deer seek with burlap, or use deer repellent.
☐	**Lawn:** Final mowing.
☐	**Winterize mower and prepare snow blower & equipment:** If applicable.
☐	**Mark walkways and driveways:** For ease of visibility during snow removal.
☐	**Before first freeze disconnect all exterior hoses:** Drain faucets and hoses including underground sprinklers. Move hoses to indoor storage to extend life. Drain and blow out sprinklers.
☐	**Pool:** Check that pool is winterized, all lines drained, pool antifreeze added if necessary, and filter drained to avoid freeze up.
☐	

Home Maintenance

	Fall Home Maintenance Checklist

Home Maintenance

	Winter Home Maintenance Checklist
	Double check pipes before the first freeze: Make sure all outside faucets have been drained and winterized as needed.
	Pipe freeze caution: If power is out for a length of time, and pipes freeze, as they thaw out watch for flooding, or have someone check if away.
	Snow: After each snow, remove snow from walkways, driveway, and consider clearing a path around home for ease of access, especially in an emergency.
	Use snow melt that's safe for cement: If slippery check labels on salt or other ice melts before using to be certain they will not damage your walks, driveway, and cement. **Many salts, including road salt on vehicles will eat up cement, as it drops on the driveway.**
	Use either roof heat cables, or snow rake: To remove two to three feet of snow above the roof edge to avoid ice dams in the gutters.
	Ice gutter dam: If ice builds up in the gutters an option is to try a snow melt or salt in a long tube sock, tied to a rope. Toss to land in gutter by down spout.

Home Maintenance

	Winter Home Maintenance Checklist

Chapter 14

Energy & Money Savings

Most of us wouldn't think of holding a $1, $5, $10 or larger bill in the air and lighting it on fire to go up in smoke. This though, is exactly what we do when we waste money, lots of money day in and day out around the home. The only difference is we don't see the immediate burning of money, it's wasted in the larger check we send in to pay the utility bill received next month. Children are quick to point out what was learned in school about the (sometimes controversial) topic of global warming. So now, when a TV or room light is left on, it's easier to use the save the planet approach along with the wasting of money. Keep an eye out continuously for places to save around the house such as:

Dryer

Vacuum out the lint filter to keep the dryer running efficiently and for dryer safety. Dryer fires account for one of every 22 home structure fires reported to US Fire Departments from 2006 to 2010 (National Fire Protection Association, NFPA.org) Aside from safety, a clean filter can save up to 30% annually in electric usage savings.

Run dryer loads back to back: To avoid dryer cooling between loads.

Don't over dry: Which causes more electric use and damages clothing materials.

Energy & Money Savings

Clothes line and drying rack: Cut the annual cost of running a dryer 20 to 50% or more by using a drying rack in your home, possibly in a laundry room or a safe distance nearby heating system. Install wire shelves to hang clothes. An exterior clothes line if allowed by local ordinances and homeowners association rules is also a great way to avoid using the dryer. Place in as inconspicuous an area as possible.

Electric Bill/Usage

Check bill as received and compare cost of bill as well as amount of electricity used to the same period a year ago.
Keep in mind adjusting for unusually hot or cold months. If bill is unusually high it may be due to a defective electric meter. Contact your electric company.
Meter appliances: Many electric companies will test an appliance that may be drawing too much electricity by plugging in an individual meter to say your refrigerator. This may locate the cause of spikes in an electric bill.

Appliances

Energystar.gov: As appliances are upgraded, check out the www.energystar.gov website to buy more efficient models. There may be rebates, for example $50 recently for turning in an old air conditioner that worked, when buying a new more energy efficient model.

Refrigerator

Vacuum the coils and condenser behind or at bottom of the refrigerator to make more efficient. Use brush attachment on

Energy & Money Savings

your vacuum or coil cleaning brush available at hardware & home centers, being careful not to damage the coils.

Set temperature: At 35 to 38 degrees F in refrigerator, 0 to 5 degrees F in freezer.

Dollar test the door seals: These wear out, as sure as the dollar bills it costs to run with old seals. Close a bill in the door seal and gently try to pull. If it pulls out to easy you may need to change the leaky seal.

Keep it full: Your fridge and freezer will run more efficiently when full. As room permits, keep bags of ice in the freezer and gallons of water in the fridge.

Replace old refrigerator: Look for rebates with energystar efficient models, but don't run the old, already inefficient model in a hot garage or near the furnace.

Electric Saving Tips

Vampire electric use: Be aware (or *beware*) of vampire use of many appliances driving up your electric bill. TV's are designed to turn on instantly, due to power constantly being drawn by the set. Up to 75% of the electric cost to operate electronics in the household is due to this vampire usage. A power strip can be used to turn the entire set off causing no electric use, especially when away or in rooms not frequently used. Most newer appliances have memory chips that resets settings when powered back up.

Use motion detectors: Install light fixtures and switches in rooms that automatically turn lights on and off.

Air conditioners: Keep air conditioner filters clean and replace as needed. Follow manufacturers' recommendations to service,

Energy & Money Savings

tune up and lubricate motor as needed. Plant tall shrubs, trees or fence/lattice to shade central a/c unit from direct sun to reduce cost up to 10%, being careful not to block air flow.

Filters: Purchase air conditioner, heating, water and other filters in bulk for the year. Label each with the month/day they are scheduled to be changed as a reminder for the coming year. Dirty filters are less efficient. They don't clean the air as well, and have reduced air flow causing the system to work harder to move less air - at an increased cost to operate.

Vents: Make sure vents aren't blocked for maximum efficiency. Additionally, they should be opened or closed as needed seasonally, and covered when not in use. Leaving a ceiling vent open in winter that's used only for summer air conditioning is allowing a great deal of heat loss up and out the vent. Install magnetic covers available in most home centers to seal in off season. Vacuum all ductwork as needed.

Baseboard: Make sure sofas, beds and other furnishings aren't blocking baseboard for maximum efficiency. Vacuum baseboard fins regularly for maximum efficiency.

Unused rooms: Some systems work most efficiently when all rooms are heated and cooled as designed. If applicable in your home, reduce heating and cooling costs by closing vents or baseboard in rooms that aren't being used and close the door. Be careful not to cause extreme temperature change that can freeze visible or hidden pipes or damage walls & paint.

Open drapes and shades on sunny winter days: To let in the sun's warmth. Close at night to retain heat and insulate the windows.

Energy & Money Savings

Fireplace

Damper: When not in use during winter season close damper, and if for extended period block with insulation to avoid sending your heat up the chimney. Include an indicator/instruction on the fireplace so all know damper is closed or insulated prior to starting next fire. Fireplaces are very inefficient, and convert only 15% of wood energy into heat. The heated interior air is being used to fuel the fire. A crackling fire looks nice, especially around the holidays but keep in mind that as the fire is dying out the damper can't be closed. Tuck in bed for the night and all the household heat is heading up the flue.

Install a woodstove insert: Normally generate more heat than a fireplace, and door can be closed to avoid household heat loss as fire dies out.

Convert to gas: Gas Fireplaces have energy efficient ratings as high as 77%.

Hot Water Use

A large part of household utility cost is in the producing of domestic hot water. To lower this cost:

Water temperature: Is the water temperature out of your faucets so hot you need to constantly adjust with cold water? Check the temperature setting on your domestic hot water heater. Many water heaters are set at well over 140 degrees. To save money and avoid scalding adjust to 140 degrees. Some people adjust to 120 degrees; the concern though is that if set below 140 degrees bacteria causing legionnaires disease can develop. This is a health concern, especially to seniors, children and individuals with a compromised immune system. Review the water heater page at energy.gov http://energy.gov/energysaver/projects/savings-project-lower-water-heating-temperature.

Timers: Use a timer to turn electric water heater on and off according to your schedule. Some have multiple daily settings to turn on say one hour before you wake in the morning, off all day while away and on in the evening until bedtime. You can override the setting as needed. Why heat water constantly if not being used?

Doing Dishes

Hand washing: Instead of doing dishes by running faucet continuously which uses **27 gallons of water** (3 to 5 gallons **per minute**,) try first scraping off the dishes then briefly rinse excess. Do dishes with a stopper to fill sink with hot soapy water as dishes are washed, rinsing to allow many to soak as being washed. **This method of efficient hand washing uses up to only 8 gallons of water.**

Dishwasher: Load to capacity prior to running. Some dishwashers state no rinsing is required. If rinsing first try scraping, then rinse with cold water to save energy dollars heating water. According to the National Resources Defense Council website: http://www.nrdc.org/living/stuff/great-dishwasher-debate.asp New Energy-Star qualified dishwashers use **as little as 3 gallons of water** and 1 kWh per load; older machines up to 15 gallons and 2-3 kWh.

Energy & Money Savings

Most efficient: The most efficient method to wash dishes is to use a new energy star machine, filled to capacity; and the next best is efficient hand washing. A combination of these methods may work for some, efficient hand washing as needed when there won't be enough dishes for a full load for a while.

	Water	Electricity
1. New Energy Star machine	3-5 gallons	1 kWh
2. Efficient hand-washing	Up to 8 gallons	1 kWh
3. Older machine	Up to 15 gallons	2-3 kWh
4. Regular hand-washing	27 gallons	2.5 kWh

Washing machine: If you currently wash all loads in hot water consider washing in warm. A thermometer can be used to check the temperature. Many detergents are designed to clean well with temperatures between 65 to 85 degrees. If the type of load permits wash in warm water, and rinse with cold.

Water heater: Install energy saving insulating blanket around the heater to lower energy cost.

Install a mixing valve: If you don't already have a mixing valve, and your system would benefit speak to a plumber about any benefits to having one installed. This adds cold water to the hot off the furnace to use less hot water.

Energy & Money Savings

Heating, Ventilation Air Conditioning & Cooling

Energy savings workshops: Many state or non-profit cooperative extension agencies hold these seminars. By attending you'll get lots of money saving tips and often handouts and free energy saving devices.

Lower the heat: Instead of keeping the heat 2-3 degrees warmer than comfortable, keep the heat a couple of degrees cooler than at first may be comfortable, your body will normally adjust to the lower setting. This can also be done gradually to adjust your body to it. Wear a sweater of thermals if it helps.

Lowering the heat:

- Lowers your energy bill saving money.
- Health: Don't freeze yourself and get sick, but the body being too warm is a contributing factor to obesity, according to a 2014 study in Trends in Endocrinology & Metabolism. Being a little on the cold side activates your brown fat and spurs your metabolism to keep warm.

Raise the A/C temp: Instead of setting the temperature to keep the home 2-3 degrees cooler than comfortable, raise the thermostat to keep the home 2-3 degrees warmer. The range of 5 degrees in temperature will save money.

Furnace: Have serviced annually prior to winter season and check for energy efficiency. Tuning up can save money.

Heating oil: If you heat with oil, shop the price and weigh options with service provider. See if company's offer a price lock to prepay oil for the season. Some oil suppliers offer an option that if the price of oil drops you get the lower price.

Programmable thermostat: Install to automatically increase and decrease temperatures at desired days and times. Read the instructions to fully understand how to maximize its benefits and cost savings.

Insulation

See http://energy.gov/energysaver/energy-saver for lots of great information. Also, attend energy saving workshops held throughout the country.

Home energy audit: Get an audit specific to your home by a certified company. Check your state's resources for qualifications and list of approved companies. Often free through state grants, you'll get a list of money saving ideas, payback in years, and will make your home more comfortable.

Attic: This is a source of the bulk of heat loss and additional cost to cool a home. You should have at least 6 inches of insulation in the attic, much more in the colder climates. Many homes, especially older homes are lacking, install more if needed.

Ducts: Seal leaks in any ducts, especially at elbow connections. Check while running to feel any drafts leaking.

Floor joists: Insulate where the floor joists sit on foundation, a major cause of winter heat loss.

Outlets: Install insulating covers behind switch plates to reduce energy cost and drafts.

Seal air leaks: Great Stuff brand of spray insulation is available at most hardware and home centers in two types.

Energy & Money Savings

Around windows use the type that does not expand to avoid pressure making them hard to open.

Water pipes: Wrap hot water pipes with insulation as water loses heat as it travels from the water heater to your faucets. Available in 8+ ft. lengths of various pipe diameters at most home centers; the foam is pre-slitted the length to fit over pipes easily, cutting to fit as needed. Start with the pipes nearest the heater first to get immediate savings and work away to reach all exposed pipes.

Window shades: Keep a home cooler and save energy by closing to block the sun in warm months. In heating season shades save money by blocking cold air at the window. Insulated shades (some roller shades slide up and down on tracks) cost more but lower heating bills dramatically. Closing curtains as needed provides similar benefits. The attached 8 page provides details on methods and savings.
http://www.human.cornell.edu/dea/outreach/upload/Energy-saving-wind-trtmnts-f-sht.pdf

> "A house is made of walls and beams;
> a home is built with love and dreams."
>
> William Arthur Ward
> Writer 1921 - 1994

Fans

Make the home more comfortable and save BIG on cooling costs. When used in conjunction with closing shades to avoid sun and good window use, closing to avoid hot mid-day air and opening top and bottom when screens permit for circulation reduces and may eliminate the need to use air conditioning.

Attic Fans

Roof fan: Mounting a roof fan will exhaust hot air out of the attic

Gable fan: If your home has gable end vents, mounting gable fan with temperature control sensor is an inexpensive way to exhaust hot air out of the attic and house. A quick fix is mounting an inexpensive box fan in the attic to blow air out of an existing vent.

Whole house fan: Normally installed in a hall area, on an upper floor if more than one story. Whole house fans appear as a large louvered vent in the ceiling. Turned on, the vents pop open and the fans exhausts hot air out of the home. Be sure to seal in winter months to avoid heat loss.

Energy & Money Savings

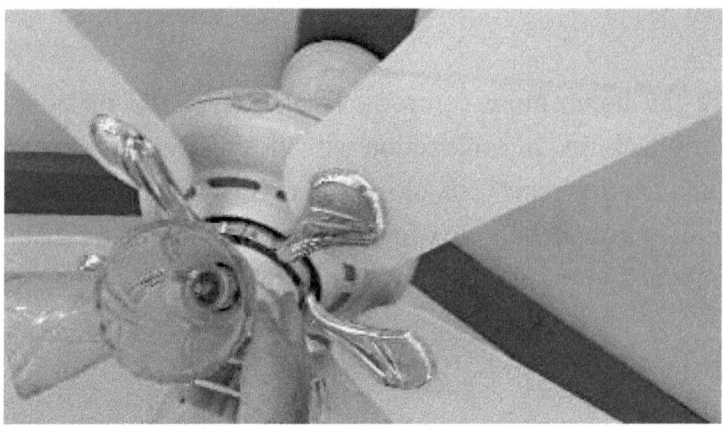

Ceiling fans: Save money and are helpful in most rooms, especially those with high or cathedral ceilings. Fans are a low energy use way to keep air moving in your home as they use only about 60 watts of energy, much less than over 3,000 watts of an air conditioner. They are an important part of a home as energy prices rise, and are on many home buyers wish list so they will add to your homes resale value. Fans keep you cooler in the summer; allowing thermostat to be set a few degrees higher; and warmer in the winter, with thermostat set a few degrees lower. Most fans have switches to reverse fan direction and air flow. They should be 7 to 8 feet off the floor, so if your ceiling is low buy a hugger fan that is flush mounted. Fans should have an angle to the blades to cause air movement, not flat or near flat. The greater the angle, the more air movement; too much angle and you'll spend more time picking up all the papers flying around, energystar.gov website suggests:

Energy & Money Savings

Turn ceiling fans off when not in the room: Ceiling fans cool people, not rooms. If the room is unoccupied, turn off the ceiling fan to save money.

Use the ceiling fan year round: If fan has switch to reverse, set direction for counterclockwise in summer, clockwise in winter as follows:
- **Summertime high *Counterclockwise:*** Set the fan to run at higher speed causing the air to blow down below the fan for a cool breeze.
- **Winter slow *Clockwise:*** Reverse the motor and operate the fan with the blades spinning clockwise. Air will be pulled up in the center of the room, pushing it down near the edges to the occupied space. This will mix warm air that would trap high in the room and cool air that settles towards the floor for a more consistent temperature. The warm air may be most noticeable near the walls of the room. Energy and dollar savings could be realized with this simple step!
https://www.energystar.gov/index.cfm?c=ceiling_fans.pr_ceiling_fans_usage

Fans are Opposite of "Spring Ahead, Fall Back"

A way to remember seasonal fan direction is to think of it as the *reverse of the time and clock changes* each year. We think "Spring Ahead, Fall Back" for the clocks to change. Instead of turning the clock ahead - clockwise; think of *the fan going Counterclockwise in the Spring.*

Window fans: That are reversible are inexpensive to buy and quick to pop in a window. They often have two small fans with accordion sides. These save by exhausting hot air out of

Energy & Money Savings

room, or blowing cooler outside air, say in the evening into a warm room.

Lighting

Exterior motion activated lights: Instead of leaving outside lights on all eve while you are out, use motion detectors on exterior fixtures. Consider also low voltage solar exterior lighting: Though not always consistently bright after frequent overcast days, solar lighting is an inexpensive way to accent the house, walkways and light up a flag. Solar lights normally have a rechargeable battery that charge as sunlight is absorbed in the small solar grid. They're especially good installed in areas such as an area of the yard where there is no electric plug nearby.

Switch to compact fluorescent light bulbs: Switching to CFL's is one of the quickest things to do to start saving money over the long run. They use significantly less energy than incandescent bulbs to give off the same amount of light. Install where appropriate. Lower wattage per bulb generates higher amount equivalent of light. A 15W CFL may generate equivalent of a 60 watt light bulb. CFL's generate less heat than incandescent bulbs, which give off 90% of their energy as heat per energy.gov (which is why incandescent bulbs are used in kids easy bake ovens.) Many light fixtures end up with crispy, very unsafe wires over years of light bulb heat.

Upgrading 15 incandescent bulbs to CFL: could save $50 per year per energy.gov. Initially, the cost to purchase these is higher than traditional incandescent bulbs. The longer life should generate the additional savings.

Energy & Money Savings

Use the CFL warranty: With the added cost of CFL bulbs keep manufacturer to their promise of bulb life by saving receipts and original packaging. Either write on the packaging, or receipt which device it was installed & date, or write date with permanent marker on the bulb. Warranties normally go by the date purchased, not when installed so don't wait to install. When a bulb fails send the receipt and portion of packaging with barcode to manufacturer. Save copy until coupon is received for replacement. They may replace one bulb claimed for warranty with a 6 pack if this was purchased. **Be careful handling CFL's as they contain small amounts of mercury, which is hazardous. Stores like Home Depot and Lowes accept these for recycling.**

Incandescent bulbs: Where these are still being used, one higher watt bulb will use less energy than two or more low watt bulbs in the same room.

Maximize natural light: When possible open the blind or curtains for natural light in rooms. In addition to money savings, natural sunlight helps you absorb stress reducing Vitamin D and is known to improve a persons' mood.

Balance the benefits with extra cooling cost when A/C is running, along with potential to sun fade carpets and textiles.

Task lighting: Instead of lighting an entire room, consider utilizing task lighting for the project at hand. For example a reading lamp directed where you are sitting reading a book.

Dimmer switches: Reduce energy use by utilizing dimmer switches. Turning bulbs on gradually may also increase its filament life, instead of the sudden burst on at full power. Be sure to use bulbs that are dimmable, and never plug other

Energy & Money Savings

items such as a cell phone, TV etc., as they may be damaged by lack of full power.

Holiday lighting & decor: For those that decorate the house for the holidays, consider some tastefully placed exterior lighting. Some types of 100 light strings of holiday bulbs only use 40 watts of power. Trimming your hedges to provide greens for wreaths and roping, with bows may create a festive holiday décor without spinning the electric meter driving up your utility bill.

Water Usage and Bill

Homes that have municipal water and sewer are normally billed for the sewer portion based on gallons of water used. Saving water also reduces the sewer portion of bill. According to the United States Environmental Protection Agency (EPA,) "10% of homes have leaks that waste 90 gallons of water or more a day. The average US household's water leak can account for more than 10,000 gallons of wasted water per year; do your part for the environment to fix water leaks that waste more than 1 trillion gallons annually nationwide."
http://www.epa.gov/WaterSense/pubs/fixleak.html

Check for leaks by checking your meter: Check your water meter before and after a two hour period when no water is being used. If the meter does not read the same you probably have a leak.

Promptly fix water leaks: The longer a leak is delayed being fixed, the more money is wasted that could have been used to buy a small part or pay a plumber. Act right away to avoid more expensive repairs and potential for in some cases mold and water damage.

Fix leaky faucets: A drip at the rate of one drip per second can waste more than 3,000 gallons per year. That's the amount of water needed to take 180 showers!

Toilet water leak: Check for any water which may be seen running, or heard as a slow hissing sound. To test for leaks, place a drop of food coloring in the toilet tank and wait 15 minutes without flushing. If the color shows up in the bowl after 15 minutes without flushing you have a leak. Flush immediately to avoid staining the tank. Promptly repair any leaks to save water. Home Water Works, a project of the Alliance for Water Efficiency: http://www.home-water-works.org/

Replace toilets with WaterSense: Replacing an older toilet that uses 3.50 gallons per flush (gpm) with a High- Efficiency Toilet (HET) that uses 1.28 gpf will save 2.22 gallons for each flush. The EPA WaterSense program labels efficient toilets that use a maximum 1.28 gallons per flush. If the toilet is flushed an average of 6 times a day it will save 13 gallons per day, or 4,745 gallons per year. Some older toilets may use as much as 7 gallons per flush. Replacing old high water use toilets in a house with WaterSense, water efficient models can save a family nearly $2,400 in water and wastewater bills over the lifetime of the toilets.

Add a brick: Old toilets that use lots of water can be made a little more water efficient by putting a brick in the water tank. Be sure not to put it in the way of the flushing mechanism.

Laundry: Always do full loads. Conventional washers built before 2011 use about 40 gallons per load. Newer, resource efficient models may use as little as 15 gallons per load.

Energy & Money Savings

Adjust washer water level: to the amount needed for the load. Some new efficient washers will do this automatically.

Dishwashing: Fill the sink with water rather than continually running the tap.

Turn off the faucet: When lathering hands, shaving or brushing teeth.

Hoses: Make sure hoses have a shutoff nozzle when washing cars or gardening to not waste water by running continuously.

Running water: If it takes a while for the hot water to reach your faucet, fill up watering cans to use the water for other uses, like watering house plants.

Rain barrels: Buy or make a rain barrel out of 55 gallon drum or large plastic trash can to catch rainwater from downspouts. Use to water lawn and plants.

Pump from water: If there is access to a stream, pond, or pool with excess water use a small pump connected to a hose to water the lawn if regulations allow. Saves water and sewer use charges. When pools need to be pumped anyway, making use of the water on the lawn saves. To pump on a regular basis from a water source, weigh the cost of water and sewer versus the cost of electricity used to pump.

Point well: Can be installed to pump water out of the ground. Check regulations, and call your local utility to verify safe location to drive a point well.

While it is being environment friendly to conserve, consider also if buying materials is cost effective. Know your cost per gallon of water and/or sewer fees, and determine how long the savings of buying a rain barrel or pump will take to pay itself back. Consider also cost of electricity running pump.

"The most important work you and I will ever do will be within the walls of our own homes."

Harold B. Lee
US Mormon Clergyman
1899 - 1973

Chapter 15

Home Improvements

Be cautious not to overdo major renovations until you have a good emergency fund, and are on track with your investment goals. Often, living in a home a while prior to doing major renovations will help put clarity into the essentials of projects. As you get to know your home you may find little idiosyncrasies that arise, adding to the wish list of improvements you'd like to make. The question is, do you learn to live with them, or correct? **Safety items** should rank high in priority for property improvements. **Improvements that save money** such as energy saving furnace, domestic hot water, and energy efficient doors and windows may also be wiser investments.

If a major renovation simply isn't in the budget and an emergency fund isn't in place it may not be the priority it appeared to be. Consider other options:

Inexpensive paint and décor can go a long way. Look into websites and TV Shows such as HGTV's Design on a Dime: http://www.hgtv.com/design-on-a-dime/show/index.html

Outdated kitchen cabinets can be painted or stained, touches like country wallpaper added inside a raised panel creates a cozy country kitchen for a fraction the cost of a full kitchen remodel. If needed, individual projects can be included such as adding additional GFI protected outlets.

Home Improvements

Your Home's Solar Orientation

If planning renovations, additions, new windows and other changes, keep in mind thoughts on the orientation of your home in relation to which exposures face north, south, east, and west as well as the present floor plan. While you probably won't be moving an existing house; additions, new window installations and future new construction can keep these points in mind in order to increase comfort and reduce energy bills. Many are familiar with the fact that the sun rises in the East and sets in the West; and it is higher in the summer and lower in the sky in the winter. Depending on your climate, the "quick answer" to the orientation of homes was traditionally considered that:

Southern Exposure has more windows to let the sun shine in. Ideally, the long front side of the home with more windows face south. Deciduous trees planted on the south side of the home provide shade from the summer sun, and loose leaves to provide free solar warmth in the winter.

Resources on tree planting distance and height to compliment building orientation in Chapter 17 Lawn and Garden.

Northern Exposure that has cold north winds in the winter has less windows, and may possibly have the garage on this side, as well as evergreens or pine trees to shield the cold winter winds.

North facing homes give the back yard more sun for gardening in the summer. **South** facing homes make the back yard shady

Home Improvements

and cooler during hot summer afternoons; which many may appreciate.

East and West Exposure: Take advantage of Mother Nature's help reducing energy bills by planting deciduous trees that will lose their leaves. These trees provide good shade in the summer with leaves on; and in the winter with leaves off will provide solar warmth and sunlight to the home.

Taking the simplified orientation from a step further, it actually gets more technical to pinpoint use of the sun better.

http://www.nachi.org/building-orientation-optimum-energy.htm

Use of glass and length of overhangs:
http://greenpassivesolar.com/passive-solar/building-characteristics/orientation-south-facing-windows/

Orientation and amount of window area on north, south, east, west:
http://www.ecowho.com/articles/6/The_importance_of_building_orientation.html

Renovation Considerations

Don't over improve for the neighborhood: Keep in mind that if you do home improvements that make your home more expensive than most homes in your neighborhood, you may not recoup your investment. In appraisal terminology, **regression** brings the value of your home down when you are one of the most expensive homes in the neighborhood. **Progression** brings your value higher when your home is less expensive than others in the area.

Garage Addition Planned? Pay attention to your homes layout. Do you want the garage nearer to the kitchen to avoid carrying all shopping packages across the length of the house?

Projects Payback: Are you considering renovations such as a new kitchen, bath, heating system, siding, or deck, among others? Check out Remodeling Magazine's annual survey of pay back of projects by region to determine if the project will add enough value to your home to justify the expense. If doing the work yourself the cost may be lower than shown. If not cost effective you may want the improvement mainly for personal enjoyment, as it's ultimately your decision. Your Realtor may also have helpful advice.

Many home improvement projects simply do not increase a home's value as much as the cost of the improvement, with most only adding 50 to 85% of the improvements cost to a home's value. The interactive online survey can be reviewed by region nationally to give a better sense of improvement values in your area.

According to the Remodeling 2015 Cost vs. Value Report (www.costvsvalue.com) as a national average, of 35 projects, 17 home improvements increased their cost value ratio and 18 reduced their ratio in their change from 2014 to 2015. After adjusting for the increased year to year cost of a pro doing the job only five improvements saw their cost-value ratios rise in the 2015 report. Of note the midrange roofing replacement was

Home Improvements

the largest gainer rising 5.9% and midrange garage door replacement, up 5.6%. Confirming the importance of curb appeal as well as energy savings the 20-gauge steel replacement entry door rose 5.4% and the sole increase for upscale projects: a fiberglass replacement entry door, saw a 1.7% increased ratio.

Backup Generator: According to the report, the biggest gainer in last year's 2014 report, installation of a backup generator had the biggest 2015 decrease of 11.3%. 2014 reflected the market's response to that year's unpredictable weather and multiple large storms which were fresh in Realtor's minds:

© 2015 Hanley Wood, LLC. Complete data from the Remodeling 2015 Cost vs. Value Report can be downloaded free at www.costvsvalue.com.

In addition to what the report indicates as payback on improvements consider also the negative impact a severely deteriorated kitchen or bath has on resale price and marketability of a home. If the kitchen or bath is in very bad condition, to the point that buyers have no interest in the home unless as a "handyman special," a modest improvement may generate a better payback than doing the same to a kitchen or bath that may have functioned good without the expense.

Choosing a Contractor

Complaints against contractors normally rank high among the types of complaints investigated by the authorities annually.

Home Improvements

Many a "Help Me Howard" type news reporter is shown knocking on the door of a builder trying to get a homeowners' $25,000 deposit back for a kitchen that was demolished months ago without a new kitchen in sight. Hiring the first contractor that knocks on your door, you Google or see in the yellow pages may not be the best choice. In any case, check references fully.

- To find a reputable contractor, ask family and friends for recommendations, ask local suppliers that you may be doing business with, check with the better business bureau, and ask the contractor for several references.
- Find out how long they have been in business, as well as their level of experience. Google searches of the name may also generate positive and negative reviews, but be leery of possible planted good reviews. A poor contractor may have a difficult time getting even one good reference. Check the references, and see if the job may have similarities to yours. Probe with questions further to ask how the reference heard about the builder (is he his brother in law?) how the job site was left daily, and so forth. Keep in mind that a family, friend or past reference may have a different idea of a good job than you have.
- Get at least three estimates for the job in order to find a match with a contractor you're comfortable with. This also helps generate ideas, and perhaps a better project.
- A contractor who is known and active in the community may be a good choice, with more of a reputation to uphold locally than one from out of town.

Licensed? Some cities and towns require builders, electricians and or plumbers to be licensed with the municipality. Verify

Home Improvements

what is needed, as well as what work you are allowed to do yourself as a homeowner if desired.

Insured and Bonded? Verify the builder is insured, and to what limits. Many a "Sanford and Son" (referring to the old sitcom) clunker of a pickup truck has the words "Fully Insured" painted on the door, but insurance brokers know the difference: What is fully insured? Do they have minimum liability coverage on just their truck, a minimum liability business insurance policy?

What level of liability insurance limits? Is there workers compensation insurance on every worker on the job site in case they are injured? Many builders claim on the books that each worker is "not" their employee, paying them as a subcontractor to avoid the expense of workers compensation insurance. Some successfully duck their audits and get by without paying premium on them, but should an injury or fatality occur on the job the proverbial stuff hits the fan. Many states hold the property owner liable too for unsafe job sites.

Certificate of Insurance: Should be obtained listing all insurance in place, and review to be certain it is sufficient.

Bonded: Having the builder post a performance bond to give assurance with an insurance company on the hook if the contractor doesn't complete the job. If the builder defaults, the insurance company will pay another builder to finish the job. Insurance companies do some due diligence on the builder, possibly including a credit check before issuing a bond. This gives a little more assurance the builder at least was bondable.

The cost of the bond though will normally be added to the job cost.

Uninsured: There are contractors that work without liability insurance due to the cost. Keep this in mind when comparing estimates. A bid for a job from a roofer or electrician without insurance should be much less than a bid from contractor without insurance. Companies with insurance in place may tend to be more established, and may provide a warranty for their work. This warranty though would only be as good as them staying in business to honor it.

Warranty: How long will the builder guarantee their workmanship to you, and is the guaranty transferrable to a new buyer? This can be a selling point should you sell your home.

Hands on Contractor? Depending on the scope and complexity of the project, consider if your contractor will be physically on the job swinging the hammer. Some builders are out meeting with customers and bidding jobs, leaving the work to be done by a crew, possibly with a job foreman. Sometimes items discussed with the contractor don't get conveyed to the foreman, or the instructions get lost in the translation.

Subcontractors: Some builders bid an entire job, say for an addition, but have no crew of their own. Once you hire the builder as the general contractor he or she may "sub" all or part of the individual jobs out to subcontractors. A masonry company for the foundation, framer for the structure, roofer, drywall company, painting contractor, and heating/ac, electrical may all be separate companies that are hired by the builder. Does it make a difference to you? If the job is done correctly and everyone gets paid it may possibly not be a concern. The concern that arises though is when something goes wrong and fingers get pointed, or when you've paid the builder in full when done, and you receive a lien from a subcontractor. For example, the heating system that was delivered may never have been paid for. Ask for a list of subcontractors before the job starts to verify all have been paid. Even a good honest contractor may develop financial difficulties, or someone that owes the contractor money may default with a ripple effect to you.

Trade Association Memberships: Is the builder a member of groups such as The National Association of Home Builders, National Association of the Remodeling Industry, or National Kitchen and Bath Association? If so, for how many years? Some associations have membership criteria that may indicate a builder is more established.

The Contract

Trust, but verify: It's commendable to be old school and believe a handshake is good enough. The concern though is that even with the best of intentions your idea of the job and the builders may be different, especially should unexpected work be encountered. This can open the door for disagreements, and potential lawsuits. Consumer complaints against contractors normally rank high in the number of victims in many communities. The Federal Trade Commission has resources for hiring a contractor: www.consumer.ftc.gov/articles/0242-hiring-contractor

Home Improvements

LEGAL ADVICE: If you are in doubt or the job is very expensive, the time to talk to your lawyer is before you sign on the dotted line. That's when it's easiest and least expensive to address any problems.

GET A WRITTEN AGREEMENT: Contract requirements vary by state. Even if your state doesn't require a written agreement, ask for one. It should be clear and concise and include the who, what, where, when, and cost of your project.

STANDARD CONTRACTS are probably more favorable to the party presenting it, the contractor, than to the consumer.

CONTRACTS ARE NEGOTIABLE: Language can be crossed out and changed, as long as both parties initial each change.

CONTRACTS CAN BE as casual as a piece of paper, and often job proposal you received is signed by you, which then becomes a contract.

DON'T SIGN an agreement unless you fully understand, and the other party may not be the best person to explain what you are signing.

BLANK SPACES: Sign no contract that has blank spaces. Draw a line or place an x in them.

CONSIDER SIGNING in blue ink, to distinguish originals from copies.

Some contractors seek to keep the contract as simple as possible, avoiding specifics. Consider including:

- **Date signed by homeowner & builder.**
- **Contractors name**, address, phone, and license number (if required.) Specify if the contractor is sole proprietor, partnership, or corporation.

Home Improvements

- **Homeowners name & address**
- **Contract price.**
- **Right to cancel:** A written statement of your right to cancel the contract within three business days if you signed it in your home or at a location other than the seller's permanent place of business.
- **Down payment** should be as small as possible. Some state laws limit the amount of money a contractor can request as a down payment. Contact your state or local consumer agency to find out the law in your area.
- **Don't pay cash:** For smaller projects, you can pay by check or credit card (if accepted.) Many people arrange financing for larger projects.
- **Financing contingency:** If the project cannot be completed without securing financing, include this contingency in the contract.
- **Scope of work:** Does the agreement state that the builder will provide "all labor, materials, and services necessary to complete the project." or will there be a lot of extra charges?
- **Estimated start & completion dates:** If appropriate consider including a bonus if completed earlier than scheduled, as well as a penalty if not completed on time.
- **Permits/licensing & zoning:** Contractor's obligation to get all necessary permits and approvals, or who is responsible.
- **Materials detailed list**: Including each product's color, model, size, and brand. If some materials will be chosen later, the contract should say who's responsible for

choosing each item and how much money is budgeted for it (this is also known as the "allowance.")

- **Contractor's responsibilities:** Is site clean-up and trash hauling included in the price? Ask for a "broom clause" that makes the contractor responsible for all clean-up work, including spills and stains. Is cleanup done daily?
- **Promises made** during conversations or calls. If they don't remember, you may be out of luck, or charged extra.
- **Materials & equipment storage/theft:** Who is responsible if stolen? Will builder or homeowner need to submit an insurance claim? Be certain insurance covers first.
- **Progress payment schedule** for the contractor, subcontractors, and suppliers. Contractors don't expect to be paid entirely in advance, but they also don't expect to wait until all work has been done. It's customary to pay one third upon signing a contract to allow the contractor to buy supplies and get started. In smaller projects, two payments may suffice; with larger jobs, plan to make payments contingent upon completion and approval of each of the defined major phases of work. This way, if the work isn't going according to schedule, the payments to your contractor also are delayed.
- **Change orders:** A change order is a written authorization to the contractor to make a change or addition to the work described in the original contract, and could affect the project's cost and schedule. Since very few jobs go exactly as planned, the contract should

Home Improvements

have a provision that enables it to be amended simply and easily, without invalidating the contract.

- **Warranties:** Covering materials and workmanship, with names and addresses of who is honoring them: the contractor, distributor, or manufacturer. Contract should assure that the materials are new, the length of the warranty period and any limitations also should be spelled out.
- **Final payment:** Make your final payment as large as possible, usually at least 10%; and don't make the final payment or sign an affidavit of final release until work is inspected you're satisfied. You also need to know that subcontractors and suppliers have been paid, all liens cancelled and all warranties are in proper hands. Laws in your state might allow them to file a mechanic's lien against your home to satisfy their unpaid bills, forcing you to sell your home to pay them. Protect yourself by asking the contractor, and every subcontractor and supplier, for a lien release or lien waiver.

Building Permits

Verify if your city or municipality requires building permits. Often, the person obtaining the permit is responsible to complete the work. Many towns issue permits charging a permit application fee based on the cost of the improvement. If there is a range in the cost of the improvement, consider if some items that perhaps may not be done initially, and are not part of the major capital improvement on the home may not

Home Improvements

need to be part of the cost of the major improvement. Clarify who will pay the expense of the permit fee.

Assessment: Often, many municipalities will have the building permit application details sent to the assessor, in order to raise the property assessment due to the value of the improvement.

Certificate of Occupancy/Compliance: When the work is complete - or periodically throughout the project, the building inspector will inspect the job in order to issue a Certificate of Occupancy (C/O) or a Certificate of Compliance (C of C) to show the work was done satisfactorily.

Home Tip: Sellers often come across the concern selling a home where lack of a Certificate of Occupancy delays a closing. After months marketing a home, finding a homebuyer that loves it, everyone packing and getting ready to close it is delayed. Home improvements may have been done over the years without proper permits, now requiring an inspection in order to secure the C/O. This concern may also arise for a homeowner getting a new mortgage.

Taxable Status day: When securing the final C/O, many towns also have what may be known as a taxable status day. If the improvement isn't quite done, instead of rushing to get the C/O, sometimes a few days, or weeks can be the difference of not paying increased taxes on the improvement for an entire year. For example, from the New York State website: **www.tax.ny.gov/pit/property/learn/proptaxcal**

Home Improvements

Valuation Date: Is the date upon which the value of your property is based. In most communities, Valuation Date is July 1 of the prior year. For instance, assessments on the 2011 assessment roll (typically made public on May 1, 2011) were between Tentative Roll Date and Valuation Date enables based on the value of property as of July 1, 2010. The lag assessors and taxpayers to use all available sales before AND after the Valuation Date to estimate the value of property.

Taxable Status Date vs. Valuation Date: The assessments published on the tentative and final assessment rolls are: Based on the **value of the property** on **Valuation Date**, and based on the **property's condition and ownership** as of **Taxable Status Date.** Examples:

- Your home was destroyed by fire in February, 2011 leaving only a vacant lot.
- Because the property burned down prior to Taxable Status Date, your 2011 assessment was based on the vacant lot only.
- Your 2011 assessment was based on the value of your vacant lot on July 1, 2010 (Valuation Date).
- Your September 2011 school taxes and January 2012 town/county taxes are based on the value of the vacant lot.
- Your home burned down on March 15, 2011 leaving only a vacant lot.
- Because the property burned down after Taxable Status Date, your 2011 assessment was based on your property with your home intact.

Home Improvements

- Your 2011 assessment was based on the value of your home on July 1, 2010 (Valuation Date.)
- Your September 2011 school taxes and January 2012 town/county taxes are based on the value of your home.

If the Valuation Date is approaching and the home improvement isn't fully complete it may pay not to rush completion until after the valuation date. Likewise, if you are demolishing a structure, it may be to your benefit to have it completed before valuation date.

Your Home's Market Value

Keep your eye on your home's value by watching comparable home prices. Be cautious not to over improve if the market will not sustain the price should you decide to sell. In Real Estate Appraisal, over improving your home results in regression in the home's value. Having the most expensive home on the block may tend to pull the price of your home down. Whereas having the least expensive home on the block causes progression and may tend to increase your home's value. Want that new custom kitchen with granite counter tops? If the neighborhood doesn't warrant the investment you may want to know that you are making the improvement because it's something you want to enjoy, and not for the investment potential. You may want to keep your eye on the local classifieds, watch the open houses, and check out these sites as well as your local MLS if available for public access. It's a good idea to "keep your finger on the pulse" of your real estate market for many reasons. You may want to refinance, you may have enough equity in the home to request the PMI

Home Improvements

(private mortgage insurance) premium on your mortgage be dropped. Major improvements should be weighed with the neighborhood values, and should you decide to sell you'll know some track record of sales in the area.

www.realtor.com
www.zillow.com

Chapter 16

Safety and Security

In the movie *Meet the Parents* with Ben Stiller, the wedding ceremony was to take place under a canopy to symbolize the home the couple will build together; to become their sanctuary from the outside world. Our homes are the places we return to after a busy day to find comfort and security. Many people in hazardous occupations all day return home for that peace and relaxation. Homes though, are also the place where 20,000 accidental injuries - sadly causing fatalities take place a year. Making homes the second most common location for accidental death, behind only cars. By being aware of common concerns steps can be taken to reduce or minimize. The 5 most common types of fatal home injuries are:

1. **Falls**
2. **Poisoning**
3. **Fire and Burns**
4. **Airway Obstruction**
5. **Water – Drowning and Submersions**

These are accidental injuries that in many cases **may have been avoidable.** Keep the following precautions in mind:

Safety and Security

1. Falls

The leading cause of unintentional home injury deaths, claim 6,000 lives per year.

WHAT TO DO: Make bathrooms No Slip Zones: Install grab bars and non-slip appliqués and mats in tub and shower, to avoid falling against the hard surface. Clean up water spills right away.

Safety Proof Stairs & Walks: Remove clutter from stairs and walkways; and stairs should have secure railings on both sides and have good lighting. Use hardware mounted safety gates at top *and* bottom of stairs (not pressure mounted.)
Landings, Balconies, Lofts need guards: On banister if a baby can slip through.
Windows: On upper floors need window guards with quick release mechanisms in case of fire. Screens are not strong enough to prevent falls. Keep furniture away from windows, and always watch kids around windows.
Ladder Safety: There are 164,000 ladder accidents a year and 300 deaths, which have tripled in the past year. Most deaths are from falls of 10 feet or less. Follow manufacturers' specs for ladder use and capacity. Falls are categorized in 3 ways:

- Using wrong ladder for the job
- Ladder in poor condition
- Ladder used improperly

Causes of accidents are: Holding objects with one or both hands, wet, greasy or oily shoes, ladder not braced/secured, and lack of inspecting ladder for defects.

Do: Keep one hand on the rail at all times, keep your body centered with your belt buckle between the rails, keep body straight and close to the ladder, and move slowly and carefully. Get and use a bigger ladder if the job requires.
Don't: Lean over or reach too far in any direction. Don't try and jump to move the ladder while on it, instead go down to the ground and safely reposition.

2. Poisoning

Claims about 5,000 lives a year. Can be caused by overdosing or combining medicines, including being followed by an alcoholic drink to create an accidental death. Additionally, around the home poisonings occur by accidentally ingesting garden products and fertilizer, detergents, cleaning agents, many household products including cosmetics, as well as carbon monoxide poisoning.

WHAT TO DO:
Buy products with child safety lids whenever possible.
Keep products in original containers. Always label, and store up high and in locked cabinet. Don't store medicines in pockets, purse or drawers.
Don't mix cleaning agents and chemicals: For example bleach and ammonia mixed together creates a toxic gas that'll require quickly evacuating the home.

Safety and Security

Carbon Monoxide is odorless and tasteless. Make sure garage is sealed, with wall joints spackled and taped. Never run car in garage, and pull in garage so exhaust aims out. Don't back in causing exhaust to blow in when motor runs.

Have stoves, heaters and fireplaces checked by professionals annually.

Never use barbecue grill inside home, garage, interior spaces, especially during power outages; this has been the cause of many of the fatalities during storms.

Favor Natural Products whenever possible.

CO_2 Detectors: Are available at home centers. In many municipalities they are required. Required or not they are a must for safety in every home. Some plug in a household outlet, others mount like a smoke detector or are available as a combo unit with a smoke detector. There are models that display the CO_2 reading on screen.

Poison Control Hotline
1 (800) 222-1222

PSA Ads are run often with this phone number as a jingle Say it by singing it a few times to remember it.

- Program in all home and cell phones
- Put a sticker on or near each phone, in garage and areas chemicals and medicines are stored.

3.   Fire and Burns

Are the cause of 3,000 deaths a year. The fires start and spread quickly, and *working* smoke alarms reduce the chance of dying in a fire by 50%.

WHAT TO DO: Install Smoke Detectors
Many are incorrectly installed by homeowners without reading the directions.

Install smoke detectors in each bedroom or near bedroom areas per manufacturers recommended location. If yours weren't professionally installed verify they were placed correctly. Smoke alarms are sold with specific directions of where to install including distance from edge of ceiling. *Many are incorrectly installed by homeowners without reading the directions.* These can be hard wired to your electrical circuit with a battery backup or be battery operated only. Some "talk to each other," so that if one downstairs detects a fire, both it and others in the house will all sound the alarm, providing occupants an earlier warning.

Are yours over 10 Years Old? If you are unsure of the age of your smoke detectors replace with new or check with manufacturer. Many detectors are only good for up to 10 years. A properly installed and maintained smoke alarm is the first thing in your home that can alert you and your family to a fire 24 hours a day, seven days a week. Home fire sprinklers can also alert you, but are a few seconds slower than smoke alarms. Whether you're awake or asleep, a working smoke alarm is constantly on alert, scanning the air for fire and smoke.

According to the National Fire Protection Association, almost two-thirds of home fire deaths resulted from fires in properties without working smoke alarms. A working smoke alarm significantly increases your chances of surviving a deadly home fire. There are many brands of smoke alarms on

Safety and Security

the market, but they fall under two basic types: **ionization** and **photoelectric**. Ionization and photoelectric smoke alarms detecting different types of fires. Since no one can predict what type of fire might start in their home, (the US Fire Administration) USFA recommends that every home and place where people sleep have both ionization *and* photoelectric smoke alarms; or Dual Sensor Smoke Alarms, which contain both ionization and photoelectric smoke sensors.

There are also alarms for people with hearing loss. Many of these alarms have strobe lights that flash and/or vibrate to alert those who are unable to hear standard smoke alarms when they sound.

False Alarms - Rate of Rise Detectors: If smoke detectors are always being set off in the kitchen area, look into rate of rise detector for the kitchen. These are triggered by the rising change in temperature.

Smoke alarms are powered by battery or by your home's electrical system. If the smoke alarm is powered by battery, it runs on either a disposable 9-volt battery or a non-replaceable 10-year lithium ("long-life") battery. Alarms that get power from your home's electrical system, or "hardwired," usually have a back-up battery that will need to be replaced once a year. Smoke alarms are not expensive and are worth the lives they can help save.
Source:
http://www.usfa.fema.gov/prevention/outreach/smoke_alarms.html

Safety and Security

Central Station Alarm: Some fire alarm systems are set up to be monitored by a central station 24/7.

Verify you receive insurance discounts with smoke detectors, and normally larger discount if central station monitored.

Install Fire Hoses: If not already in place, it's a good idea to have hoses installed in your home for convenience, and if needed to extinguish a small non grease fire. Having larger diameter hoses with high volume nozzles on opposite sides of the home say in a garage and laundry room, so both can reach all areas of house may provide peace of mind.

Install Fire Extinguishers: Have readily available on each floor of your home, for example in kitchen, laundry room, garage, and/or basement areas. Different types of fires require different types of extinguishers. A grease fire and an electrical fire require the use of different extinguishing agents to be effective and safely put the fire out. Use of water on a grease fire can cause the grease with fire to spread across the water. Review important information at the FEMA US Fire Administration website:
http://www.usfa.fema.gov/citizens/home_fire_prev/extinguishers.shtm

Types:
Class A Extinguishers put out fires in ordinary combustible materials such as cloth, wood, rubber, paper, and many plastics.

Class B Extinguishers are used on fires involving flammable liquids, such as grease, gasoline, oil, and oil-based paints.

Safety and Security

Class C Extinguishers are suitable for use on fires involving appliances, tools, or other equipment that is electrically energized or plugged in.

There are also multi-purpose fire extinguishers, such as those labeled "B-C" or "A-B-C" that can be used on two or more of the above type fires.

Study up on fire safety. For example, according to FEMA, when a pan initially catches fire, it may be safer to turn off the burner, place a lid on the pan, and use an extinguisher. By the time the fire has spread, however, these actions will not be adequate. **Only trained firefighters can safely extinguish such fires.**

Fire Safety Do's and Don'ts

- **Don't keep flammable items like paper towels and potholders near cooking areas.**
- **Don't leave food unattended on the stove.**
- **Don't smoke in bed, if dozing on sofa/easy chair or leave cigarettes unattended.**
- **Don't empty ashes in trash can, there may be embers.**
- **Do keep matches & lighters away from children.**
- **Do have a family escape plan and practice every 6 months.**
- **Do install sprinklers in the home if feasible.**

Candle Fires: Average of 42 reported every day, over 15,000 per year causing 1,200 injuries and 165 deaths a year.

Safety and Security

- Over half start because candle is too close to combustible materials.
- 20% start when candles are unattended.
- 1/3 start in the bedroom.
- ½ deaths occur between midnight and 6am.
- Top Five Days for Home Candle Fires are:
  1. Christmas Day
  2. Christmas Eve
  3. New Year's Day
  4. Halloween
  5. December 23
- Use battery operated or electric flameless candles and fragrance warmers.
- If you must burn candles, use sturdy metal, glass or ceramic holders placed where they will not knock down or tip over.
- Avoid in bedrooms, and extinguish before going to sleep. Keep 12 inches from anything that can burn, and out of reach from children and pets.
- Never use candles where oxygen is being used to avoid large fire.
- Never put candles on a Christmas Tree.
- Never leave candles unattended.
- Use flashlights, not candles for emergency lighting.

More resources at:
http://www.usfa.fema.gov/citizens/home_fire_prev/candle.shtm

Battery Safety: A seldom discussed safety concern is storage of household batteries. Save original packaging and store batteries so the tips don't touch together or contact item such as a metal can. Batteries have been known to cause fires due to improper storage. Some have noticed that a coffee can full of batteries creates heat and fire hazard.

4. Airway Obstruction

Cause 1,000 deaths a year due to choking and suffocation.

WHAT TO DO: Reduce choking hazards. Don't leave plastic bags where kids can play causing accidental suffocation. Be cautious of any objects that are small enough to fit through a toilet paper holder as they are also choking hazards.
Watch for coins that fall in and around sofas and chairs.
Learn about baby safety, with no items that could cause suffocation in the crib.
Button Batteries Cause 2,800 ER Visits Annually: Button batteries are used in remote controls, greeting cards, calculators, key fobs, jewelry and a host of other products. Keep all these products out of reach of children, and lock up loose batteries.

5. Water – Drowning and Submersions

Pools are a fantastic addition to homes. They provide recreation, exercise, and a gathering place. Owning a pool also comes with the responsibility to have precautions in place. 3,600 people die each year from non-boating unintentional drowning. Many more non-fatal accidents result in injuries, in cases with severe long term disabilities, brain damage and sometimes vegetative state. Children 1 to 4 have the highest drowning rates. We don't want the woulda, coulda, shoulda's if something were to happen. Insurance companies call items like a pool "an attractive nuisance." This, because the pool draws people, and kids towards the water. The CDC, Center for Disease Control offers information and suggestions.

WHAT TO DO: For personal, family and friends safety, read the CDC fact sheet as well as other available water safety information:
 http://www.cdc.gov/HomeandRecreationalSafety/Water-Safety/waterinjuries-factsheet.html

Swimming Pool Safety Tips

Every year, approximately 300 children under the age of 5 drown in swimming pools and spas. Thousands more are hospitalized, some with lifelong disabilities. Every one of these deaths and injuries is preventable.

Safety and Security

According to the government website http://www.poolsafely.gov/ these 7 steps need to be followed:

Step 1: Supervision
Step 2: Fencing
Step 3: Pool & Spa Covers
Step 4: Alarms
Step 5: Safety Drain Covers
Step 6: Swimming Lessons
Step 7: Learning CPR

Pool Fencing: Should enclose all four sides of the pool, without counting the house as one side. A child should not be able to walk out the back door directly to the pool. Gates must be self-closing and with child proof latches out of kids reach.
Consider automatic door locks, door alarm, and pool alarm to detect movement in the water. Meet or exceed your code requirements.
Remove toys, balls and floats from pool area to avoid kids being attracted near pool.
Learn CPR
Teach all to swim: Kids and adults should all know how to swim.
Touch supervision: Kids should always be within reach.
Have life preserver with rope poolside along with long reach pole.
Nearby water concerns: Are there any other streams, ponds, or neighbors pools in the area? In addition to pool safety in your home, pay attention to concerns at neighborhood pools and other natural sources of water in the area.

Safety and Security

Additional Safety Items Around the Home

Emergency preparedness, pack a *Go Bag*

Visit Ready.gov and register if desired, selecting the type of updates you'd like to receive. Pack a basic go bag for you and your family if ever needed. Water can be replaced as you shop, keeping your back up fresh in your go bag. There are a lot of helpful instructions and links throughout the website: http://www.ready.gov/kit A basic emergency supply kit should include the following recommended items:

- Water, one gallon of water per person per day for at least three days for drinking and sanitation.
- Food, at least a three day supply of non-perishable food
- Battery-powered or hand crank radio and a NOAA Weather Radio with tone alert and extra batteries for both
- Flashlight and extra batteries
- First aid kit
- Whistle to signal for help
- Dust mask to help filter contaminated air and plastic sheeting and duct tape to shelter-in-place
- Moist Towlettes, garbage bags, and plastic ties for personal sanitation
- Wrench or pliers to turn off utilities
- Manual can opener for food
- Local Maps
- Cell phone with chargers, inverter or solar charger

Flood Preparedness: https://www.floodsmart.gov/floodsmart/
Hurricane Preparedness http://www.ready.gov/hurricanes

Safety and Security

When high winds or hurricanes are expected be sure to take any items that can become projectiles indoors or secure as needed.

Hurricane roof straps can be installed in the attic to avoid roofs blowing off in excessive winds FEMA offers guidance at www.fema.gov

Hurricane Shutters: To avoid the need to plywood up the home when a hurricane is expected, installing hurricane shutters helps to secure the home in the event of the threat of hurricanes and tornados.

Neighborhood Watch Programs http://www.nnw.org/
Can help you get your finger on the pulse of the neighborhood. One of the foundations of a neighborhood watch program is for neighbors to get to know each other. It builds a stronger, safer community. From the nnw.org: "Our nation is built on the strength of our citizens. Every day, we encounter situations calling upon us to be the eyes and ears of law enforcement.

Not only does neighborhood watch allow citizens to help in the fight against crime, it is also an opportunity for communities to bond through service. The Neighborhood Watch Program draws upon the compassion of average citizens, asking them to lend their neighbors a hand." See if your neighborhood has a program, or consider starting one to avoid future concerns.

Appliance Recalls Check the model and serial number of all appliances. Consumer Reports Magazine reports that 150,000 residential fires each year are caused from faulty appliances; resulting in 3,670 injuries, 150 deaths and $547 million in property damage. Roughly half the fires were due to faulty appliances. www.recalls.gov

Safety and Security

Garage Doors

Garage Doors are the largest moving object in your home. For personal and family safety they must be installed properly and tested for safety. Not properly adjusted, the door with or without an automatic opener can cause serious, sometimes fatal injuries. See useful information at:
http://www.doors.org/AboutIDA/MediaRoom/ConsumerLiterature/ConsumerSafetyGuide.aspx

Refer to your garage door and opener's manual for details. Then check the operation of your garage door and automatic opener. Routine Maintenance Can Prevent Tragedies

Discuss garage door safety with your children. Explain the danger of being trapped under the door. Don't let children play with or use the transmitters or remote controls. Always place and store them out of the reach of children. Teach children to keep their hands and fingers clear of section joints, hinges, tracks, springs and other door parts. Contact with a moving door or its hardware could cause serious injury. These injuries
can also happen with garage doors that don't have automatic openers.

Pushbutton wall control should be out of the reach of children (at least 5 feet from the floor) and away from all moving parts. Mount and use the button where you can clearly see the moving garage door.

Reversal Test: Make sure your opener has a reversing feature. If a reversing feature is not present, the opener should be repaired if possible to include or replaced.

Safety and Security

Garage door openers manufactured after January 1, 1993 are required by federal law to have advanced safety features which comply with the latest U.L. 325 standards: Contact your manufacturer or installer for additional information. If the door does not reverse, have it repaired or replaced. Have a qualified individual adjust, repair or replace the opener or door.

Lead Paint: Homes built prior to 1978 contain some lead based paint, which is known to be hazardous if disturbed incorrectly. Prior to 1950 lead based paint was used more extensively. Care should be taken when scraping and sanding older lead based paint. Proper handling procedures must be followed. Children should especially not be present when lead paint is disturbed, and not be allowed to inadvertently eat loose paint chips. More at:
http://www.cdc.gov/nceh/lead/
http://leadsafeamerica.org/

Most Old Homes Contain Lead-Based Paint

- Most homes built before 1978 contain some lead-based paint. Lead-based paint is more common and was used more extensively in homes built before 1950.

Probability of a House Containing Lead

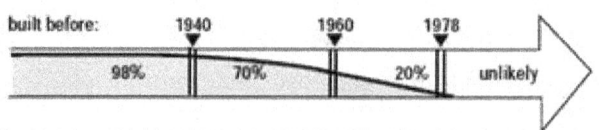

- Homes built before 1950 also used paint that had a higher concentration of lead.

Source: HUD.gov

Safety and Security

Locks: Secure, strong locks along with a separate deadbolt will help ensure a safer home. As a new homeowner, consider changing all door locks for peace of mind, not knowing how many keys made over the years may be around.

Deadbolt Locks: Are an additional lock that bolts deeper into the door jamb. They should be on all exterior doors. There is a saying though that locks are meant for honest people. The more secure one or more locks are the more an intruder is slowed down. If locks are secure enough the intruder may get discouraged and move on. The secure locks should be installed correctly along with a solid door, hinges, screws and jamb.

Radon Gas: According to the United States Environmental protection Agency (EPA) Radon is a cancer-causing, radioactive gas which you can't see, smell or taste. Radon is estimated to cause many thousands of deaths each year; because when you breathe air containing radon, you can get lung cancer. The Surgeon General has warned that radon is the second leading
cause of lung cancer in the United States today. Only smoking causes more lung cancer deaths. If you smoke and your home has high radon levels, your risk of lung cancer is especially high. Radon can be found all over the U.S.; and comes from the natural (radioactive) breakdown of uranium in soil, rock and water and gets into the air you breathe. It can get into any type of building: homes, offices, and schools, and result in a high indoor radon level. But you and your family are most likely to get your greatest exposure at home, where you spend

most of your time. You should test for radon as it's the only way to know if you and your family are at risk. EPA and the Surgeon General recommend testing all homes below the third floor for radon. Testing is inexpensive and easy, and should only take a few minutes of your time. Millions of Americans have already tested their homes for radon.
http://www.epa.gov/radon/pubs/citguide.html

The EPA Recommends:
- Test your home for radon, it's easy and inexpensive.
- Fix your home with radon mitigation if your radon level is 4 picocuries per liter, or pCi/L, or higher.
- Radon levels less than 4 pCi/L still pose a risk, and in many cases may be reduced.

Weekend Warrior Injuries: With all the concerns of safety at the home, it's no wonder Monday's have historically been the day most workers compensation injury claims are filed at the workplace. No doubt due to all the weekend warriors overdoing projects at home, and then dragging themselves to work to avail themselves of on the job workers compensation benefits by stating the injury was caused on the job.

Indoor Air Quality

According to the American Lung Association, indoor air *can be even more polluted* than the air outdoors. Air pollution causes or aggravates many breathing problems including asthma. To breather cleaner air in the place you spend most of your time:
- Make sure no one smokes in the home.

Safety and Security

- Keep rain, moisture and humidity outside.
- Use air conditioner or dehumidifier as needed, with clean filters, keeping humidity levels under 50%
- Vent anything that burns gas outside.
- Fix all leaks or drips to avoid mold growth.
- Don't use scented candles or fragrances to hide odors. Figure out what is causing the odor, clean up and ventilate to add fresh air.
- Use exhaust fans in kitchen and bath, or open window.
- Have furnace, dryer, water heater and appliances serviced as required and inspect at minimum annually.
- Install carbon monoxide detector near bedrooms.

Breathe cleaner air. Read further at:
www.lung.org/healthy-air/home/healthy-air-at-home

Household and Garden Chemicals

Over use of toxic household and garden chemicals has become a growing concern, causing a multitude of health concerns including chemical poisoning in some. We discussed accidental poisoning earlier, knowing that unsecured hazardous chemicals around the house can be dangerous if ingested. Additional concerns arise just by having some chemicals in the home. If you can smell the chemicals in your garage, closet or shed there's a concern. If the chemicals come in contact with your skin, your health can be impacted. Today, we have chemical cleaners made and marketed for every task inside and outside the home. We have chemical based cleaners for the floor, windows, counters, and tub; as well as chemicals for the lawn for every season. Our homes are stocked with chemicals, and it costs us both financially and in our health. The difference though is that while not accidentally swallowed requiring poison control, we are being *slowly* poisoned. An out of publication book by Sally Pringle titled *This Could Happen to You* (1990) tells Sally's story of chemical poisoning using cleaning products while in her job. Serious health concerns developed included rashes and Sally's tongue splitting open. We don't always know reasons why cases of asthma, allergies, complaints of migraine headaches, and dreaded diseases like cancer are caused. We can, though, do what's possible to minimize exposure to chemicals that have a page long list of warnings and side effects. Just because it's legal to sell these products, doesn't mean we have to buy them. Businesses, including chemical companies are in business to make money, not necessarily to do what's best for your health. Consider your use of cleaning supplies, household lawn and garden products:

- If not being eliminated altogether, can steps be taken to reduce your exposure? For example, Making a 4 Step lawn fertilizer a TWO step program, and using natural products the other two? This step alone cuts your exposure to lawn chemicals in half.
- Lawn Fertilizers chemical have a long afterlife. Walking on the grass barefoot applies the chemical to the bare skin and pets paws. Consider that a little nicotine patch on skin

Safety and Security

transmits nicotine into your system. Lawn chemicals do the same on people and pets. An option is to skip the chemical fertilizer in the bare foot'n summer season, and use early spring and fall only.

- Walking over the chemical and wearing shoes in the home brings the chemical throughout the house. Tests show the residue lasts a long time. Not wearing shoes in the house helps alleviate the concern.
- Lawn and Pest Treatment: If chemicals are to be applied, are you able to be out of the house for the day or weekend to avoid initial stronger exposure?
- Use as much ventilation as possible when using chemical cleaners.

Avoid chemicals and save money by using as many natural products as possible. Find a balance that works for you.

There's helpful information on the Natural Resources Defense Council website: www.nrdc.org/health/pesticides/gpests.asp

Natural Cleaners

Instead of buying dozens of harsh, expensive chemicals and toxins for use around the home and family, try these eco-friendly solutions. This is an area that grandma's old fashioned cleaning methods are better. These also are better for the environment, while saving money at the same time. Plus there's no need to store all the extra chemicals.

Always test in an inconspicuous area first to avoid damage. Be sure to label bottles with contents of homemade mixtures.

Safety and Security

Many natural cleaning solutions include some of these basic items. Pick up a gallon of generic white vinegar for $2-$3, and a bulk bag of baking soda to have on hand.

White Vinegar, Baking Soda, Lemon Juice, Hydrogen Peroxide, Rubbing Alcohol

White Vinegar: Cleans sink, drain, appliances, glassware and most areas of the home; can be used to soak faucet handles to dissolve crusty mineral deposits, as well as shower heads that are clogged with minerals.

Window Cleaner: 2 Tablespoons **white vinegar** mixed with a gallon of water. Use in a spray bottle, to apply on the windows, and then scrub with newspaper to avoid streaks. Or use full strength lemon juice or club soda to clean instead.

Baking Soda: Has hundreds of household uses. As a cleaner, start with a bucket of warm water, dip a rag or sponge in the water and sprinkle baking soda on - then clean away. Other uses include:

Unclog drains: Pour 1/2 Cup baking soda, then 1 cup white vinegar into the drain. After the foaming stops flush with hot tap water, after 5 minutes flush with cold water. This process also disinfects, washing away odor causing bacteria.

Countertops: Mix 2 parts baking soda with 1 part water to rub out stains and buff out scratches.

Rid Odors from a dirt cellar: Sprinkle a generous amount on the floor to remove the musty smell.

Safety and Security

http://www.armandhammer.com/news/arm-and-hammer-baking-soda-countless-uses-for-less-than-a-dollar.aspx

Hydrogen Peroxide: As a disinfectant on many surfaces.

Rubbing Alcohol: Put on a soft cloth or cotton ball to remove permanent marker stains from finished hardwood flooring and countertops.

Copper and Brass Tarnish Cleaner: Put a little Ketchup on a soft cloth, first test in an inconspicuous area. Rub on copper or brass to bring out the color.

Hardwood Floors: Use warm water with a few drops of vinegar to bring out the glow in floors. Don't over saturate, use just enough to pick up the dust and shine up. Avoid heels and place protective felt pads under tables and chairs.

Stickers and Bumper Sticker Removal: Try warming with a blow dryer to heat and loosen the glue first, then peeling. Or, tape and stickers can be removed by covering corners and sides with white vinegar (test in an inconspicuous area) then scrape carefully with plastic such as an expired credit card. Clean residue with white vinegar.

Club Soda: To shine up a stainless steel sink

Cornstarch: To clean grease spills on carpet. Pour on spots and vacuum after 15 to 30 minutes.

Fresh lemon: Instead of tossing fresh lemons that may have been used to cook or for lemonade, they can be used to shine

Safety and Security

the faucets! Then, if you have a garbage disposal, ground up they will deodorize the drain.

Get more ideas, Google Natural Cleaners, or Frugal Cleaning Ideas for lots of great websites like Good Housekeeping's *Hints from Heloise*:
http://www.goodhousekeeping.com/home/heloise/
and The Frugal Girls:
http://thefrugalgirls.com/homemade-cleaners

Stink Bug Trap: Virginia Tech researchers found that simple, homemade traps work better than more sophisticated commercially sold traps. Fill a large pan with soapy water, and shine a desk lamp into the water. Stink bugs are attracted to the light at night, fall into the soapy water and drown.
http://vimeo.com/92354801

Yellow Jacket Trap: Dissolve 1/2 cup sugar in 1/2 cup water into an empty 2 liter soda bottle. Add 1 cup apple cider vinegar, and push a banana peel through the opening into the

Safety and Security

bottle. Cap and shake it. Cut or drill a 3/4 inch hole in the side of bottle near the top for the bees to enter. Hang from bottle neck in a tree near where bees are active. Check weekly, discard when full and replace.

Walnuts: Keep your home spider free by putting out whole walnuts in their shell in corners, on windowsills, or wherever spiders are seen. Walnut shells contain a chemical toxic to spiders so they'll stay away from them. Careful with young children as size may be a choking hazard.

Moths and Insects: Put 1 1/2 Cups Apple Cider Vinegar in a bowl, and add a few drops of liquid dish detergent. Leave for a week then discard.

Fruit Flies: Fill a jar half way with apple cider. Punch holes in the lid and cover. The insects check in but don't leave.

Snake Trap: There are many homemade options to trap snakes. Google "Homemade Snake Trap" for lots of options, such as this YouTube video made with screen.
  http://www.youtube.com/watch?v=L11IQoDr5Wg

Google "Natural Pest Control" or Frugal Pest Control" for more great money saving - and healthier, chemical free ideas. Such as this article on BobVila.com:
http://www.bobvila.com/get-rid-of-flies/44356-pests-be-gone-10-natural-ways-to-make-your-home-critter-free/slideshows#.VDCQpZXQOUk

Safety and Security

Notes

Chapter 17

Lawn and Garden

Find Your Balance

Many of us love a lush beautiful lawn; perhaps eying those that appear perfect with awe and an appreciation for their effort. The reality though is that the picture perfect lawn takes an investment of time, natural resources in the use of water, and money. The EPA estimates that 30 to 60 percent of urban fresh water (depending on the city) is used for watering lawns. The idyllic lawn is also achieved by many with an excessive amount of chemicals, weed and feed and fertilizer. These chemicals are extremely toxic, and contain cancer causing ingredients. Chemicals make their way into our streams, homes, affect our health as well as the health of our pets, which walk barefoot outside too. The afterlife of chemicals tracked into the home may last years.

On the plus side, this lush established lawn and landscape adds to the value of your home and makes it more marketable when it's time to sell. It's also nice coming home to a yard you can be proud of. Following a 4 Step weed and feed plan each season adds a lot of chemicals to your environment and expense to the budget. Homes with chemically treated lawns that rely on well water have all those chemicals seeping into the water supply. To all this, consider finding your balance. If not fully able to fully eliminate chemicals, can you spot treat areas as needed?

www.epa.gov/greenacres/wildones/handbk/wo8

Pesticides: Be aware of pesticides used in and around the home and seek natural alternatives whenever possible. Nice to have the nicest lawn but the chemicals seep into well drinking water, tracks on shoes and pet paws into the home.

Consider fertilizing twice a year instead of with a 4 Step Program. It's healthier to be personally a little more tolerant of occasional weeds. Calculate if you can use less fertilizer. For example can you get by using 2 smaller 5,000 sq. ft. bags instead of one larger 15,000 sq. ft. bag? Mulching grass clippings onto the lawn can also take the place of adding a fertilizer treatment.

Garden chemicals around foundation: Be careful using harsh chemicals around the foundation if planting vegetables in the soil.

Keep Grass Higher: For a strong, disease resistant lawn, set the mower to cut a little higher at around 3". Even though a freshly cut lawn initially looks nicer it slows root growth and reduces the roots ability to absorb water. Root depth also increases with grass height. Taller grass shades out annual weeds before they can become established, and protectively shades the roots of grass, especially in the heat of summer.

This allows cooler soil temperature for grass to grow. The concern to balance though with grass height is not to have so high that it becomes a breeding ground for ticks.

Fall Leaves: Allowing fallen leaves to sit and pack on the lawn blocks sunlight and creates mold spores.

Composting: If space permits, consider creating a composting pile, pick up a bin, or use a snow type fence to make a small round or square area. This will provide a place for extra grass clipping and leaves, giving you rich topsoil for use in your lawn and garden as needed. Creating a compost pile with clippings may be used to fertilize the lawn. Mix browns (leaves) and greens (grass clippings) to allow proper breakdown.

Consider a Mulching Mower to save time and money. A mulching mower leaves more finely shredded clippings directly on the lawn, instead of needing to compost the clippings or bag and haul away. Mulching directly on the lawn saves a couple of steps' eliminating you as the middleman and a lot of work the extra work. The clippings generate enough nitrogen to eliminate one fertilizer application, such as in the fall. Fall leaves can also be raked to spread out then mulched as the lawn is cut. The combination of browns and green tends to create excellent compost, feeding the lawn. Some mowers can also be retrofitted with mulching blades.
www.ehow.com/how_8012920_diy-mulching-blades

Lawn and Garden

Pull weeds early in the season before they flower and spread. Weed when the ground is wet after a rain so the full root is removed easier in the moist soil.

Watering Lawn and Garden is best during the morning or daytime to allow leaves to dry in the sun, and avoid watering when it's windy. Watering late in the evening encourages disease on the wet leaves. A soaking rain or watering is best as a light watering encourages roots to grow towards surface where they can burn in the hot sun.

Golf Shoe Lawn Aerating: Got an old pair of golf shoes? Wear them while mowing the lawn or for yard work. The spikes are great for aerating the lawn, and are helpful for the extra grip pushing the mower uphill - especially when grass is damp.

Drainage/French Drain: Direct rainwater away from the house and foundation by pitching the earth and having it drain into a gravel bed.

Reduce Trim Time with Edging: Do it once, take the extra time to bury drain pipe, edge block, and patio below lawn height. Saves time and decreases landscaper cost for years to come with easier mowing without trimming around these areas. Sometimes a little extra work now while you're young can make life a lot easier when you are older.

Brush around house fire: Avoid accumulation of brush, dry bushes and dry grass near the house to avoid fire spreading quickly to the home; especially in wildfire prone areas.

Lawn and Garden

Painting the Little House
Norman Rockwell 1921

Garden

Dividing Hostas

Divide many varieties of perennial plants: Create a lush, landscaped yard without breaking the bank. Consider swapping with family and friends. Learn which plants shouldn't be split and which can and how often:
 http://www.bhg.com/gardening/dividing-perennials/
and
http://www.finegardening.com/10-tips-dividing-perennial-plants

Plant Perennial Veggies and Herbs that will return crops year after year.
http://www.goodhousekeeping.com/home/gardening/perennial-vegetables-460410

http://home.howstuffworks.com/perennial-herbs.htm

Plant as small or large a garden as time permits.

Vegetable Gardens are a great way to connect with nature and provide freshly grown produce. Check with your local garden center to see what grows well in your zone. Plant what you enjoy, and grow as little or as much as you have time for. Planting even just a few potted vegetables in a sunny spot nearby an exterior hose lets you enjoy the bounty of a small harvest.

Garden Seeds Before tossing out what may appear to be an old pack of seeds, try putting 10 in a plastic baggie with a wet paper towel and leave in a warm spot. Within two weeks, if half or more sprout the bulk of the seeds may be worth planting. Many seeds are good for one or two seasons, some last over 5 years.

Lawn and Garden

Trees

The Council of Tree and Landscape appraisers states a mature tree can add $1,000 to $10,000 resale value to a home. Many cooperative extensions and county agriculture offices offer discounted seedling sales annually.

Plant Wind Break Trees: Evergreens planted as windbreaks on the north and northwest sides of the home can cut winter heating bills up to 30 percent.

Plant Shade Trees: On the south side where the sun is the strongest. A single shade tree properly placed can equal the cooling power of 15 air conditioners. Shade trees will shade in the warm months, and lose leaves to allow sun to warm the house in winter. The best time to plant was 20 years ago; and the next best time to plant is today. Research best types of trees to plant, avoid too close to house and roof, and avoid roots to close to septic, drain pipes foundation and walks.

According to the Utah State University Extension
http://forestry.usu.edu/htm/city-and-town/tree-selection/planting-trees-for-energy-conservation-the-right-tree-in-the-right-place

"Shade from trees reduces air conditioning needs and makes non-air conditioned homes more comfortable. Plant deciduous trees so they will shade east-facing walls and windows from 7 to 11 a.m. and west-facing surfaces from 3 to 7 p.m. during June, July, and August. Trees with mature heights of at least 25 feet should be planted 10 to 20 feet east and west of the house. Plant smaller deciduous or evergreen trees with lower limbs northwest and northeast of the building to provide late afternoon and early morning shade. Trees planted to the southeast, south, or southwest will only shade a building in the summer if they extend out over the roof. In the winter, when maximum sun is desired, such trees will provide too much shade. Even deciduous trees that have dropped their leaves cast quite a bit of shade in the winter. Additionally, "To avoid winter shading, locate trees no closer than 2-1/2 times their mature height to the south of a building. Trees planted to the southeast or southwest should be about four times their mature height from the building.

Additional resources:
www.arborday.org/trees/tips/finding-a-tree.cfm

Arbor Day Tree Wizard helps select best trees for your zone.
www.arborday.org/shopping/trees/treeWizard/intro.cfm

Tree Removal and Trimming: When looking to have a tree removed or trimmed when time is not of the essence to have done immediately: Get a price asking if it will help to have it done in between their scheduling during a slow period, or when they have trucks nearby for other jobs to save travel expense. In addition, if there are tree service trucks nearby doing other jobs often stopping to talk can arrange a good deal done same or next day. Offering cash may help, and always check references.

Lawn and Garden

"I think that I shall never see A poem lovely as a tree"

Alfred Joyce Kilmer, Noted Poet
Trees 1913, Excerpted

Natural Lawn & Garden Solutions

Epsom Salt can be used to green up the lawn as it adds magnesium and iron to your soil. Add 2 tablespoons Epsom Salt for each 1 gallon of water. Spread on the lawn, then water in with regular household water to allow it to soak into the lawn. Or, to save time and money apply the Epsom Salt just prior to expected rains.

Weed & Poison Ivy Killer
1 Gallon White Vinegar 2 Cups Epson Salt
1/4 Cup Dish Soap (Dawn brand - Blue suggested by many)
Put ingredients into a pump or spray bottle. Spray over weeds and poison ivy. Most online reviewer's state works well in direct sunlight on a hot summer day, less effective on overcast, shady days. The dish soap acts as a sticking agent on the plant for the killer to work.

White Vinegar Weed Killer
As a safer alternative to chemicals, white vinegar can be an effective way to kill weeds. Mix 1 gallon of white vinegar with 1 oz. of dishwasher soap (many suggest Dawn brand) in a spray bottle or pump sprayer and spray on the weeds in direct sun. 1 cup of salt can also be added.

Lawn and Garden

Natural Pest Control Solutions

Mosquito Trap: Build inexpensively.

- 2 Liter Empty Soda Bottle
- 1 Cup Water
- 4 Tablespoons Brown Sugar
- Pinch of Yeast
- Black Construction Paper, or Black Plastic Bag
- Tape, and Knife to Cut the Bottle

Cut the top off a 2 liter bottle where the bottle starts to curve.
Heat up 1 cup of water in a pot on the stove.
Once hot, add 4 tablespoons brown sugar. Mix together until the sugar dissolves.

- Add cold water to the mix until it is merely warm.
- Once you have lowered the water temperature, add a pinch of yeast to the mixture.
- Fermenting the sugar with yeast creates carbon dioxide.
- Mosquitoes are attracted to both sugar and carbon dioxide; this mixture will attract them to the trap.
- Pour the mixture of sugar, water, and yeast in the bottom half of the bottle.
- Take the top half of the bottle, turn it upside down so it points down, and insert into the lower half of the bottle.
- Push the lower half down as far as it will go without touching the liquid, just to be sure, you want the upper and lower half to seal off completely, with no opening but the place where the cap used to be.

Lawn and Garden

- Cover the outside of the trap with black construction paper.
- Pick a cool spot outside to place the trap, shade is best.
- Check the trap every 1-2 weeks and replace the mixture.

Fabric Softener Sheets: Repel mosquitoes.

Apple Cider Vinegar: In a bowl outdoors near food, but away from people attracts insects and mosquitoes to take their last swim.

Additional Natural Pest Control Solutions

Lawn and Garden

Avoid Garden Pesticides

Attract Beneficial Insects: Avoid using pesticides on the produce you'll be eating. Plan your garden to include pollen and nectar plants, along with perennial herbs such as rosemary, thyme and mint. According to OrganicGardening.com beneficials such as ladybugs feed on aphids and other soft bodied insects. Allowing plants like broccoli or kale to go to flower in the spring attracts beneficials. Straw on pathways is a good habitat for beneficials, as long as renewed once or twice in the growing season. Plants such as Parsley, Dill, Sunflowers, Fennel, and Anise will attract beneficial insects.
http://www.organicgardening.com/learn-and-grow/meet-beneficial-insects

Hose 'em: Bugs, worms, aphids, and mites can be ejected from plants with blasts from the hose, on plants that can take some water pressure.

Companion Planting: A garden with the right combination of vegetables planted together will reduce disease, improve growth, encourage beneficial insects and increase the yield of crops. Some plants thrive near certain other plants.
The size and growth patterns of plants can complement each other to avoid shading.
Onions are well planted next to beets and carrots, and will also keep bugs away.
Basil planted near tomatoes keeps worms and flies away.
Eartheasy, Solutions for Sustainable Living list of plants to plant near or away from each other at eartheasy.com

Plant the Three Sisters: Corn, pole beans and pumpkins or squash. Iroquois legend has it that these were a gift from the gods, always to be grown, eaten, and celebrated together.

Almanac.com > companion planting three sisters. According to The Farmer's Almanac each of the sisters contributes something to the planting. "Together, the sisters provide a balanced diet from a single planting. As older sisters often do, the corn offers the beans needed support. The beans, the giving sister, pull nitrogen from the air and bring it to the soil for the benefit of all three. As the beans grow through the tangle of squash vines and wind their way up the cornstalks into the sunlight, they hold the sisters close together. The large leaves of the sprawling squash protect the threesome by creating living mulch that shades the soil, keeping it cool and moist and preventing weeds. The prickly squash leaves also keep away raccoons, which don't like to step on them."

Learn how to plant the Three Sisters:
blogs.cornell.edu/garden > get activities > signature projects

Notes

Lawn and Garden

American Flag Display

Many homeowners chose to fly the American flag at their home. Often, when a number of homes on the same street fly the flag the street becomes known for having a patriotic feeling. After September 11, 2011 patriotism was strong and flags were flying all over homes and on cars countrywide.

It is the universal custom to display the flag only from sunrise to sunset on buildings and on stationary flagstaffs in the open. However, when a patriotic effect is desired, the flag may be displayed 24 hours a day if properly illuminated during the hours of darkness.

The flag should be hoisted briskly and lowered ceremoniously.

The flag should not be displayed on days when the weather is inclement, except when an all-weather flag is displayed.

The flag should be displayed on all days, especially on New Year's Day, January 1; Inauguration Day, January 20; Martin Luther King Jr.'s birthday, the third Monday in January; Lincoln's Birthday, February 12; Washington's Birthday, third Monday in February; Easter Sunday (variable); Mother's Day, second Sunday in May; Armed Forces Day, third Saturday in May; Memorial Day (half-staff until noon), the last Monday in May; Flag Day, June 14; Independence Day, July 4; Labor Day, first Monday in September; Constitution Day, September 17; Columbus Day, second Monday in October; Navy Day, October 27; Veterans Day, November 11;

Thanksgiving Day, fourth Thursday in November; Christmas Day, December 25 and **Such other days as may be proclaimed** by the President of the United States; the birthdays of States (date of admission); and on State holidays.

Lawn and Garden

"Good Fences Make (or break) Good Neighbors"

A white picket fence has long been symbolic of homeownership in America. Fences in general though can be both a source of keeping peace between neighbors - as well as a cause for arguments, lawsuits and even an occasional fist fight if things go really bad! Following the golden rule and being courteous with a neighbor over fence issues will help, and will avoid the need to "mend fences" in your relationship later.

The quote now shortened to: "Good fences make good neighbors" was first used by E. Rogers in 1640. The actual quote though ends with, "but let us take heed that we make not a high stone wall, to keep us from meeting." This omitted section actually softens the tone and encourages getting to know your neighbors. The actual quote is: "A good fence helpeth to keepe peace between neighbours; but let us take heed that we make not a high stone wall, to keep us from meeting" according to *The Concise Oxford Dictionary of Proverbs*. The quote was then popularized when Poet Robert Frost questioned whether good fences make good neighbors, in "Mending Wall." Describing a friendly argument between him and a New England neighbor as they took their annual walk along a stone wall replacing fallen stones - as Frost discussed if there was need for a wall. Frost uses the words wall and fences interchangeably:

Lawn and Garden

"Mending Wall"

Robert Frost 1914 (Excerpted)

...There where it is we do not need the wall:
He is all pine and I am apple orchard.
My apple trees will never get across
And eat the cones under his pines, I tell him.
He only says, 'Good fences make good neighbors.'
Spring is the mischief in me, and I wonder
If I could put a notion in his head:
'*Why* do they make good neighbors? Isn't it
Where there are cows? But here there are no cows.
Before I built a wall I'd ask to know
What I was walling in or walling out,
And to whom I was like to give offense.
Something there is that doesn't love a wall,
That wants it down.'
... Not of woods only and the shade of trees.
He will not go behind his father's saying,
And he likes having thought of it so well
He says again, 'Good fences make good neighbors.'

A fence publicly shows boundaries, so there's no question left unanswered between neighbors as to where the boundaries are. Often two neighbors who never had a survey both have no idea exactly where the boundaries are. Fences increase security, can keep pets and children from wandering, and avoid a yard becoming an easy cut through to get from one property through to the next.

Lawn and Garden

Who owns fences on your property? Understand and clarify if needed who owns each of any fences surrounding your property. Unless a new development, often neither neighbor knows who originally built a fence. The owner of the fence is normally responsible to maintain.

The Magic Foot-ball,
"Tommy appeared at an upstairs window."
Norman Rockwell 1914

Lawn and Garden

Surveying or Marking the Boundaries: If you had a survey done when buying your property often there is an option of having the boundaries marked visibly at an additional charge. Doing this sets the stage at the outset that this is the understanding of property lines. Often, not having a survey, a standoff occurs where neither neighbor really knows a property boundary. Having the survey done off the bat with property corners marked makes it clear. There have been instances where once surveys were done it's been found that all homes on the street were actually built half on another neighbors' lot. If not a full survey, you may be able to read your deed description and locate the reference points - such as an iron stake in the ground, or cement marker. If the deed from 1800's says to the corner at the oak tree you may have a concern if the tree has long been chopped. A surveyor may be able to mark the boundaries without doing a full survey. Over the years homeowners and neighbors may landscape and use property that isn't theirs. This may be intentional, or may have been the boundary that neighbors have been claiming over the years. A prior owner may have told a buyer incorrect boundary information. Many states have adverse possession laws that if a property is openly and notoriously used for a period of time such as ten years, the user may be able to claim ownership. Decide if the need is present to clarify the boundaries now.

Building a Fence: Discuss your fence plans with your neighbor(s), run a rope or string and agree on where edge of the fence and posts will be located. A neighbor may want to share the cost of a new fence which may allow for a nicer design.

Lawn and Garden

Follow Municipal or City Building Codes: Municipalities often have codes that apply to how high fences can be in the rear, side, and front yards. There may possibly also be setback rules requiring the fence not be installed directly on the property line, and a permit may be required. **Home Owners Association or Developers Deed Covenants:** Aside from municipal codes, the development itself may have rules to follow. This can include more stringent height requirements, fence color, and HOA's can require certain brands or styles to keep a development consistent.

Good Side Out: Many codes require the "good" side of the fence to face out - towards the street or neighbor's property. This is also a courtesy to your neighbors. Some fences are designed so that both sides are good sides.

Not following code requirements when building a fence can create concerns later. Should an injury happen, say with a pool, not having followed codes can make you more liable, even negligent. Municipal codes are normally in place for safety and security of residents.

Can delay when selling house: Should you decide later to sell your home, if the building code that was in effect at the time the fence was installed wasn't followed it can delay receiving a certificate of occupancy (C/O) in order to sell. Often, this then entails removing or redoing the fence to meet code.

Insurance and Fences: Damage to a fence is normally covered by the *Other Structures* portion of home insurance. Often though, the damage from a tree falling on a fence is below the deductible, making the claim not worth reporting unless an injury is involved.

Chapter 18

Foreclosure Prevention

You've done everything right to protect homeownership, but are now finding yourself in a position that you may not be able to make your mortgage payments. This may be due to any number of reasons we've been discussing including loss of a job, divorce, or death of a breadwinner. Normally, there's some advance indication that a situation will be changing. Often, there are warning signs that financial difficulty is brewing.

Know the red flags:

- **Credit card balances increasing, with only minimum payments being made.**
- **Bouncing checks, overdrawing the account.**
- **Emergency fund running out.**
- **Credit Score Tanking.**

You may be able to make this month's mortgage payment, but then next month it's a little more difficult and the payment is late, then it becomes even later next month. Your bank sends late notices; you receive telephone calls day and evening regarding the late payment. Then, a more official letter from your bank that you're in default of your mortgage agreement arrives. You may scrape money together a couple of times to get caught up but find the payments are slipping. The bank's attorney sends a threatening letter. Additional expenses start to pile up in the way of late charges and attorney expenses. There's stress building up in the household that doesn't go away. You wake up at 2am to a nagging feeling. You're looking for a way out, looking for help.

> "Almost any man worthy of his salt would defend his home, but no one ever heard of a man going to war for his boarding house"
>
> Mark Twain
> 1835 - 1910

People Do "Stupid" While in Financial Stress

When a person is in the position just described it often makes them grab at any hope that "magically" appears. There are people and companies that prey on homeowners going through financial difficulties. They buy lists of homeowners that are late on mortgage payments. They read foreclosure notices. The letter or telephone call you received is part of their planned marketing. Many - if not most of these companies charge large upfront fees (that could be better used by you now) and don't deliver on their promises. There may be some reputable mortgage companies contacting you but start with the premise of being over cautious. Predators are known for having "helped" homeowners, only for them to find out that the predator became the owner of the house through papers the homeowner signed. At the outset of a financial concern that may make you fall behind on your mortgage be proactive. You may be able to take a side business or part time job on to bridge an income gap. Get advice and take control of the situation before it consumes your health and life. With all good intentions, being conscientious you may want to pay all obligations. If the income isn't there to meet all your obligations - it isn't there. Set a budget up for the month and plan to pay in order of priorities. Psychologist Abraham Maslow researched and wrote of five levels of need in what is known as Maslow's Hierarchy of Needs in 1943. With this thought in mind, pay in order of your needs in relationship to available funds:

1. **You need food for you and family; basic, and on a budget. Restaurants aren't in a frugal budget unless you're working there.**
2. **Electric and utilities for lights and heat.**
3. **Roof over your head, mortgage payment.**

Credit card and other unsecured consumer loan payments may have to be intentionally not paid for the time being if the money just isn't there. Get more in depth credit counseling to seek advice particular to your situation. By taking the bull by the horns and knowing a plan is in place that you are working through you will feel much more in control. Protect your health, this is what matters most.

Talk to your Bank: Banks don't want to foreclose on homeowners. Despite the image of bankers as characterized by the grinchly Mr. Potter in *It's a Wonderful Life*, they'd rather

Foreclosure Prevention

work with you to get on track with payments; or be patient as you arrange for a buyer. Foreclosures can cost a bank tens of thousands of dollars in legal fees, along with staff time and caring for a vacant house. It also doesn't look good on their books.

Avoiding Foreclosure: The US Government has implemented a number of programs to assist homeowners who are at risk of foreclosure and otherwise struggling with their monthly mortgage payments. The majority of these programs are administered through the U.S. Treasury Department and HUD. This page provides a summary of these various programs. Please continue reading in order to determine which program can best assist you. If you are experiencing difficulties making your mortgage payments, you are encourage to contact your lender or loan servicer directly to inquire about foreclosure prevention options that are available. If you are experiencing difficulty communicating with your mortgage lender or servicer about your need for mortgage relief, there are organizations that can help by contacting lenders and servicers on your behalf.

Read FHA's brochure, "Save Your Home: Tips to Avoid Foreclosure," also published in Spanish, Chinese and Vietnamese.
Check your state website for details on foreclosure prevention. They may have a list of recommended non-profit housing counseling agencies.
Since available programs and resources change, also start with an organization such as a local affiliate of

Foreclosure Prevention

NeighborWorks America, an organization that cares deeply about affordable housing, community development and the people who benefit from them. With over 240 community development organizations, and the support structure that they have built over more than 35 years. www.nw.org

NeighborWorks America urges homeowners to avoid paying for loan modifications. Scam artists often ask homeowners for a payment or administrative "fees," usually upfront. The Federal Trade Commission issued the Mortgage Assistance Relief Services (MARS) rule which made it illegal for companies to request money upfront. But when mortgage problems arise, many homeowners are lured by the promise of help.

National Foreclosure Mitigation Counseling Program (NFMC) Housing counseling agencies funded through the National Foreclosure Mitigation Counseling Program, administered by NeighborWorks America, can provide you with the information and assistance you need to avoid foreclosure through the Homeowner Affordability and Stability Plan (HASP). **www.findaforeclosurecounselor.org**

HASP is part of a broad, comprehensive strategy to get the economy and the housing market back on track. The plan potentially could help up to 9 million families restructure or

Foreclosure Prevention

refinance their mortgages to avoid foreclosure. Borrowers that are interested in exploring their options and eligibility under HASP can contact a counseling agency for free counseling without being referred by a servicer. If it is determined they may be eligible for the loan modification or refinance program, the counselor will work with the borrower to submit an intake package to the servicer. This service is provided at a low cost or free of charge by nonprofit housing counseling agencies working in partnership with the Federal Government. These agencies will provide borrowers with the services they need to take advantage of HASP and avoid foreclosure. There is no need to pay a private company for these services.

HUD.gov has resources to avoid foreclosure; including details below, along with list of HUD approved counseling agencies
HOPE NOW is an alliance between counselors, mortgage companies, investors, and other mortgage market participants. The alliance was encouraged by The Department of the Treasury and the US Department of Housing and Urban Development to bring together diverse stakeholders to address challenges in the mortgage market and create collaborations to solve problems. Membership works towards creating a unified, coordinated plan to assist homeowners, communities and government partners to repair the mortgage market. HOPE

NOW servicers reported almost two million solutions in 2014. www.hopenow.com

Hope LoanPort®, a non-profit web-based platform bringing efficiency and transparency to the processing of all types of foreclosure alternatives (loan modifications, short sales, etc.) Homeowners and housing counselors looking to learn more about Hope Loan Port can visit **www.hopeloanportal.org**
Homeowners wishing to self-engage in the foreclosure alternative process can visit: **www.homeownerconnect.org**.
Use of Hope Loan Port and Homeowner Connect is free for borrowers and their HUD approved nonprofit housing counselors.

Homeownership Preservation Foundation
(888) 995-HOPE   www.995hope.org

Mortgage Bankers Association: Foreclosure Prevention Resource Center contains extremely helpful information foreclosure prevention, scams to avoid, tax relief and a variety of resources. www.homeloanlearningcenter.com

Foreclosure Prevention

HUD (US Department of Housing and Urban Development): Has the following information with links on their webpage:
www.hud.gov > avoiding foreclosure

Making Home Affordable

The Making Home Affordable© (MHA) Program is an official program of the Departments of the Treasury & Housing and Urban Development. It helps homeowners avoid foreclosure, stabilize the country's housing market, and improve the nation's economy. Homeowners can lower their monthly mortgage payments and get into more stable loans at today's low rates. And for those homeowners for whom homeownership is no longer affordable or desirable, the program can provide a way out which avoids foreclosure. Additionally, in an effort to be responsive to the needs of today's homeowners, there are also options for unemployed homeowners and homeowners who owe more than their homes are worth. Please read the following program summaries to determine which program options may be best suited for your particular circumstances.
www.makinghomeaffordable.gov

Modify or Refinance Your Loan for Lower Payments

Home Affordable Modification Program (HAMP): HAMP lowers your monthly mortgage payment to 31 percent of your verified monthly gross (pre-tax) income to make your payments more affordable. The typical HAMP modification results in a 40 percent drop in a monthly mortgage payment.

Foreclosure Prevention

Eighteen percent of HAMP homeowners reduce their payments by $1,000 or more.

Second Lien Modification Program (2MP): If your first mortgage was permanently modified under HAMP SM and you have a second mortgage on the same property, you may be eligible for a modification or principal reduction on your second mortgage under 2MP. Likewise, if you have a home equity loan, HELOC, or some other second lien that is making it difficult for you to keep up with your mortgage payments, learn more about this MHA program.

Home Affordable Refinance Program (HARP): If you are current on your mortgage and have been unable to obtain a traditional refinance because the value of your home has declined, you may be eligible to refinance through HARP. HARP is designed to help you refinance into a new affordable, more stable mortgage. **www.harp.gov**

Underwater" Mortgages: In today's housing market, many homeowners have experienced a decrease in their home's value. Learn about these MHA programs to address this concern for homeowners.

Principal Reduction Alternative: PRA was designed to help homeowners whose homes are worth significantly less than they owe by encouraging servicers and investors to reduce the amount you owe on your home.

Treasury/FHA Second Lien Program (FHA2LP): If you have a second mortgage and the mortgage servicer of your first mortgage agrees to participate in FHA Short Refinance, you may qualify to have your second mortgage on the same home reduced or eliminated through FHA2LP. If the servicer of your second mortgage agrees to participate, the total amount of your

Foreclosure Prevention

mortgage debt after the refinance cannot exceed 115% of your home's current value.

Assistance for Unemployed Homeowners

Home Affordable Unemployment Program (UP): If you are having a tough time making your mortgage payments because you are unemployed, you may be eligible for UP. UP provides a temporary reduction or suspension of mortgage payments for at least twelve months while you seek re-employment.

Emergency Homeowners' Loan Program (EHLP), Substantially Similar States: If you live in Connecticut, Delaware, Idaho, Maryland, or Pennsylvania.

FHA Forbearance for Unemployed Homeowners: Federal Housing Administration (FHA) requirements now require servicers to extend the forbearance period for unemployed homeowners to 12 months. The changes to FHA's Special Forbearance Program announced in July 2011 require servicers to extend the forbearance period for FHA borrowers who qualify for the program from four months to 12 months and remove upfront hurdles to make it easier for unemployed borrowers to qualify.

Managed Exit for Borrowers

Home Affordable Foreclosure Alternatives (HAFA): If your mortgage payment is unaffordable and you are interested in transitioning to more affordable housing, you may be eligible for a short sale or deed-in-lieu of foreclosure through HAFA$^{SM.}$

Foreclosure Prevention

"Redemption" is a period after your home has already been sold at a foreclosure sale when you can still reclaim your home. You will need to pay the outstanding mortgage balance and all costs incurred during the foreclosure process.

FHA-Insured Mortgages

The Federal Housing Administration (FHA), which is a part of the U.S. Department of Housing and Urban Development (HUD), is working aggressively to halt and reverse the losses represented by foreclosure. Through its National Servicing Center (NSC), FHA offers a number of various loss mitigation programs and informational resources to assist FHA-insured homeowners and home equity conversion mortgage (HECM) borrowers facing financial hardship or unemployment and whose mortgage is either in default or at risk of default.

NSC Loss Mitigation Programs home page for answers to Frequently Asked Questions about FHA's loss mitigation programs.

Contact FHA: FHA staff is available to help answer your questions and assist you to better understand your options as an FHA borrower under these loss mitigation programs. There are several ways to contact the FHA for more information: Call the NSC at (877) 622-8525, Call the FHA Outreach Center at 1-800-CALL FHA (800- 225-5342) Persons with hearing or speech impairments can access via TTY by calling the Federal Information Relay Service at (800) 877-8339.

Foreclosure Prevention

Short Sale: Should the event occur that you are selling your home, but find values are such that the amount owed on the mortgage is more than the selling price of the home it may be worth looking into possibility of a short sale with your bank. *Rather than pay the shortage which may be thousands or tens of thousands of dollars* out of savings your bank would forgive this shortage with the agreement it will not seek to recover from you. This avoids the expense to the bank of foreclosure. This will though create a negative impact on credit report and score, and is worth getting attorney and CPA advice as the shortage may be taxable to you. Before signing any agreement to hire a private company to negotiate with your bank, and especially before paying up front money to do so., have your attorney and/or a state recommended non-profit counseling agency review.

Foreclosure happens more as a death by a thousand cuts rather than suddenly. When there is a drop in income or an increase in housing expense people may experience a gradual slipping of the dream worked so hard to build. Savings are exhausted, retirement plans drained, credit cards maxed out as the financial picture grows worse. Whatever the reasons are to date that resulted in a financial hardship is in the past. We can't turn the clock back. What you can do today is to start fresh. Be proactive, and don't bury your head in the sand. Seek advice that has your best interest in mind. Having a plan in place will give you control and some needed peace of mind.

Reach out to a state approved nonprofit housing counselor early. Speak to your bank. There may be options at the outset to modify a loan to avoid unnecessary expense.

Chapter 19

_____

Selling Your Home

Start keeping track of capital improvements now to minimize or avoid capital gain tax when you sell.

With a discussion of taxes, it should go without saying that a knowledgeable CPA or tax professional should be consulted to discuss your situation. In general, when you sell your **primary residence** and meet all requirements you can make up to $250,000 in profit as a single homeowner, $500,000 if you're married.

Before listing your home for sale it's always best to get professional advice since the laws do change. As an example, say you took a job in another city and decided to rent your current - primary home out. Should you sell years later you'd be taxed on the profit if you didn't live in the home two out of the past five years. There are rules, such as that you have to actually **live** in your home two out of the past five years, not just own it.

According to the website nolo.com
http://www.nolo.com/legal-encyclopedia/taxes-when-you-convert-your-rental-property-your-personal-residence.html

"Perhaps the greatest boon in the tax law for property owners is the $250,000/$500,000 home sale exclusion. This rule permits

Selling Your Home

single homeowners to exclude from their taxable income up to $250,000 in profit realized from the sale of a personal residence. The exclusion is $500,000 for married couples filing jointly. There is no limitation on how many times the exclusion may be used during your lifetime....However, a special rule enacted in 2009 limits the $250,000/$500,000 exclusion for homeowners who initially use their home for purposes other than their principal residence, such as a rental or vacation home. The rule requires you to reduce pro rata the amount of profit you exclude from your income based on the number of years after 2008 you used the home as a rental, vacation home, or other "non-qualifying use."

Use the Capital Gains Exclusion to your Advantage

- You can take this profit on your primary home over and over again, as long as each sale is over two years apart and meet requirements.
- This allows homeowners to buy the worst house on the block, fix it up, live in it two years and sell for a tax free profit every two years if all requirements are met.

A rental home may be able to be turned into a primary residence to make part the sale eligible for capital gains exclusion if all the criteria are met. Newer rules limit this, verify with tax professional. If you own a primary residence, and a vacation home, the primary home can be sold with the $250,000 single/$500,000 married capital gain exclusion. You can then move into the vacation home for two years and sell it without paying gain tax, again if all requirements are met.

Selling Your Home

As with all tax laws there are many variables that play a role. Members of the Military are allowed exclusions to some rules. Newlyweds where one spouse recently sold and took the exclusion, death of a spouse, and other events all impact the exclusion. **Be sure to review all details with accountant *prior* to making large financial decisions.** You may be surprised to learn a large tax is owed simply because you missed the capital gain exclusion by selling your home a week shy of living in the home for the two out of the past five years.

Complete details are available in IRS Publication 523: **www.irs.gov/publications/p523/ar02.html**

Start today keeping track, be ready to calculate if a taxable profit when home is sold:

1. **Save Closing Documents** from home purchase and all receipts: Mortgage Expense, Attorney, Title, Survey.
2. **Track Home Capital Improvements** from purchase to sale.
3. **Save Receipts for Home Improvements** in your home and personal property binders, major/crucial documents in a fire & waterproof box. Some register and carbonized receipts will fade over time and may be best to photocopy.
4. **Save Closing Documents** when home is sold.
5. **Calculate Gain or Loss**

Selling Your Home

Your gain is calculated by taking the:	
Selling Price	$
Less Selling Expenses	- $
Equals Amount Realized	= $
Less Adjusted Basis	- $
Equals Gain or Loss	= $

Gain is the excess of the amount realized (the profit) over the adjusted basis of the property.

Loss is the excess of the adjusted basis over the amount realized for the property.

To calculate your adjusted basis you'll need to know your basis in your home to figure the gain or loss when you sell it. Your basis is determined by how you got the home. Generally, your basis is its cost if you bought it or built it. If you got it in some other way (inheritance, gift, etc.), your basis is normally either its fair market value when you received it or the adjusted basis of the previous owner. While you owned your home, you may have made adjustments (increases or decreases) to your home's basis. The result of these adjustments is your home's adjusted basis, which is used to figure gain or loss on the sale of your home.

Other Expenses that are added to the price of your home when it was purchased that raise its basis include: Some settlement fee/closing costs, abstract and recording fees, legal fees, survey fees, title insurance, transfer or stamp taxes,

Selling Your Home

Documenting all capital improvements to your home will increase your basis which will lower your gain and possible tax.

Home Purchase
Capital Gains Tax Worksheet
See IRS Publication 523

	Amount	Notes
Purchase Price of Home	$	
Settlement Fees or Closing Costs	$	
Abstract and Recording Fees	$	
Legal Fees	$	
Survey Fees	$	
Title Insurance	$	
Transfer or Stamp Taxes	$	
Other	$	

Home Capital Improvements

List all capital improvements that add to the home's value, such as a new kitchen, bath driveway, and additions. Repairs such as painting a room aren't a capital improvement unless in some cases part of a capital improvement to the room.

Date	Improvement	Amount	Notes

Selling Your Home

Date	Sale of Residence		
		Amount	Notes
	Selling Price		
	Less:		
	Transfer Tax/Filing		
	Sales Commission		
	Marketing Fees		
	Legal Fees		
	Other:		
	Other:		

Selling Your Home

Notes on Sale of Home

Summary

Enjoy Many Happy Years

We began **American Homeowner** offering congratulations on taking the steps to be a homeowner. Congratulations and thank you are in order now for being the type of person that takes the time to read. This shows that protecting homeownership, and all that you worked to achieve is important to you. It's hoped you found reading worthwhile; and will make use of many of the suggestions and money saving ideas. Please skim through the pages again in the future as you may think of additional items to act on. Consider also making others aware of the book, or some of the ideas that may benefit them too. Should you ever find your financial circumstances changing please seek help as soon as possible. As discussed, foreclosures don't normally happen overnight; you'll know in advance that trouble is brewing. Be proactive.

When the day comes that you may decide to sell your home your efforts maintaining and strategically done improvements will make it sell quicker and at a better price. Keep in mind when selling; your home will then be on the market with many other homes, including new homes that are in move in condition.

Enjoy Many Happy Years

To make your home more marketable when it's time to sell:

- **Turn into a model home** taking personality out.
- **Neutral paint colors** for broader appeal.
- **Home staging** shows all rooms and outdoor living areas to best advantage.
- **Declutter** basement, attic and empty closets. When you pack to move you'll have to do this anyway. Doing in advance will increase marketability.

Just as a business owner may have a team of trusted advisors, you may want to keep in touch with yours. Your **Realtor®** can keep you up to date with market values and homes for sale should friends and relatives be in the market to buy in the neighborhood. Major improvements can also be discussed with your Realtor® to determine if these will over-improve your home in comparison to neighborhood values. Keep in contact with your **banker** as you consider refinance or improvement loans, **attorney** as legal questions arise, **insurance advisor** for updates and annual reviews; and your **CPA/tax preparer** for advice before major financial transactions. Best wishes for many happy years with your home. It's our hope to have helped in some way in you're having a tremendously successful and rewarding homeownership experience. So that when you close the door for the last time you'll have had the best of memories.

Closing the Door One Last Time

As I pull the door closed one last time, a million thoughts go through my mind.

Because I know that happier memories will be hard to find.

I remember moving in this house like it was yesterday.

A little bit of work can wait, right now my family and I are going out to play.

A house, a yard, and room for the kids to roam. Paint, wallpaper, a little bit of love and this house became our home.

Family dinners with parents long gone.
And those million thoughts were memories to me fond.

I do savor every moment that comes to mind, and will the next chapter in my life be just as kind?

Bibliography

Adams, James Truslow, The Epic of America (Boston, 1st Edition 1931)

Stanley, Thomas J. PhD and Danko, William D., PhD, The Millionaire Next Door: The Surprising Secrets of American's Wealthy

Zamm, Dr. Alfred V., Why Your House May Endanger Your Health (Kingston, NY 1982)

The Concise Oxford Dictionary of Proverbs, makes a significant distinction (*Letter* in *Winthrop Papers* [1944] IV.282):

"Benjamin Franklin 1767" by David Martin - The White House Historical Association. Licensed under Public domain via Wikimedia Commons - http://commons.wikimedia.org/wiki/File:Benjamin_Franklin_1767.jpg#mediaviewer/File:Benjamin_Franklin_1767.jpg
http://www.poetryfoundation.org/poem/173530 Robert Frost

www.rhodeislandhousing.org/sp.cfm?pageid=576
Madeline Walker Act
The Madeline Walker Act of 2006 is named after an 81-year-old Providence woman who was evicted from her home in December 2005 because she had unknowingly failed pay a sewer bill of $496. Under the law, effective January 1, 2007, cities, towns, and other taxing authorities are required to notify Rhode Island Housing of delinquent liens well in advance of tax sales.

Website Resources

Homeownership Resources, Related Reading and Industry Information

To equip you with a beginning list of available resources, below are names and websites of various real estate and homeownership organizations.

National Association of Realtors Homeowner Resources
www.houselogic.com

Mortgage Information and Advice
www.fha.gov

United Policyholders
http://uphelp.org/library/resource/your-home-underinsured-8-key-points

Homeownership Preservation Foundation
www.995hope.org
1-888-995-HOPE (24 hours a day/7 Days)

Property Tax Liens
AARP April, 2014 Bulletin
http://www.aarp.org/money/taxes/info-2014/tax-liens-target-homeowners.html

Keep your energy costs down, to keep your home comfortable, and affordable.
www.energystar.gov
http://energy.gov/energysaver/projects/savings-project-lower-water-heating-temperature

US Census
http://factfinder.census.gov
Learn more about your town and neighborhood; income, education and ethnic diversity. Type your zip code or city and state to get the facts from the most recent census, also watch the US population counter update in real time.

FEMA The Federal Emergency Management Agency
www.fema.gov
Flood Information, Flood Zones and Maps.
Many floods occur in non-high risk zones. Get to know the lay of the land and take the proper precautions. Quote flood insurance and find an agent.

Additional Resources

http://www.emilypost.com/

http://en.wikipedia.org/wiki/Housewarming_party

http://www.americaslibrary.gov/jb/wwii/jb_wwii_empire_1.html Empire State Building May 1, 1931 opening

http://repaircafe.org/

http://www.home-water-works.org/

https://www.freecycle.org/

Financial & Investing

http://www.sec.gov/answers/breakpt.htm

http://www.finishrich.com

http://www.feedthepig.org/

http://www.finra.org/

http://www.letsmakeaplan.org/working-with-a-financial-planner/types-of-financial-advisors

http://www.sharebuilder.com

www.myfico.com

We'd like to hear from you!
Suggestions to make American Homeowner better?
Parts of the book you found helpful to you personally?

Please email: reader@americanhomeownerbooks.com
Your comments will help improve new editions, and receive a copy the free eBook
101 Time and Money Saving Tips

Home Interior Notes

Home Exterior Notes

Heating, Ventilation, Air Conditioning Notes

Lawn & Garden Notes

Important Document Locations		
Document	Where Located	Notes
Deed for House		
Mortgage Docs		
Survey		
Closing Statement		
Title Insurance		
Home Insurance		
Will		
Life Insurance		
Retirement Accounts		

	Name & Address	Phone
Realtor		
Insurance Agent		
Accountant		
Attorney		
Plumber(s)		
Electrician(s)		
Garage Door Service		
	Poison Control Hotline 1-800- 222-1222	

www.ingramcontent.com/pod-product-compliance
Lightning Source LLC
Chambersburg PA
CBHW071648090426
42738CB00009B/1456